THE
STEP-BY-STEP
FAMILY
COOKBOOK

MORE THAN 250 DELECTABLE DISHES

THE
STEP-BY-STEP
FAMILY
COOKBOOK
MORE THAN 250 DELECTABLE DISHES

Book Express

Quality and Value in Every Book…

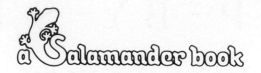

Specially produced for Book Express, Inc.
Airport Business Center,
29 Kripes Road,
East Granby, Connecticut, USA

This edition © Salamander Books Ltd., 1992

ISBN 0 86101 727 7

CREDITS

Designer: Sara Cooper
Contributing authors: Judy Bastyra, Mary Cadogan, Julia Canning,
Carole Hanslip, Jacqui Hurst, Felicity Jackson, Lesley Mackley,
Cecilia Norman, Lyn Rutherford, Louise Steele, Carol Timperley,
Mary Trewby

Typeset: BMD Graphics Ltd., Hemel Hempstead

Color separation: Contemporary Lithoplates Ltd.,
Kentscan, Scantrans Pte, Ltd

Photographers: Sue Atkinson, David Gill, Jacqui Hurst,
David Johnson, Graham Tann

Printed in Italy

Contents

Introduction

There are many pleasures associated with owning a new cookery book: first and foremost, the new ideas that it brings to our cooking repertoire, but for those interested in food, it is often a good read in itself. This book is a real feast for the eyes and the imagination's tastebuds. Food-lovers will be delighted to pour over page after page of mouthwatering recipes, all beautifully prepared and illustrated with step-by-step photographs as an additional aid to preparation.

The recipes in this delightful book take full advantage of the wonderful range of fresh foods now readily available from good supermarkets and specialty food stores. Fruits and vegetables are flown in from all over the world, enabling us to regard mangoes and melon as commonplace, whilst foods that were once seasonal, such as strawberries, are now available all the year round. There was a time when only those who lived in large cities could create authentic Chinese meals using the correct ingredients. Now even isolated communities have access to a store that sells an unbelievable selection of products. And the range of foods is growing daily, in line with our readiness to try new tastes.

This collection of recipes is a celebration of the very best recipes and ingredients from around the world. Some of the ideas in the book simply take the best of these fresh ingredients and use them in inspirational combinations to tantalize the tastebuds, for example, Cucumber & Strawberry Salad, Liver with Raspberries, Chicken & Pineapple Kabobs and Papaya & Prosciutto Starter. Many such dishes have their roots in the nouvelle cuisine movement that valued the simplicity of good food, where every ingredient was cooked to maximize its taste and texture and then combined in such a way as to exploit its characteristics to the full.

Other recipes are based on the great traditions of the world, updated to reflect today's concern over healthy eating, and taking advantage of the ingredients we have to hand. The traditions of Europe, especially those of France and Italy are well represented, with familiar dishes such as Lamb & Mushroom Blanquette, Filets de Boeuf en Croûtes, Risotto con Funghi and Pasta with Clam Sauce. Other recipes take these old ideas and turn them into something new. The roulade, for instance, is given a new lease of life with a delicious lobster and spinach filling in one recipe, a creamy mushroom and herb filling ideal for vegetarians in another, and even a delicious dessert adapting the recipe for Chestnut & Orange Roll. Filo pastry is used in the popular Greek dish, Spinakopitta, but the same pastry is filled with flounder and watercress or with blue cheese to make wonderful little parcels of goodies. In the final chapter, filo pastry is used to make delicate little cups to hold a rich mocha mousse. Crêpes, omelets, quiches, mousses, icecreams and many more basics are revolutionised in recipe after recipe to create a cuisine for today.

Yet more recipes have their roots in Asia. For those people who thought that curries were just overspiced and fiery, Spiced Lamb with Fruit has been included, to show that the subtle flavors of spices such as fenugreek, ginger, turmeric and cilantro can all be tasted, but all are harmoniously blended. And be sure to try the more characteristic fruity tastes of Singapore and Indonesia, the home of the satay and from where familiar Chinese dishes have been adapted to give their own unique flavor.

Just for good measure, there are even some British recipes in the collection. Beef Casseroled in Stout is one that has stood the test of time, along with some splendid game recipes, including Venison with Apples and Pheasant with Chestnuts. Brandy Snaps are also revived to accompany a rich Coffee Syllabub.

Browsing through this book, it is impossible not to be impressed by the skill and care that has been taken in the presentation of the food. Use the photographs as a guideline to help you to improve the presentation of your own cookery – it's amazing what a difference a few neatly arranged lemon slices, a wisp of dill or a bunch of chives can do for even everyday meals. A minute spent on the finishing touches shows your family and friends that you have taken care over the preparation of their meal and often reaps its rewards in gasps of approval and praise. Simple herb garnishes can also be most effective. If you have your own garden, cultivate a small patch of herbs and pick them as required. Alternatively, many varieties can now be bought at the supermarket or greengrocer. To keep them fresh, place in a plastic bag along with a little water. Blow the bag up as you would a balloon and knot the end securely. Kept like this, herbs will stay fresh and green in the refrigerator for several days.

Above all, enjoy this book and savor the delights it will reveal to you. Happy eating.

Glossary

There are a number of unusual ingredients in the recipes within this book, although most of them are now available in this country. The following glossary may help you to identify them. Do try them, you will be pleasantly surprised by the new tastes and textures.

Amaretti – a dry macaroon-type biscuit from Italy made from sweet and bitter almonds. (Note: Amaretti di Saronno contains apricot kernels).

Austrian Smoked Cheese – a medium fat processed cow's milk cheese that is sausage-shaped with a firm, rubbery, slightly smokey texture.

Balsamic Vinegar – a high quality wine vinegar.

Cape Gooseberries – also called *Goldenberry*, this is a yellow fruit that looks similar to a cherry, but with a seedy inside like a gooseberry. It tastes like a sweet, perfumed tomato.

Carambola – also known as *Starfruit* or *Star Apple*, this is a fruit from Malaysia with a waxy yellow green skin, which looks a little like a lantern, although when cut resembles a five-pointed star. It has a juicy, refreshing flavor.

Celeriac – an unattractive-looking root vegetable closely related to celery with a strong celery-like taste. Used in salads and as a hot vegetable.

Cep – the French name for the woodland mushrooms called *Porcini* by the Italians and *Penny Bun* by the English. They have a thick stem and a stickly brown cap. Often dried for later use, when they adopt a strong pungent flavor.

Chanterelle – a bright egg-yellow funnel-shaped mushroom that is popular in France. Sometimes found in Continental delicatessens. Available dried.

Chestnut Mushrooms – brown-capped cultivated mushroom with a fuller flavor than its paler counterpart.

Chèvre – a French cheese made from goat's milk.

Chorizo Sausage – a Spanish pork sausage heavily spiced with paprika. Usually sold dried and smoked. Available in large supermarkets and delicatessens.

Cloud Ear Mushrooms – usually purchased dried, they need reconstituting before use. They retain a chewy texture on cooking.

Crayfish – a freshwater crustacean rather like a lobster in appearance. It is the smaller English-style crayfish that is suggested in this book.

Creamed Coconut – usually sold as a bar of compressed coconut that is heated with fresh milk to form coconut cream. This is often used in Asian cooking and is available from supermarkets and Asian food stores.

Crème Fraîche – if unavailable, substitute fromage fraise or quark.

Crystallized Fruits – for instance, papaya, pineapple. Available in good health food stores and specialist food shops.

Curly Endive – also known as *frisée*, it is slightly bitter outside, lightening to pale green on the inside. It is related to chicory.

Dandelion Leaves – sometimes available commercially, this is a common weed, however, and the young outer leaves made an excellent salad green. Avoid picking dandelions anywhere where chemical pesticides and weedkillers may have been used.

Dolcelatte – Italian soft blue cheese.

Dried Fruits – for instance, mango, pears, apricots. Available in good health food stores, supermarkets and specialty food shops.

Dublin Bay Prawns – of the same species as Langostinos and shrimp.

Eddoe – sometimes known as *dasheen* or *taro*, it is a starchy staple vegetable in the West Indies, Africa and India. Treat as for potatoes.

Emmental – a hard Swiss cheese.

Feta Cheese – a Greek sheep's milk cheese with a sharp, salty flavor and a crumbly texture. Sometimes it is found marinated in olive oil and oreganum.

Frisée – see *Curly Endive* above.

Fromage Frais – a french rennet curded cheese made from cow's milk and whipped to give a thick texture. Varies from 0-10% fat, so is increasingly popular as a cream and cream cheese substitute. Quark is the German/Dutch version of the same cheese.

Garam Masala – an Indian mixture of spices used in curries.

Gorgonzola Cheese – a fairly sharp Italian blue cheese.

Green Peppercorns – unripe pepper berries sold pickled in brine.

Gruyère – a hard Swiss cheese, with a strong nutty flavor and used in cooking.

Haloumi Cheese – a semi-soft Cypriot goat's cheese with a wild, salty flavor and a rubbery texture that can be sliced and cooked.

Hoisin Sauce – a Chinese barbecue sauce.

Juniper Berries – a strong aromatic spice. It comes as a purple-colored berry and is sold in most spice ranges.

Kumquat – a tiny citrus-like fruit with a sweet skin and a bittersweet flesh containing many small seeds. It can be eaten whole and is used in both sweet and savory dishes.

Mangosteen – a purplish round fruit that contains segments of juicy white flesh with a delicate, fragrant flavor. Eat only the flesh.

Mascarpone Cheese – Italian soft cow's milk cheese that has the consistency of soft butter. Substitute fromage frais if unavailable.

Mooli – or *daikon* is closely related to the radish, but it is shaped like a giant white carrot with a crisp texture and a mild flavor.

Morels – considered to be one of the finest edible mushrooms. Available canned, dried and occasionally fresh, from delicatessens and gourmet food shops. Morels are a creamy color and look like natural sponges on stems.

Oyster Mushrooms – one of the varieties of mushrooms now widely cultivated and often available in large supermarkets. Shaped like an oyster, they have a rich taste.

Passata – creamed tomatoes.

Petit Suisse Cheese – a French soft cheese with a very high fat content – around 65%. The cheese is very runny and sold in portion-sized paper-wrapped cylinders. Substitute the creamier varieties of fromage frais.

Pipo Crème – a creamy soft blue cheese.

Prosciutto – Parma ham.

Raddicchio – a red salad vegetable also known as red chicory with a similar flavor to chicory.

Ramutan – a small, brownish fruit covered in long, hairy spines, that when removed reveal a succulent opaque fruit similar to the lychee.

Rocket – a salad green native to the Mediterranean. Sometimes available in Italian or Greek food stores. Use sparingly for its strong, unusual taste.

Roquefort Cheese – the gourmet's favorite blue cheese from France.

Sapodillas – or *Sapote*, a tropical fruit that looks like a cross between a potato and a kiwi fruit. Inside, the pulp is brown and granular and very sweet, rather like toffee.

Scorzonera – or *Black Salsify*, a long thin root vegetable with a black skin. The inside is white with a delicate oyster-like flavor.

Sharon Fruit – a variety of Persimmon. Looking like a rough yellowish tomato with a slightly tart, seedless pulp.

Shittake Mushrooms – sometimes available fresh, but these Oriental mushrooms are most often purchased dried. The dried ones are very strong. Four to six reconstituted mushrooms will flavor a dish. Substitute small button mushrooms for fresh.

Sorrel – a wild European leaf vegetable with a highly prized flavor. Occasionally available in gourmet produce stores. Otherwise, substitute spinach.

Straw Mushrooms – popular in Chinese cookery, these long, thin mushrooms are available dried, canned or sometimes fresh, in Chinese food markets.

Sweet Potatoes – usually a red-skinned potato-like vegetable with a sweet, starchy flesh when cooked. Available in supermarkets and ethnic food stores.

Tahini – a paste made from sesame seeds, used particularly in Eastern Mediterranean cooking. Available in large supermarkets and ethnic and health food stores.

Tamarind – fruit pods of an African tree, sold for their sour juice, which is used as a flavoring in curries.

Tamarillo – an egg-shaped, reddish-yellow fruit which can be treated like tomatoes. Used in salads and sweet dishes.

Teriyaki Sauce – a Japanese soy-based sauce used for flavoring meat and fish.

Tofu – compacted soya bean curd which is high in protein and low in fat. Sold in health food stores and oriental food stores.

Topaz Oranges – a hybrid orange.

Tortillas – Mexican corn or wheat pancakes. Available in large supermarkets.

Truffles – strong-flavored gourmet food added to dishes in small quantities. Available in high class delicatessens.

Wild Rice – a wild grass with a blackish seed that is boiled or baked like rice. It has a nutty taste and a chewy texture.

Yabbies – small, Australian freshwater crayfish.

Zywiecka Sausage – a spicy Mid-European sausage.

Soups

Cream of Mushroom Soup

3 tablespoons butter
1-1/2 pounds mushrooms (see *Note*),
    coarsely chopped
1 shallot, finely chopped
1/2 garlic clove, chopped
2 tablespoons all-purpose flour
1/2 cup white wine
3 cups stock (see *Note*)
1/2 cup whipping cream
Salt and pepper to taste

To Garnish:
1/4 cup whipping cream
Parsley sprigs

In a large saucepan, melt butter. Add mushrooms, shallot and garlic; cook a few minutes, stirring. Stir in flour and cook, stirring, 1 minute. Add wine and stock, a little at a time, stirring well after each addition. Bring to a boil; then reduce heat, cover and simmer 20 minutes.

In a food processor or blender, puree soup (in batches, if necessary); return soup to pan. Over low heat, stir in 1/2 cup cream, then add salt and pepper.

Transfer to warmed soup bowls. Swirl 1 tablespoon cream atop each bowlful; garnish with parsley sprigs.

Makes 4 servings.

Note: Button mushrooms give this soup a good color. If wild mushrooms are available, include some of them, too; they'll add a superior flavor. Fairy rings, morels, and meadow or horse mushrooms are good choices.

If possible, use mushroom stock for this soup; otherwise, use vegetable or chicken stock.

Carrot Soup with Croûtons

2 tablespoons butter
1 small onion, finely chopped
1 pound carrots, sliced
1 (2-inch) piece fresh gingerroot,
    chopped
3-3/4 cups chicken stock
1 bay leaf
Pinch of freshly grated nutmeg
1/3 cup whipping cream
3 tablespoons brandy
Salt and pepper to taste

Mushroom Croûtons:
1/4 cup butter, room temperature
3 ounces mushrooms, finely chopped
2 teaspoons finely chopped parsley
1/2 small garlic clove, pressed or
    minced
8 slices French bread

To Garnish:
Cilantro or parsley sprigs

In a large saucepan, melt butter; add onion and sauté about 5 minutes or until softened and golden. Add carrots and ginger and cook 2 to 3 minutes. Pour in stock and bring to a boil; add bay leaf and nutmeg. Reduce heat, cover and simmer 20 to 25 minutes or until carrots are soft. Remove bay leaf.

In a food processor or blender, puree soup (in batches, if necessary); return soup to pan. Over low heat, stir in cream, brandy, salt and pepper.

To make croûtons, mix room-temperature butter, mushrooms, parsley and garlic in a small bowl. Toast bread on one side only; turn slices over and spread other sides with mushroom butter. Just before serving, toast slices under the broiler until hot and golden.

Serve soup in warmed wide soup bowls; float 2 croûtons on each serving and garnish with cilantro or parsley sprigs.

Makes 4 servings.

Note: The soup may be prepared in advance and reheated; the croûtons may be spread with mushroom butter, then toasted at the last minute.

Crab, Corn & Mushroom Soup

3-3/4 cups chicken stock
1 (1-inch) piece fresh gingerroot,
    coarsely chopped
2 green onions, coarsely chopped
About 1 cup cooked corn kernels
3 tablespoons peanut oil
4 ounces button mushrooms,
    quartered
6 ounces lump crabmeat, flaked into
    small pieces
2 eggs, lightly beaten
Salt and pepper to taste

To Garnish:
Fresh cilantro leaves

In a large saucepan, combine stock, ginger and green onions. Bring to a boil; then reduce heat, cover and simmer 15 minutes.

Meanwhile, in a food processor or blender, smoothly puree half the corn kernels.

Strain stock; discard ginger and onions.

In same pan, heat oil; add mushrooms and sauté 2 minutes or until softened. Stir in remaining corn kernels, corn puree and strained stock. Bring to a boil; then reduce heat and simmer, uncovered, 10 minutes.

Just before serving, stir in crabmeat and bring to a gentle simmer. Pour in beaten eggs in a slow stream, stirring constantly; add salt and pepper.

Serve in warmed soup bowls, garnished with cilantro.

Makes 4 servings.

Note: This soup may be prepared in advance up to the point when the crab and eggs are added.

Chicken Soup, Chinese Style

5 dried shiitake mushrooms
3 cups chicken stock (use strong
    stock)
2 slices plus 1/4 teaspoon finely
    chopped fresh gingerroot
2 cilantro sprigs
1 (4-inch) piece lemon grass
Pinch of sugar
2 green onions, shredded
2 teaspoons soy sauce
2 tablespoons dry sherry or rice wine
4 ounces cooked chicken, cut or torn
    into small strips
Szechuan pepper to taste (see *Note*)

Place mushrooms in a small bowl; cover with warm water and let soak 20 minutes. Drain, reserving soaking liquid. Rinse mushrooms well; trim off tough stems and slice caps. Set aside.

In a large saucepan, combine stock, mushroom liquid, ginger slices, cilantro sprigs, lemon grass and sugar. Bring to a boil; then reduce heat,

cover and simmer 30 minutes. Strain through a fine sieve; discard ginger, cilantro and lemon grass. Return stock to pan and add mushrooms, chopped ginger and remaining ingredients. Bring to a boil; then reduce heat, cover and simmer 10 minutes. Adjust seasoning. Serve piping hot, in warmed soup bowls.

Makes 4 servings.

Note: You can buy Szechuan peppercorns—tiny, pungent-tasting, reddish-brown berries—in Asian markets and well-stocked supermarkets. Before using the peppercorns, bring out their flavor by toasting them in a dry frying pan over medium-high heat 5 minutes. Then grind, using a mortar and pestle.

Potato & Mushroom Soup

3 tablespoons butter
1 onion, finely chopped
1-1/2 pounds potatoes, peeled, cut
    into 1/2-inch cubes
2 bacon slices, diced
12 ounces brown or chestnut
    mushrooms, quartered
3-3/4 cups beef or chicken stock
1-1/4 cups whole or extra-rich milk
Sprinkling of freshly grated nutmeg
Salt and pepper to taste

To Garnish:
Crumbled crisp-cooked bacon
Snipped chives

In a large saucepan, melt butter; add onion and sauté about 5 minutes or until pale golden. Stir in potatoes, diced bacon and mushrooms; cook 1 minute. Add stock, milk and nutmeg. Bring to a boil; reduce heat, cover and simmer 20 minutes or until potatoes are soft, stirring occasionally.

In a food processor or blender, puree half the soup; then return to remaining soup in pan. Season with salt and pepper.

Pour into warmed soup bowls; garnish with crumbled bacon and chives.

Makes 6 servings.

Chilled Fruit Soup

6 ounces red currants
6 ounces black currants
6 ounces cranberries
1/2 cup sugar
1-1/2 cups medium-dry white wine
1 (2-inch) cinnamon stick
Finely grated peel and juice of 1 orange
1-1/4 cups water
1 tablespoon crème de cassis liqueur
2/3 cup dairy sour cream
TO DECORATE:
Black currant leaves, if desired

1. In a large saucepan, combine currants, cranberries, sugar, wine, cinnamon stick, orange peel and juice and water. Bring to a boil, lower heat and cook gently 15 minutes, until fruit is tender.
2. Discard cinnamon stick. Puree mixture in a blender or food processor, then press through a nylon sieve into a bowl to remove seeds. Cool, then chill 1-1/2 hours.

3. Stir crème de cassis into chilled soup. Pour into 4 to 6 chilled bowls. Carefully add a spoonful of sour cream to each bowl of soup. Use a skewer to feather sour cream in an attractive pattern. Serve immediately, decorated with black currant leaves, if desired.

Makes 4 to 6 servings.

Watercress Soup with Marigolds

2/3 cup garbanzo beans
3 thyme sprigs
3 tablespoons olive oil
1 leek, finely chopped
2 zucchini, cubed
1 carrot, sliced
2 tablespoons finely chopped
   parsley
4-1/2 cups chicken stock
3 cups finely chopped watercress

To Garnish:
3 marigold flowers

Put garbanzo beans in a bowl, cover with cold water and let soak 2 hours. Put into a large saucepan with soaking liquid and thyme. Add water to cover beans by about 4 inches. Bring to a boil and boil steadily 10 minutes. Lower heat, cover pan and simmer 30 to 40 minutes or until soft. Drain beans and discard thyme.

In another saucepan, heat oil. Add leek, zucchini, carrot, parsley and beans. Cover and cook over gentle heat 10 minutes to soften vegetables. Pour on chicken stock and simmer 15 to 20 minutes or until vegetables are tender. Add watercress.

Puree soup in a blender or food processor until smooth. If too thick, thin with a little hot chicken stock.

Serve immediately, garnished with marigold petals.

Makes 6 servings.

Potato & Herb Soup

1 tablespoon butter
1-1/2 lbs. potatoes, cubed
1-3/4 cups chicken stock
1-3/4 cups milk
Salt and pepper to taste
1 egg yolk, if desired
1/4 cup finely chopped mixed
   seasonal herbs
1 tablespoon whipping cream, if
   desired

To Garnish:
Parsley sprigs or other herbs

In a large saucepan, melt butter over low heat. Add potatoes, cover and let stand 5 minutes to allow potatoes to absorb butter.

In another saucepan, heat chicken stock and milk; pour over potatoes and season with salt and pepper. Simmer gently, stirring occasionally, about 15 minutes or until potatoes are cooked.

The soup is equally good served hot or chilled. If it is to be served hot, return to pan and reheat gently. Beat egg yolk in a soup tureen, then gradually add hot soup. Sprinkle with chopped herbs and swirl in cream, if desired. Garnish with herbs and serve immediately.

If soup is to be chilled, pour into a tureen and chill until required. Add cream, if desired, and herbs just before serving.

Makes 4 servings.

Note: Use four or five different herbs, including a balance between the sharper varieties such as thyme, and mellower flavors—basil and parsley—for example.

White Stilton & Leek Soup

3 leeks, about 12 ounces total, thinly
  sliced
1 small potato, diced
3 cups homemade chicken stock
4 ounces white Stilton cheese,
  crumbled
Pepper, to taste
2 tablespoons half and half

To Garnish:
Parsley sprigs or a few reserved leek
  rings

Put leeks into a large saucepan with
potato and stock and cook about 20
minutes or until vegetables are soft.

Puree vegetables and stock in a
blender or food processor fitted with
the metal blade until smooth. Return
soup to pan and add Stilton. Heat
gently, stirring constantly or until

cheese melts; season with pepper.

Divide soup among individual
bowls and spoon over a little cream.
Create a feathered effect using a
wooden pick or a small skewer. Garnish each portion with parsley sprigs,
or leek rings (see note).

Makes 4 to 6 servings.

Note: It is important to use a good
homemade stock as bouillon cubes
are not suitable for this recipe.

To garnish with leek rings it is important to blanch the leek first, otherwise the flavor will be too strong: add
to boiling water, leave 2 minutes,
drain, then refresh under cold running water.

Cheese & Artichoke Chowder

2 tablespoons butter
1 small onion, sliced
1 pound Jerusalem artichokes, sliced
  into water with 1 tablespoon lemon
  juice added
8 ounces carrots, sliced
5 teaspoons all-purpose flour
2-1/2 cups chicken or vegetable stock
1-1/4 cups milk
8 ounces Gruyère cheese, shredded
  (2 cups)
1/2 teaspoon dry mustard
Salt and pepper, to taste

Julienne Garnish:
1 Jerusalem artichoke
1 carrot
1 leek
Chervil leaves

In a large saucepan, melt butter, add
onion and cook 1 minute, stirring

constantly. Drain artichokes; add to
pan with carrots. Cook 2 minutes.
Add flour, then gradually add stock.
Cover and simmer 20 minutes.

Meanwhile, prepare julienne garnish. Cut artichoke, carrot and green
part of the leek into julienne strips.
Blanch in boiling water 1 minute; refresh in cold water and set aside.

Blend soup in a blender or food
processor fitted with the metal blade
until smooth. Add milk, cheese and
seasonings and blend again. Pour
into a clean pan and reheat gently; do
not boil.

Pour into individual soup bowls
and garnish with the prepared vegetables and chervil leaves.

Makes 4 servings.

Tarator Soup

2/3 cup walnut pieces
2 garlic cloves
2 tablespoons olive oil
1-1/4 cups milk
1-1/4 cups plain yogurt
Salt and pepper, to taste
1/4 cucumber
TO GARNISH:
Dill sprigs

1. Put walnuts and garlic in a food processor fitted with the metal blade and process until finely chopped.
2. With motor running, gradually add oil through the feed tube until a smooth puree forms. Pour in milk and process until smooth. Put yogurt in a large bowl. Gradually pour in blended mixture, stirring until thoroughly mixed. Season with salt and pepper to taste.
3. Peel and chop cucumber; stir into soup and refrigerate 2 hours. Pour into individual soup bowls and garnish with dill.

Makes 4 servings.

Variation: Replace walnut pieces with hazelnuts.

Cashew & Fennel Soup

4 white bread slices, crusts removed
2/3 cup water
1 cup cashews
1 to 2 garlic cloves
3 tablespoons lemon juice
1-3/4 cups milk
Salt and pepper, to taste
2 tablespoons chopped fennel
CROÛTONS:
2 white bread slices, crusts removed
Vegetable oil

1. Put bread in a medium-size bowl and add 2/3 cup water; let soften 5 minutes. Put cashews in a food processor fitted with the metal blade and chop finely. Add soaked bread and water, garlic to taste, lemon juice, 3/4 cup milk and seasoning; process until smooth, then turn into a bowl.
2. Stir in remaining milk and fennel, cover and refrigerate 1 hour.
3. To make croûtons, cut bread into 1/4-inch cubes. Heat oil in a small skillet and fry bread, turning occasionally, until pale golden-brown. Remove with a slotted spoon and drain on paper towels. Pour soup into individual soup bowls and sprinkle with croûtons to serve.

Makes 4 servings.

Chestnut & Madeira Soup

2 carrots
1 onion
2 celery stalks
1 tablespoon vegetable oil
1 tablespoon all-purpose flour
3 cups vegetable or chicken stock
1 bouquet garni
2 chervil sprigs
Salt and pepper, to taste
1 pound peeled, cooked chestnuts, sieved
2/3 cup half and half
1/3 cup medium-dry sherry
TO SERVE:
3 tablespoons half and half
Chervil sprigs
Croûtons

1. Dice the carrots, onion and celery. In a medium-size saucepan, heat oil and cook onion until softened. Stir in flour, then add celery, carrots, stock, bouquet garni, chervil and seasoning. Bring to a boil, stirring, then cover, reduce heat and simmer gently 20 minutes, until vegetables are tender.
2. Remove bouquet garni. Pour into a blender or food processor fitted with the metal blade and process until smooth; return half to saucepan. Add sieved chestnuts and half and half to remaining soup in blender or food processor and process until smooth.

3. Pour into the saucepan with sherry and simmer 5 minutes, until heated ·hrough. Pour into individual soup bowls and swirl a little half and half into each one. Garnish with chervil and serve with croûtons.

Makes 6 servings.

Note: A 15-1/2-ounce can unsweetened chestnut puree can be used instead of fresh chestnuts.

Bouquet garni: 1 sprig each of thyme and parsley and 1 bay leaf tied in cheesecloth.

Iced Avocado Soup

1 tablespoon sunflower oil
6 green onions, thinly sliced
4 teaspoons all-purpose flour
1-3/4 cups chicken stock
2 ripe avocados
2 teaspoons lemon juice
1-3/4 cups milk
2/3 cup dairy sour cream
Salt and white pepper to taste
2 good pinches red (cayenne) pepper
TO GARNISH:
Dairy sour cream
Chives

1. In a medium-size saucepan, heat oil. Add green onions and sauté 2 minutes, stirring frequently. Stir in flour and cook 1 minute, then gradually stir in stock and bring to a boil, stirring constantly. Reduce heat and simmer gently 10 minutes; cool.
2. Cut avocados in half, peel and remove seeds. Slice off a little for garnishing, brush with 1 teaspoon of lemon juice and set aside. Cut up remaining avocados. In a blender or food processor fitted with the metal blade, process avocados and cooled

sauce mixture until smooth.
3. Add remaining lemon juice, milk and sour cream and blend thoroughly to combine. Season with salt and white pepper and red pepper and mix well. Chill at least 2 hours before serving.

Pour into 4 individual serving bowls and garnish each with sour cream, reserved slivers of avocado and a few chives.

Makes 4 servings.

Spiced Pumpkin Soup

1-1/2 pounds pumpkin
1 (1-inch) piece gingerroot
2 tablespoons butter
1 large Spanish onion, chopped
1/4 teaspoon garam masala
1 tablespoon all-purpose flour
2-1/2 cups chicken or vegetable stock
Salt and pepper to taste
1 tablespoon snipped chives
1 tablespoon chopped cilantro
1/4 cup half and half
TO GARNISH:
Sprigs of cilantro

Fava Bean Soup Gratinée

1 tablespoon olive oil
3 tablespoons butter
1 garlic clove, crushed
1 Spanish onion, halved and sliced
3 large lettuce leaves, shredded
1 tablespoon all-purpose flour
2-1/2 cups chicken stock
1 pound shelled fava beans
Salt and pepper to taste
4 slices French bread, about 1 inch thick
1-1/2 teaspoons Dijon-style mustard
1 cup shredded Gruyère cheese (4 oz.)
TO GARNISH:
Snipped chives

1. Cut unpeeled pumpkin in even pieces; remove seeds. Place pumpkin in a steamer, cover and steam about 30 minutes or until tender. Cool slightly, then scrape away pulp from skin and mash well or puree in a blender or food processor fitted with the metal blade.
2. Peel gingerroot and chop very finely. In a large saucepan, melt butter. Add onion and fry gently 5 minutes. Stir in gingerroot and garam masala and cook 2 minutes, stirring constantly. Add flour and cook 1 minute. Gradually stir in stock and bring to a boil, stirring constantly. Reduce heat, then add pumpkin and season with salt and pepper.
3. Cover and simmer gently 10 minutes. Stir in herbs and half and half. Remove from heat and adjust seasoning, if necessary. Serve hot, garnished with cilantro sprigs.

Makes 4 to 6 servings.

Note: This soup is also good served garnished with toasted pumpkin seeds or finely shredded Cheddar cheese.

1. In a large saucepan, heat oil and 2 tablespoons of butter. Add garlic, onion and lettuce and sauté 3 minutes, stirring frequently. Stir in flour and cook 1 minute. Stir in 1-1/4 cups of stock and bring to a boil, stirring frequently. Reduce heat and add fava beans. Cover and simmer 25 minutes.
2. In a blender or food processor fitted with the metal blade, process 1/2 of mixture until smooth; return to pan. Repeat with remaining mixture. Stir in remaining stock and season with salt and pepper. Reheat, stirring constantly, until piping hot. Transfer to 4 individual flameproof soup bowls and place on a broiler pan. Preheat broiler.
3. Spread French bread with remaining butter and mustard and press down into soup. Sprinkle with cheese and broil under preheated broiler 6 to 8 minutes, until golden and melted. Sprinkle with chives and serve immediately.

Makes 4 servings.

Note: For a chunky soup, puree 1/2 of mixture only in step 2. For a thinner soup, add a little extra stock.

Clam Chowder

3/4 cup dry white wine
2 pounds small clams in shells
2 tablespoons butter
3 bacon slices, diced
2 leeks, shredded
2 celery stalks, thinly sliced
1 pound potatoes, peeled, chopped
1 cup milk
1/2 cup whipping cream
2 tablespoons chopped parsley
Salt and pepper, to taste
TO SERVE:
Garlic Croûtons (see below)

1. Put wine and 1 cup water in a large saucepan. Add clams, cover tightly and cook over high heat 3 to 4 minutes, until shells have opened. Drain, reserving liquid; discard any clams that have not opened. Remove clams from shells and set aside.
2. In a large saucepan, melt butter, add bacon and fry until lightly colored. Add leeks and celery and fry 5 minutes. Add potatoes and strain clam cooking liquid into pan. Bring to a boil, cover and simmer about 20 minutes, until potatoes are tender.
3. Add milk, cream, parsley, clams, salt and pepper and simmer 5 minutes. Serve with Garlic Croûtons, as a light meal.

Makes 4 servings.

Garlic Croûtons: Fry 1/2-inch cubes of crustless white bread in hot oil flavored with a crushed garlic clove until crisp and golden. Drain on paper towels.

Fisherman's Soup

2 pounds mussels, cleaned
2 cups dry white wine
2 tablespoons butter
1 leek, white part only, chopped
1 pound tomatoes, peeled, seeded and chopped
Strip of lemon peel
1 pound sea scallops
Salt and pepper, to taste
4 ounces peeled shrimp, thawed if frozen
1/4 cup whipping cream
2 tablespoons chopped fresh mixed herbs (e.g., fennel, chives, tarragon, dill)

1. Put mussels into a large saucepan with wine and 1 cup water. Cover and cook over high heat, shaking pan, 3 to 4 minutes, until shells have opened; drain, reserving cooking liquid. Discard any that have not opened. Remove mussels from shells and set aside.
2. In a large saucepan, melt butter, add leek and cook gently about 5 minutes, until softened. Add tomatoes, lemon peel, half the scallops and 1/2 cup reserved cooking liquid. Bring to a boil, reduce heat, then simmer 10 minutes; remove lemon peel. Transfer mixture to a blender or food processor and purée until smooth.
3. Return purée to a clean pan and add remaining cooking liquid. Bring to a boil and season with salt and pepper. Detach corals, if present, from remaining scallops and cut the white part of each scallop into 4 pieces. Add scallops, corals, shrimp and mussels to the pan and simmer 5 minutes. Just before serving, stir in cream and herbs and warm through.

Makes 4 servings.

Variation: Replace mussels with clams.

Appetizers

Smoked Salmon Pâté

9 ounces smoked salmon, thinly
**   sliced**
5 tablespoons butter
9 ounces button mushrooms, sliced
About 1/3 cup yogurt or dairy sour
**   cream**
1-1/2 teaspoons lemon juice
2 teaspoons chopped fresh chervil
Salt and pepper to taste

To Garnish:
Chervil sprigs
Lemon slices

To Serve:
Melba toast or other crisp crackers

Using two-thirds of the salmon slices, line bottoms and sides of 4 (1/2-cup) ramekins. Set aside. Coarsely chop remaining salmon.

In a large saucepan, melt butter. Add mushrooms; sauté about 5 minutes or until soft. Transfer to a food processor or blender and let cool; then add chopped salmon and puree until mixture is smooth. Transfer to a bowl and fold in yogurt or sour cream, lemon juice, chopped chervil, salt and pepper.

Divide pâté among prepared ramekins, folding any overhanging salmon slices over top. Cover each ramekin with plastic wrap and chill at least 1 hour.

To serve, turn out salmon-wrapped pâté onto serving plates and garnish with chervil sprigs and lemon slices. Serve with melba toast.

Makes 4 servings.

Oyster Mushroom Beignets

Vegetable oil for deep-frying
1 pound oyster mushrooms

Tangy Dip:
2/3 cup dairy sour cream
1 tablespoon lemon juice
1/2 garlic clove, pressed or minced
1 teaspoon honey
1/4 cup finely chopped fresh lemon
**   balm or mint**
Salt and pepper to taste

Beer Batter:
1 cup all-purpose flour
1/2 teaspoon salt
2 eggs, separated
2/3 cup beer
2 tablespoons olive oil

To Garnish:
Lemon balm or mint sprigs

Prepare dip by mixing all dip ingredients in a small bowl; set aside. To prepare batter, sift flour and salt into a bowl; add egg yolks, then gradually whisk in beer to form a smooth batter. Stir in oil. In a clean bowl, whisk egg whites until they hold soft peaks; then fold into batter.

In a deep, heavy saucepan, heat 3 or 4 inches of oil to 350F (175C). Dip mushrooms into batter to coat; lower into hot oil, a few at a time (do not crowd pan). Cook 2 to 3 minutes or until crisp and golden. Drain on paper towels and keep hot while cooking remaining mushrooms.

Spoon dip into a small serving bowl; garnish with lemon balm or mint sprigs. Serve beignets with dip.

Makes 4 servings.

Variation: Substitute button mushrooms or chanterelles in place of oyster mushrooms.

Bagna Cauda

1-1/4 cups whipping cream
3 garlic cloves, pressed or minced
2 (2-oz.) cans anchovy fillets, drained, chopped
1/4 cup unsalted butter, cut into pieces

To Garnish:
Parsley sprigs

To Serve:
Whole button mushrooms
Radishes
Cubes of crusty bread

In a small saucepan, combine cream, garlic and anchovy fillets. Bring to a boil; then reduce heat and simmer gently, uncovered, 12 to 15 minutes or until smooth and thickened. Add butter; stir until melted.

Transfer to a serving dish and garnish with parsley sprigs. Serve with mushrooms, radishes and bread cubes for dipping.

Makes 4 servings.

Note: This dish comes from the Piedmont region of Northern Italy, where it was traditionally served as a dip for cardoon, a locally grown edible thistle. I think it is superb with firm white button mushrooms. Keep the dip hot at the table over a candle or alcohol flame.

Marinated Mushrooms

6 tablespoons virgin olive oil
1 teaspoon coriander seeds, lightly crushed
1/2 teaspoon cracked bay leaves
1 pound whole large cultivated or button mushrooms
Finely grated peel of 1/2 lime
Juice of 1 lime
1 garlic clove, pressed or minced
2 tablespoons white wine or cider vinegar
Pinch of sugar
Salt and pepper to taste

To Garnish:
1 tablespoon chopped parsley
Lime slices
Parsley sprigs

To Serve:
Crusty French bread

In a large saucepan, heat 3 tablespoons oil. Add coriander seeds and cook 1 minute. Stir in bay leaves and mushrooms; cook over low heat 5 to 7 minutes or until mushrooms are just tender. Remove from heat and add lime peel, lime juice, garlic, vinegar, sugar, salt and pepper. Mix well, then transfer to a shallow bowl and let cool. Cover and chill at least 2 hours.

Adjust seasoning. Garnish mushrooms with chopped parsley, lime slices and parsley sprigs. Serve with crusty French bread.

Makes 4 servings.

Variation: To give the dish a hint of anise flavor, substitute fennel seeds for coriander seeds.

Quail Eggs on a Nest

Chicory leaves
1/4 cup walnut oil
1/2 garlic clove, pressed or minced
4 very large (about 4-inch-diameter) cultivated mushrooms
12 uncooked quail eggs (available at some gourmet markets)
3 bacon slices, cut into short, thin strips
1 tablespoon plus 2 teaspoons white wine vinegar
Salt and pepper to taste

To Garnish:
2 teaspoons snipped chives
Whole chives

Line 4 individual serving plates with chicory; set aside. In a large nonstick frying pan, heat 2 tablespoons oil; add garlic and mushrooms. Cook over low heat about 5 minutes or until mushrooms are just tender. Place one mushroom, stalk side up, atop chicory on each plate.

Add remaining 2 tablespoons oil to pan. When oil is hot, add quail eggs, in 4 batches; cook each batch about 30 seconds. Carefully arrange eggs over mushrooms.

Add bacon to pan and cook over medium-high heat until crisp. Deglaze pan with vinegar, stirring to scrape up browned bits; season with salt and pepper.

Pour hot dressing equally over salads and sprinkle with snipped chives; add a few whole chives alongside each mushroom "nest." Serve immediately.

Makes 4 servings.

Morels & Oysters in Brioches

4 small brioches (available at many bakeries)
6 ounces fresh morels
1/4 cup butter
1/2 small onion, finely chopped
1/4 cup dry white wine
3/4 cup whipping cream
6 freshly shucked oysters, halved
1 teaspoon cornstarch blended with 2 teaspoons water
2 to 3 teaspoons lemon juice
Salt and pepper to taste

To Garnish:
Assorted salad greens

Preheat oven to 325F (160C).

Cut tops from brioches; carefully hollow out each brioche (you can reserve the centers to make bread crumbs). Place brioches and tops on a baking sheet and set aside.

To prepare morels, slice in half lengthwise and place in a bowl of salted water. Let soak 15 minutes, then rinse carefully. Blanch in boiling water 2 minutes; drain.

In a medium-size saucepan, melt butter; add onion and sauté 2 minutes or until softened. Stir in wine and mushrooms and cook, stirring, over high heat until almost all liquid has evaporated. Add cream and oysters. Reduce heat; cook until edges of oysters just begin to curl and cream is almost boiling. Stir in cornstarch mixture; cook, stirring, until thickened. Add lemon juice, salt and pepper.

Divide mixture among brioches. Set brioche tops in place and bake 15 to 20 minutes or until hot. Serve immediately, garnished with salad greens.

Makes 4 servings.

Variation: Cultivated mushrooms can be used in place of morels. Cut into quarters or slices before cooking.

Chèvre & Mushroom Croustades

5 ounces wild mushrooms (see *Note*)
1 to 2 teaspoons sesame oil
2 tablespoons butter
2 cups fresh white bread crumbs
1 tablespoon plus 1 to 2 teaspoons
    sesame seeds
6 ounces soft chèvre (goat cheese)
1 tablespoon finely chopped
    sun-dried tomatoes (see *Note*)
1 tablespoon chopped fresh basil
1 tablespoon virgin olive oil

To Garnish:
Fresh basil leaves
Assorted salad greens

Preheat oven to 400F (205C). Chop mushrooms coarsely unless they are very small; set aside. Brush 4 (3- to 4-inch) tartlet pans with sesame oil and set aside.

In a small saucepan, melt butter; stir in crumbs and 1 tablespoon sesame seeds. Divide crumb mixture evenly among tartlet pans, pressing it firmly against pan bottoms and sides. Bake 12 to 15 minutes or until pale golden and crisp.

Meanwhile, in a small bowl, mix chèvre, sun-dried tomatoes and

chopped basil; set aside.

In a small frying pan, heat olive oil; add mushrooms and sauté 1 minute. Reserve a few mushrooms for garnish, then divide the rest equally among baked croustade shells. Top with chèvre mixture, spreading it evenly to fill shells. Top with reserved mushrooms and sprinkle with remaining 1 to 2 teaspoons sesame seeds. Return to oven; bake 10 minutes or until filling is hot.

Serve hot or warm, garnished with basil sprigs and salad greens.

Makes 4 servings.

Note: Use chanterelles, fairy rings, horse mushrooms, cepes (porcini), oyster mushrooms or a mixture of wild mushrooms; or use sliced button mushrooms.

Sun-dried tomatoes are available in many delicatessens and gourmet food shops. They're sold in jars, preserved in olive oil, with or without salt. For this recipe, unsalted tomatoes are best.

Ravioli with Three Cheeses

12 flat-leaf parsley leaves
2 tablespoons butter, melted
1 to 2 tablespoons freshly grated
    Parmesan cheese

Egg Pasta:
1 cup all-purpose flour
1 egg
1 teaspoon olive oil
Pinch of salt

Cheese Filling:
1 ounce dried cepes (porcini)
6 tablespoons ricotta cheese
3 ounces smoked mozzarella or
    provolone cheese, finely chopped
2 tablespoons whipping cream
Pepper to taste

To make pasta, sift flour onto a work surface. Make a well in center; add egg, oil and salt and beat with a fork to blend. Gradually work flour into egg mixture; then knead together, adding a little water if dough seems dry. On lightly floured work surface, knead dough at least 5 minutes or

until smooth and elastic. Wrap in plastic wrap and set aside 1 hour.

To make filling, place cepes in a small bowl; cover with warm water and let soak 20 minutes. Drain; rinse well to remove any grit. Chop coarsely, place in a clean small bowl, and mix in cheeses, cream and pepper.

On a lightly floured surface, roll out dough paper-thin; cut into 24 squares. Divide filling among 12 squares and place a parsley leaf on each; cover with remaining pasta squares. Parsley should be visible through pasta. Press edges of each ravioli to seal; trim edges, then crimp with a fork. Let stand 10 minutes to dry slightly before cooking.

Cook in a large saucepan of boiling salted water 3 minutes; drain well. Allow 3 ravioli per person; drizzle with butter and sprinkle with Parmesan cheese.

Makes 4 servings.

Goat Cheese with Mint

6 ozs. goat cheese
1/3 cup milk
1 tablespoon olive oil
1 teaspoon lemon juice
1/2 red bell pepper, seeded
4 teaspoons chopped mint
Salt and pepper to taste

To Garnish:
Mint sprigs

To Serve:
Crackers, if desired

Press goat cheese through a nylon sieve into a bowl. Add milk, oil and lemon juice and blend well until mixture is smooth and creamy. Cut bell pepper in thin strips 2 inches long. Fold into cheese mixture with chopped mint. Season with salt and pepper.

Mold cheese mixture into a flat round 6-inch dish. Place on a serving plate, cover with plastic wrap and chill at least 4 hours to allow flavors to mingle.

Uncover cheese and garnish with mint sprigs. Serve with crackers, if desired.

Makes 4 servings.

Note: A delicious starter which may alternatively be served at end of meal in place of cheese.

For a more decorative effect, mold cheese in a heart or diamond shape.

Prosciutto & Sage Crespellini

4 slices prosciutto, cut in half
8 large sage leaves
2 eggs
3/4 cup all-purpose flour
Pinch salt
1/3 cup milk
Vegetable oil for frying

Wine Sauce:
1/4 cup butter
1 tablespoon all-purpose flour
1/3 cup white wine
Salt and pepper to taste
4 teaspoons whipping cream
3 tablespoons grated Parmesan cheese

Tomato Sauce:
2 teaspoons olive oil
8 ozs. tomatoes, skinned, seeded, chopped
1 garlic clove, crushed
Salt and pepper to taste

To make crespellini, mix eggs, flour, salt and milk in a blender or food processor. Chill 1 to 2 hours.

Heat oil in a crepe pan. Using 2 tablespoons batter, tilt pan to spread batter. Cook on both sides. Makes 8 crespellini.

To make wine sauce, melt butter. Add flour and cook, stirring, 1 to 2 minutes to form a roux. Add warm wine, stirring. Season and simmer 20 minutes, stirring occasionally. Remove from heat and stir in cream and Parmesan.

Meanwhile, prepare tomato sauce. Heat oil and add remaining ingredients. Simmer 15 to 20 minutes.

Preheat oven to 350F (175C). Cover bottom of a baking dish with a thin layer of wine sauce. Place a half slice of prosciutto, a sage leaf and 2 teaspoons tomato sauce on each crespellini. Fold over and place in baking dish. Pour over remaining wine sauce and bake 15 minutes.

Makes 4 servings.

Gail's Artichokes

4 artichokes
1 lemon

Bread Crumb Stuffing:
1 cup dried bread crumbs
1/2 cup grated Parmesan cheese
4 teaspoons caraway seeds
1/2 teaspoon salt

Shrimp Stuffing:
1/3 cup olive oil
6 ozs. shrimp, peeled, deveined,
  chopped
1 shallot, finely sliced
2 teaspoons capers
1 tablespoon chopped parsley

To Garnish:
Parsley sprigs

Wash artichokes thoroughly in several changes of water; drain. Trim leaves and scoop out choke, rub cut surfaces with lemon.

To prepare bread crumb stuffing, mix together bread crumbs, Parmesan cheese, caraway seeds and salt.

To prepare shrimp stuffing, in a small saucepan, heat 1 tablespoon oil and fry shrimp, shallot, capers and parsley a few minutes.

Put a spoonful of shrimp stuffing in the center of each artichoke; fill gaps between leaves with bread crumb stuffing. Put artichokes in a saucepan large enough to hold them tightly in a single layer. Pour over remaining olive oil. Add 1 inch of water, cover pan tightly and cook 1-1/4 hours or until artichokes are tender.

Carefully lift out artichokes. Drain thoroughly and serve immediately, garnished with parsley sprigs.

Makes 4 servings.

Variation: Aniseed or fennel seeds may be used instead of caraway seeds.

Chicken Livers & Fennel

2 tablespoons butter
1 small fennel bulb, thinly sliced
2 shallots, finely chopped
8 ozs. chicken livers, each cut in
  4 to 6 pieces
2 teaspoons dry sherry
1 tablespoon chopped walnuts
Salt and pepper to taste
2 teaspoons chopped fennel
  leaves

Croûtes:
4 thin slices bread, crusts
  removed
Melted butter

To Garnish:
Fennel leaves

Preheat oven to 375F (190C).

To prepare croûtes, cut bread in half diagonally. Brush both sides with melted butter. Place on a baking sheet and bake in oven about 10 minutes, until golden.

Meanwhile, in a skillet, melt butter. Add fennel and shallots and saute until fennel is beginning to brown. Remove vegetables with a slotted spoon and keep warm.

Add chicken livers to skillet and cook about 4 minutes—they should remain pink inside. Push to one side of pan. Add sherry and stir into cooking juices, then cook rapidly about 1 minute. Lower heat and return fennel and shallots to pan. Add walnuts and stir in chicken livers, seasoning and chopped fennel leaves.

Spoon chicken livers and fennel onto croûtes and serve immediately, garnished with fennel leaves.

Makes 4 servings.

Note: If fennel leaves are unavailable, use feathery tops of fennel bulb or substitute dill weed.

Danish Dip

2/3 cup half and half
2/3 cup dry white wine
2 egg yolks
4 ounces Danish blue cheese, coarsely
crumbled
2 teaspoons finely chopped dill weed

To Garnish:
Dill sprigs

To Serve:
Selection of raw vegetables, including
julienne strips of carrot, red and
yellow bell peppers and zucchini;
celery sticks; cauliflowerets; and
blanched asparagus spears

In a bowl, blend together half and half and wine; immediately beat in egg yolks. Stir in cheese. Pour into the top section of a double boiler set over barely simmering water. Cook a few minutes, stirring constantly or until thick and smooth. Remove from heat and stir in dill weed. Let cool. Pour into a serving dish, cover and chill until required.

To serve, place the dish of cheese dip in the center of a serving platter, garnish with dill and surround with prepared vegetables.

Makes 1-1/4 cups.

Horseradish Dip

1/2 cup fromage frais or plain yogurt
4 teaspoons prepared horseradish
1/4 teaspoon ground pepper
1/4 teaspoon garlic salt

To Serve:
Pretzels
Poppadums
Cheese Straws (see note)

In a bowl, blend together all the ingredients. Cover and refrigerate 3 to 4 hours for the flavors to develop, then pour into a serving dish. Accompany with pretzels, poppadums and Cheese Straws.

Makes 2/3 cup.

Note: To make cheese straws, roll out some ready-made puff pastry on a lightly floured surface. Using a sharp knife, cut into finger-size rectangles. Brush with beaten egg and sprinkle with grated cheese and sesame, poppy or caraway seeds.

Put the pastry rectangles on a dampened baking sheet and bake in a preheated oven 400F (205C) about 10 minutes or until puffed and golden brown. Transfer the cheese straws to a wire rack to cool.

Avocado with Mascarpone

4 avocados, ripe but firm, halved
3 tablespoons freshly squeezed lemon
  juice
4 ounces mascarpone cheese
1 or 2 teaspoons French-style mustard
1 garlic clove, crushed
Few drops hot pepper sauce
Salt and pepper, to taste

To Garnish:
1/4 cup (1 oz.) sliced almonds
Parsley sprigs
Chive flowers (optional)

Carefully scoop out avocado using a teaspoon, making sure skins remain whole; set skins aside. Roughly chop the flesh, put into a bowl and sprinkle with 1 tablespoon of the lemon juice, to prevent discoloration.

In a separate bowl, blend cheese with mustard to taste, garlic and remaining lemon juice. Season with hot pepper sauce, salt and pepper. Add chopped avocado and mix in carefully. Pile into avocado shells and chill about 20 minutes.

Garnish with almonds, parsley and chive flowers if available, and serve in individual dishes.

Makes 8 servings.

Note: This tasty dish can be served, with French bread, as a light lunch for 4 people.

Chaource Mousse & Chive Sauce

4 large crisp lettuce leaves
1 teaspoon butter
1/4 cup chopped button mushrooms
1 celery stalk, very finely chopped
1 shallot, chopped
4 ounces chaource cheese, white rind
  removed, crumbled
3 tablespoons fromage frais or plain
  yogurt
2/3 cup cold chicken or vegetable
  stock
2-1/2 teaspoons gelatin powder,
  dissolved in 2 tablespoons stock
2 teaspoons snipped chives
2 teaspoons chopped parsley
Pinch of dry mustard
Salt and pepper, to taste

Sauce:
1 egg white
1 tablespoon crème fraîche
1 tablespoon snipped chives

To Garnish:
A few lettuce leaves
Carrot julienne
Melba toast

Put lettuce leaves into boiling water, then immediately into cold water. Drain on paper towels. Use to line 4 oiled ramekins.

In a small saucepan, melt butter, add mushrooms, celery and shallot and cook 1 minute. Remove from heat and set aside.

Put cheese, fromage frais and stock into a blender or food processor fitted with the metal blade and process until smooth. Slowly add dissolved gelatin and blend again. Stir in cooked vegetables, herbs and seasonings.

Spoon the mixture into prepared ramekins, arranging the leaves over the filling to enclose it. Chill until set.

Make sauce a few minutes before serving: in a small bowl, whisk egg white until soft peaks form, fold in crème fraîche and chives.

Turn the mousses onto 4 individual plates and spoon over a little sauce. Garnish with lettuce leaves and carrot. Serve with melba toast.

Makes 4 servings.

Grilled Chèvre with Walnuts

4 (3-oz.) chèvre slices
1/2 head chicory, broken into pieces
Few radicchio leaves, broken into pieces
1 head Belgium endive, cut diagonally into 1/2-inch slices
Handful of rocket leaves
1/4 cup (1 oz.) chopped walnuts

Dressing:
3 tablespoons walnut oil
2 teaspoons white wine vinegar
1/2 teaspoon honey
Salt and pepper, to taste

Place chèvre on a piece of oiled foil in a broiler pan. Preheat broiler.

Put chicory, radicchio, endive and rocket leaves in a bowl.

Put all dressing ingredients in a small jar with a lid and shake vigorously until blended. Pour over salad, toss thoroughly and arrange on 4 individual plates.

Put the chèvre under preheated broiler 1 to 2 minutes or until melting; place 1 slice on each salad.

Sprinkle with walnuts and serve immediately.

Makes 4 servings.

Note: Chèvre may also be bought in (6-1/2-oz.) rolls. Buy 2 rolls and cut them into 6 slices each. Serve 3 slices per person.

Baked Haloumi in Vine Leaves

8 ounces haloumi cheese
16 to 20 vine leaves, packed in brine
Olive oil

Sauce:
1 tablespoon cornstarch
1-1/4 cups tomato juice
2 teaspoons lemon juice
1/4 teaspoon ground pepper
1/4 teaspoon sugar
1/4 teaspoon ground thyme
1 teaspoon shredded basil leaves

To Garnish:
Basil leaves

Pat haloumi dry with paper towels and cut into 16 to 20 (1/2-inch) slices; divide into small bars and set aside.

Soak vine leaves in a large bowl of cold water 30 minutes to remove brine. Drain, then place one at a time into a large pan of boiling water and blanch 2 minutes. Drain and pat dry with paper towels.

Preheat oven to 450F (230C).

Brush a shallow ovenproof dish liberally with oil.

Place a piece of cheese near stalk end of each vine leaf; fold in sides and roll up to form small packets. Pack stuffed vine leaves closely together in a single layer in prepared dish. Brush generously with olive oil and bake 15 to 20 minutes or until crisp.

To make sauce, blend cornstarch with a little of the tomato juice, stir in remaining juice, then place all sauce ingredients in a heavy saucepan over medium heat. Whisk constantly until thickened.

Serve stuffed vine leaves hot on a pool of sauce, garnished with basil leaves.

Makes 8 to 10 servings.

Note: This dish can also be served with rice as a main course for 4 to 5 people.

Deep-Fried Cambazola

8 ounces firm cambazola (or similar
   blue brie type cheese)
1/2 cup all-purpose flour
Salt and pepper, to taste
2 eggs
1/2 cup dry bread crumbs
Vegetable oil for deep-frying

To Garnish:
4 plums, sliced

To Serve:
1/2 cup Chinese plum sauce

Using a small sharp knife, remove
white rind and cut cheese into 3/4-
inch cubes.

Season flour with salt and pepper.
Beat eggs in one bowl; put bread
crumbs in another.

Dip cheese cubes in seasoned flour,
coating each piece well; shake off excess. Next dip in beaten eggs, then
bread crumbs to coat well, firmly pat-
ting them into place. Refrigerate 20
minutes.

Fill a deep-fryer one-third full with
vegetable oil and heat to 360F (180C)
or until a 1-inch bread cube turns
golden brown in 1 minute. Using a
slotted spoon, carefully lower cheese
cubes one at a time into hot oil; do not
overfill pan—cook cubes in batches.
Deep-fry 3 to 4 minutes or until gold-
en brown; remove with a slotted
spoon and drain on paper towels.
Serve immediately on warmed plates;
the melted cheese oozes out on stand-
ing. Garnish with sliced plums and a
little Chinese plum sauce.

Makes 4 to 5 servings.

Note: Chinese plum sauce is available
from Chinese stores, some supermarkets and delicatessens.

Roquefort Purses

About 3 sheets filo pastry
1 tablespoon butter, melted
1-1/2 ounces Roquefort cheese, cut
   into 12 cubes
12 chives
Vegetable oil for deep-frying

To Garnish:
Chives

Cut pastry into 24 (3-inch) squares.
Pile on top of each other and cover
with a slightly damp cloth to prevent
drying out.

Brush one square with butter;
place another on top to make an 8-
pointed star, then brush with butter.
Put a cheese cube in the center. Bring
up edges of pastry to cover cheese
and pinch together into a money bag
shape—the butter will help pastry to
stick together. Tie a chive around top.
Repeat with remaining pastry, cheese
and chives.

Heat oil in a deep-fryer to 360F
(180C) or until a 1-inch bread cube
turns golden brown in 1 minute.
Place purses in basket and deep-fry 1
minute or until crisp and golden
brown. Drain thoroughly on paper
towels.

Garnish with chives and serve immediately on individual plates.

Makes 12 appetizers.

Note: Serve 2 or 3 of these purses as a
pretty starter. Or, serve as part of a
buffet with drinks.

Cashew & Blue Cheese Dip

2 ounces cashews
6 chervil sprigs
2 ounces blue cheese
3 ounces fromage frais or plain yogurt
Salt and pepper, to taste
Milk (optional)
CRUDITÉS:
6 quail eggs
1 head Belgian endive
2 ounces snow peas
2 ounces baby carrots
1/2 fennel bulb
1 bunch of radishes
4 ounces cherry tomatoes
1 red apple, quartered and cored
1 teaspoon lemon juice

1. Put nuts and chervil in a food processor fitted with the metal blade and chop finely. Add cheese, fromage frais and seasoning and process to a puree, adding a little milk if necessary. Turn into a serving bowl.
2. To prepare crudités, boil quail eggs 2 minutes, put into cold water, remove when cool and shell.
3. Prepare vegetables: divide Belgian endive into leaves; remove ends and any strings from snow peas; peel carrots; cut fennel into thin wedges; leave tops on radishes and tomatoes. Slice apple and brush with lemon juice to prevent discoloration. Place the bowl of dip in the center of a large serving dish; arrange crudités around dip.

Makes 4 to 6 servings.

Variation: Use almonds or hazelnuts instead of cashews if you prefer.

Walnut, Stilton & Pear Salad

2 ripe pears
1/4 head chicory
Few radicchio leaves
Handful of arugula leaves
4 ounces Stilton cheese, cut into cubes
1/2 cup chopped walnuts
MELBA TOAST:
4 thin slices white bread
DRESSING:
2 tablespoons walnut oil
2 teaspoons cider vinegar
Salt and pepper, to taste

1. First make Melba toast: preheat oven to 350F (175C). Toast bread, then remove crusts. Slice toast in half horizontally and place toasted side down on a baking sheet. Bake in the oven 5 minutes, until curled.

For the dressing: put all ingredients in a jar with a lid and shake thoroughly until well mixed; pour into a bowl.
2. Quarter pears, remove cores and slice into dressing; mix gently to coat with dressing, which will prevent them from discoloring.
3. Break chicory and radicchio into bite-size pieces and add to bowl with arugula leaves, Stilton and walnuts; toss thoroughly. Serve on individual plates with Melba toast.

Makes 4 servings.

Note: If arugula is unavailable, substitute a few lettuce leaves.

Avocado & Grapefruit Salad

2 pink grapefruit
1 large avocado, halved and pitted
1 teaspoon lemon juice
WALNUT SAUCE:
2/3 cup walnut pieces
1 tablespoon walnut oil
1 teaspoon lemon juice
1/4 cup plain yogurt
Salt and pepper, to taste
TO GARNISH:
Dill sprigs

Mediterranean Pine Nut Salad

2 eggplants, sliced
Salt
6 tablespoons virgin olive oil
2 garlic cloves, chopped
1 red bell pepper, seeded and sliced into rings
4 large tomatoes, peeled and chopped
2 tablespoons chopped parsley
Pepper, to taste
TO GARNISH:
Thinly sliced onion rings
1/4 cup pine nuts, toasted
1 tablespoon chopped parsley
6 ripe olives, halved and pitted

1. Peel grapefruit with a serrated knife and cut into sections, removing all pith and membrane.
2. Peel each avocado half and slice lengthwise; brush with lemon juice to prevent discoloration. Arrange alternate, overlapping slices of avocado and grapefruit on 4 individual serving plates.
3. To make sauce, place all ingredients in a blender or food processor fitted with the metal blade and process until smooth; turn into a bowl. Spoon a little sauce on the side of each plate. Garnish with dill and serve accompanied by Melba toast.

Makes 4 servings.

1. Put eggplants in a colander, sprinkle with salt and leave 30 minutes. Rinse well and pat dry with paper towels. This will rid them of their bitter juices, and prevent them from absorbing too much oil during frying.
2. In a large skillet, heat a little oil and fry eggplant slices in batches until golden on both sides, adding more oil as necessary. Drain on paper towels.
3. Heat a little more oil in the pan, add garlic and bell pepper and cook 1 minute. Add tomatoes, parsley and fried eggplant, season with salt and pepper, cover and simmer 10 minutes, stirring occasionally. Turn into a shallow serving dish, arrange onion rings on top, then sprinkle with pine nuts, parsley and olives.

Makes 6 servings.

Tomato Salad with Pesto

1 pound tomatoes
2 tablespoons ripe olives, halved and pitted
3 ounces Feta cheese, crumbled
PESTO VINAIGRETTE:
2 tablespoons each chopped fresh basil and parsley
1 small garlic clove, crushed
1/4 cup pine nuts
2 tablespoons grated Parmesan cheese
2 tablespoons lemon juice
1/3 cup olive oil
Pepper, to taste
HERB LOAF:
1 French bread loaf
1/4 cup butter, softened
3 tablespoons chopped mixed herbs (parsley, chives,
thyme, marjoram)
Salt and pepper, to taste

1. First make vinaigrette: put herbs, garlic, pine nuts and Parmesan cheese in a food processor fitted with the metal blade and chop finely. With the motor running, gradually pour in lemon juice and oil through the feed tube; add pepper, to taste.
2. Slice tomatoes and arrange in 6 individual serving dishes. Pour vinaigrette over tomatoes. Sprinkle olives and cheese over the top and let stand 1 hour before serving, for the flavors to mingle.
3. To make herb loaf, preheat oven to 400F (205C). Slice bread diagonally, but not quite all the way through. Cream butter with herbs and seasoning; spread some on each side of every cut. Wrap in foil and bake 15 minutes; loosen foil at the top and bake 5 minutes, to crisp. Slice and serve hot with the tomato salad.

Makes 6 servings.

Scallop & Asparagus Croustades

1 (8- to 9-inch) unsliced sandwich loaf
3 tablespoons sunflower oil
FILLING:
4 ounces asparagus
6 scallops, cleaned
1/2 cup white wine
Bouquet garni
1 small onion, chopped
4 ounces button mushrooms, sliced
1 tablespoon plus 1 teaspoon all-purpose flour
3 tablespoons whipping cream
1 ounce pine nuts, toasted

1. Preheat oven to 400F (205C). Cut 6 (1-1/4-inch) slices from the loaf; cut into 3-inch squares. Cut out the center, leaving a bottom and a 1/4-inch border. Brush all over with 2 tablespoons oil, place on a baking sheet and bake in the oven 10 minutes, until crisp and golden.
2. Meanwhile, for the filling, cut asparagus into 1-1/2-inch lengths. Cook stalks in boiling water 5 minutes; add tips and cook 3 minutes. Drain, reserving 1/4 cup liquid. Cut each scallop into 4 pieces.
   Put wine, reserved liquid and bouquet garni in a saucepan and bring to a boil. Add scallops, cover and cook gently 3 minutes; remove with a slotted spoon. Boil cooking liquid until reduced to 2/3 cup.
3. In a pan, heat remaining oil and fry onion until softened; add mushrooms and cook 2 minutes. Remove from heat, stir in flour, then gradually stir in reduced liquid. Bring to a boil and cook, stirring, 2 minutes, until thickened. Add cream; return scallops and asparagus to pan with pine nuts and heat through. Spoon into warmed croustades and serve.

Makes 6 servings.

Asparagus & Nut Dressing

1 pound asparagus
Salt
MACADAMIA DRESSING.
2 ounces macadamia nuts
6 large chervil sprigs
1/4 cup hazelnut oil
1 tablespoon lemon juice
1/4 teaspoon honey
Salt and pepper, to taste

Gruyère & Walnut Tartlets

PASTRY:
1-1/4 cups all-purpose flour
6 tablespoons butter, chilled
1/3 cup walnut pieces, ground
1 to 2 tablespoons ice water
FILLING:
6 ounces asparagus
2 eggs
2 ounces cream cheese
2/3 cup half and half
1 cup shredded Gruyère cheese (4 oz.)
1/2 cup chopped walnuts
1 tablespoon chopped fresh tarragon
Salt and pepper, to taste
TO GARNISH:
Salad leaves

1. Bend lower end of asparagus so that it snaps—it will do this naturally at the point where it becomes tough. Tie asparagus in a bundle and put upright in an asparagus steamer or tall saucepan, with sufficient boiling salted water to come 2 inches up stems.
2. Cover, making a lid with foil and doming it over asparagus tips if necessary, so that the heads cook in steam. Simmer until tender: 15 minutes for small asparagus, 20 to 30

minutes for thicker stems. Lift asparagus from pan, drain very carefully and arrange on a serving platter.
3. To make dressing, place nuts and all but 1 small sprig of chervil in a blender or food processor fitted with the metal blade; chop finely. Add remaining ingredients and process until smooth. Spoon dressing over asparagus and garnish with remaining chervil.

Makes 4 servings.

1. To make pastry, sift flour into a bowl. Cut in butter until mixture resembles bread crumbs. Add ground walnuts and 1 to 2 tablespoons ice water, mixing to a smooth firm dough. On a lightly floured surface, knead lightly, then wrap in plastic wrap and refrigerate 15 minutes. Roll out pastry thinly and divide into 6 pieces. Roll into circles and use to line 6 (3-1/2-inch) individual flan pans; prick the bottoms. Refrigerate 15 minutes. Preheat oven to 400F (205C).

2. To make filling, cut asparagus into 1/2-inch lengths, cook in boiling water 5 minutes, then drain. In a medium-size bowl, mix eggs and cottage cheese together until smooth; add half and half, cheese, chopped walnuts, asparagus, tarragon and seasoning.
3. Spoon into pastry shells and bake 25 minutes, until puffed and set. Garnish with salad leaves to serve.

Makes 6 servings.

Goat Cheese & Walnut Parcels

2 sheets filo pastry
2 tablespoons butter, melted
1 (6-1/2-oz.) roll goat cheese, 1-3/4-inch diameter
2 tablespoons chopped walnuts
6 chives
Vegetable oil for deep-frying
TOMATO SAUCE:
1 tablespoon olive oil
1 small onion, chopped
1 garlic clove, crushed
1 pound tomatoes, peeled, seeded and chopped
2 teaspoons tomato paste
Salt and pepper, to taste
TO GARNISH:
Chervil sprigs

Crab Cocktail

8 ounces cooked crabmeat
1 celery heart, finely chopped
1 hard-cooked egg, finely chopped
2 tablespoons whipping cream
1 teaspoon tomato paste
8 drops hot-pepper sauce
1 Galia melon
1 large avocado
1 tablespoon lime juice
Salad leaves to garnish
LIME MAYONNAISE:
1 egg
1 tablespoon lime juice
1 teaspoon dry mustard
Salt and pepper to taste
1-1/4 cups olive oil

1. Cut filo pastry into 12 (6-inch) squares; pile on top of each other and cover with a clean towel to prevent pastry drying out. Brush 1 pastry square with butter, lay another square on top and brush again with butter.

2. Cut goat cheese into 3/4-inch slices and lay a slice in the center of pastry square; sprinkle with chopped walnuts. Bring up edges of pastry and pinch together into a "money" bag shape—butter will help the pastry to stick. Repeat with remaining pastry, cheese and walnuts. Tie a chive around the top of each.

3. To make sauce, heat oil in a small pan, add onion and fry until softened. Add garlic, tomatoes, tomato paste and seasoning, cover and simmer 10 minutes. Sieve, then reheat.

In a deep pan, heat oil until a cube of bread turns brown in 1 minute. Put 3 parcels in the hot oil and deep-fry 2 minutes, until crisp and golden-brown, turning once. Repeat with remaining parcels.

Serve immediately, accompanied by the sauce and garnished with chervil.

Makes 6 servings.

1. To make lime mayonnaise, in a blender or food processor, combine egg, lime juice, dry mustard, 1 teaspoon salt and a generous sprinkling of black pepper. While machine is running, gradually add olive oil in a thin steam through lid; blend until mayonnaise is thick and shiny.

2. In a large bowl, mix crabmeat, celery and hard-cooked egg. Stir in 3 to 4 tablespoons of mayonnaise, whipping cream, tomato paste, hot-pepper sauce and salt and pepper. Chill.

Cut melon in quarters, discarding seeds. Set aside.

3. Peel, pit and thinly slice avocado, then toss in lime juice to prevent discoloration. Cut melon in slices, same size as avocado slices. Cut away melon skin.

Spoon crab cocktail onto individual plates and arrange a fan of alternating melon and avocado slices on each. Garnish with salad leaves and serve immediately, accompanied by remaining mayonnaise.

Makes 6 servings.

Papaya & Prosciutto Starter

2 small papayas
4 ounces Prosciutto
4 small crisp lettuce leaves
Strip of pared lime peel
DRESSING:
1 papaya
1/2 cup crème fraîche
Juice of 1 lime
Few drops of hot-pepper sauce
Salt and pepper to taste
TO GARNISH:
Lime slices, if desired

Fig, Ham & Mozzarella Salad

6 smoked ham slices
6 fresh figs
4 ounces mozzarella cheese, thinly sliced
8 ounces mixed salad leaves (such as radicchio, curly endive or frisé, oak leaf, lamb's lettuce or mâche)
DRESSING:
1 garlic clove, crushed
1 teaspoon English mustard
1 teaspoon sugar
1/4 cup wine vinegar
1/4 cup plus 2 tablespoons olive oil
2 tablespoons hazelnut oil
Salt and pepper to taste

1. To make dressing, cut papaya in quarters. Remove skin and seeds, then coarsely chop pulp. In a blender or food processor, blend chopped papaya, crème fraîche, lime juice, hot-pepper sauce and salt and pepper until smooth, then set aside.

2. Cut each small papaya in half, then cut each half in 3 slices, removing skin and seeds. Cut each piece of prosciutto in half lengthwise. Arrange 3 parallel papaya slices on each in-dividual serving plate, then weave 3 strips of prosciutto through, forming a lattice.

3. Place a lettuce leaf on each serving plate and spoon dressing into center of each leaf. Cut lime peel in fine julienne strips and sprinkle over papaya. Garnish with lime slices, if desired. Serve immediately.

Makes 4 servings.

1. Preheat broiler. Divide ham among 6 individual gratin dishes or other shallow ovenproof dishes. Cut each fig in quarters lengthwise and place on top of ham. Cover with moz-zarella cheese.

2. To make dressing, in a large salad bowl, mix garlic, mustard and sugar. Stir in vinegar, then gradually add olive oil. Add hazelnut oil, then salt and pepper. Add salad leaves to dressing and gently toss, ensuring all leaves are coated.

3. Place ovenproof dishes under grill about 3 minutes or until cheese has completely melted. Serve im-mediately with tossed salad leaves.

Makes 6 servings.

Tamarillo & Pasta Salad

1 pound pasta shells
1/3 cup olive oil
3 tamarillos
6 ounces goat's cheese, sliced or crumbled
DRESSING:
1/2 cup olive oil
1/2 cup red-wine vinegar
2 garlic cloves, crushed
1 green bell pepper, seeded, chopped
1 small onion, chopped
1 (4-oz.) can pimento, drained
3 tablespoons chopped parsley
3 tablespoons chopped basil
Salt and pepper to taste
TO GARNISH:
Sprigs of basil

Pear & Roquefort Quiches

1 cup all-purpose flour
Pinch of dry mustard
Salt and pepper to taste
1/4 cup margarine, diced
1/2 cup shredded Cheddar cheese (2 oz.)
1 to 2 tablespoons water
3 Comice pears
2 ounces Roquefort cheese
1/4 cup cream cheese (2 oz.), softened
2 eggs, beaten
1/2 cup whipping cream
1 tablespoon chopped tarragon
1 tablespoon butter, melted
DRESSING:
1 ounce Roquefort cheese
2 tablespoons sunflower oil
1 tablespoon tarragon vinegar

1. In a large saucepan, cook pasta in boiling salt water 8 to 10 minutes or until just cooked (al dente). Drain, rinse under tepid water and drain thoroughly. Transfer to a large bowl and pour olive oil over pasta, tossing pasta to ensure it is evenly coated. Cover with plastic wrap and refrigerate 30 minutes.
2. To make dressing, put all ingredients in a blender or food processor and process until smooth. Pour dressing over pasta and toss well.
Peel tamarillos and cut in thin slices.
3. Add tamarillos and goat's cheese to pasta and toss very gently. Transfer to individual serving plates and garnish with basil sprigs. Serve immediately.

Makes 6 servings.

1. Sift flour, mustard and a pinch of salt into a bowl. Add margarine and cut in until mixture resembles bread crumbs; stir in Cheddar cheese. Mix in water to make a soft dough. Wrap in plastic wrap and chill 30 minutes. Preheat oven to 400F (205C). Roll out pastry thinly and line 4 greased deep 3-inch tartlet pans.
2. Peel, core and chop 1 pear. Beat Roquefort and cream cheese, then beat in eggs, whipping cream, tarragon and salt and pepper. Stir in chopped pear. Spoon into pastry cups. Peel and slice remaining pears. Arrange a few slices in a fan pattern on each tartlet. Brush with melted butter and bake in oven 20 minutes. Let stand a few minutes, then remove from pans.
3. To make dressing, in a bowl, cream Roquefort cheese until smooth, then beat in oil and vinegar. Season to taste with salt and pepper.
Serve tartlets warm or cold with a little dressing drizzled over.

Makes 4 servings.

Camembert with Rhubarb Preserve

8 individual portions of Camembert
1/2 cup all-purpose flour
2 eggs, beaten
1/2 cup toasted sesame seeds
Vegetable oil for deep-frying
Sprigs of herbs to garnish
PRESERVE:
1 pound rhubarb
2 tablespoons sunflower oil
1 large onion, sliced
1/3 cup cider vinegar
1/2 cup superfine sugar
1 (3-inch) cinnamon stick
3 whole cloves
1 (1-inch) piece fresh gingerroot, finely chopped

Mango & Shrimp Bundles

1 large mango, peeled, halved
12 ounces cooked peeled shrimp
2 green onions, finely chopped
6 large iceberg lettuce leaves
DRESSING:
1/2 cup mayonnaise
1 garlic clove, crushed
1 tablespoon mango chutney, sieved
2 teaspoons finely chopped cilantro
Salt and pepper to taste
TO GARNISH:
Lime slices
Sprigs of cilantro

1. To make preserve, cut rhubarb in 2-inch slices. In a saucepan, heat sunflower oil, add onion and cook 5 minutes, until softened. Add rhubarb and cook, stirring frequently, 5 minutes. Pour vinegar over rhubarb and bring to a boil. Add sugar, cinnamon stick, cloves and gingerroot. Lower heat, cover pan and simmer 40 minutes, stirring occasionally, until all liquid is absorbed. Cool slightly, then discard cinnamon stick and cloves. Puree mixture in a blender or food processor. Transfer to a serving dish and cool.

2. Coat each portion of cheese with flour and then beaten egg. Roll in sesame seeds.
3. Heat oil in a deep skillet. When hot, deep-fry cheese, a few at a time, 30 seconds. Remove with a slotted spoon and drain on paper towels. Serve immediately, garnished with herbs and accompanied by rhubarb preserve.

Makes 4 servings.

1. From 1 half of mango, cut 6 thin slices; set aside for garnish. Cut remaining mango pulp in small cubes; place in a bowl with shrimp and green onions.
2. To make dressing, in a bowl, mix mayonnaise, garlic, chutney, cilantro and salt and pepper. Pour dressing over mango and shrimp and toss gently to ensure all ingredients are evenly coated.
3. Lay lettuce leaves on a work surface. Divide mango and shrimp mixture among them. Gently fold leaves over to form bundles, enclosing filling. Arrange bundles on individual plates, folded sides underneath.

Garnish with reserved mango slices, lime slices and cilantro sprigs to serve.

Makes 6 servings.

Crudités with Skorthalia

3 slices day-old white bread, crusts removed
2 or 3 garlic cloves, crushed
1 tablespoon white wine vinegar
1/2 teaspoon each salt and pepper
1/3 cup olive oil
1 tablespoon lemon juice
1/4 cup ground almonds
1 tablespoon chopped fresh mint
1 head Belgian endive
1 red bell pepper
2 medium-size zucchini
2 stalks celery
12 radishes
1/4 head medium-size cauliflower
1 ripe olive, cut in slivers
Sprig of mint

Salmon & Guacamole Terrine

1 tablespoon butter
2 tablespoons all-purpose flour
1 (7-1/2-oz.) can salmon
5 teaspoons lemon juice
1-1/2 (1/4-oz.) envelopes unflavored gelatin (4-1/2 teaspoons)
5 tablespoons mayonnaise
4 teaspoons tomato paste
1/4 cup whipping cream
Few drops Worcestershire sauce
Salt and pepper to taste
2 ripe avocados
1 garlic clove, crushed
1 teaspoon olive oil
2 pinches red (cayenne) pepper
TO GARNISH:
Sprigs of dill

1. Cut bread in cubes and place in a bowl. Add enough cold water to cover; soak 5 minutes. Spoon into a sieve and, using a wooden spoon, press bread against sieve to extract water. In a blender or food processor fitted with the metal blade, process bread, garlic, vinegar and salt and pepper until smooth.
2. With motor running, gradually add olive oil in a thin stream and blend until completely absorbed. Blend in lemon juice, ground almonds and chopped mint. Adjust seasoning, if necessary. Spoon into a serving bowl and chill at least 1 hour.

3. To prepare crudités, divide Belgian endive in separate leaves. Cut bell pepper in strips. Slice zucchini lengthwise, then cut in sticks. Cut celery in small sticks. Discard leaves from radishes and trim bottoms. Break cauliflower in bite-size flowerets. Wash all vegetables, drain and pat dry on paper towels. Chill until needed.

Place dip in center of a large serving platter. Arrange prepared vegetables in groups around bowl. Garnish dip with olives and mint.

Makes 4 to 6 servings.

1. In a saucepan, melt butter, add flour and cook 1 minute. Drain salmon, reserving liquor; add enough water to measure 3/4 cup. Stir liquor into pan and bring to a boil, stirring; cook 2 minutes. Remove from heat. Flake salmon finely; stir into sauce.

In a bowl, mix 1 tablespoon lemon juice and 2 tablespoons water; sprinkle over gelatin and let stand 5 minutes. Set bowl in a pan of hot water; stir until dissolved. Let stand until cool but not set.
2. Add 1/4 cup of mayonnaise, tomato paste, cream and Worcestershire sauce to salmon mixture; season and mix well. Stir in gelatin; chill 15 min-

utes. Peel, seed and thinly slice 1 avocado; brush with 1 teaspoon of lemon juice. One-third fill a dampened 8" x 4" loaf pan with salmon mixture. Cover with 1/2 of avocado; repeat layers, finishing with salmon. Chill at least 2 hours.
3. Peel, seed and mash remaining avocado in a bowl. Add remaining lemon juice and mayonnaise, garlic, oil, red pepper and salt. Chill.

Dip terrine into very hot water 2 to 3 seconds, then turn out onto a serving plate. Swirl guacamole sauce over top. Garnish with dill.

Makes 6 to 8 servings.

Globe Artichokes à la Grecque

4 large globe artichokes
SAUCE:
2 tablespoons tomato paste
1/4 cup olive oil
2/3 cup dry white wine
2/3 cup water
1 small onion, finely chopped
1 garlic clove, crushed
1 teaspoon chopped oregano
2 sprigs of thyme
2 ripe tomatoes, peeled and chopped
Salt and pepper to taste
TO GARNISH:
Lemon wedges
Sprigs of oregano

Sesame-Glazed Asparagus

1 pound asparagus
4 tablespoons butter
6 green onions, thinly sliced diagonally
Finely grated peel of 1/2 small lemon
1 tablespoon lemon juice
Salt and pepper to taste
Pinch of red (cayenne) pepper
1 to 2 tablespoons sesame seeds, lightly toasted
1 teaspoon sesame oil
TO GARNISH:
Lemon slices
Sprigs of flat-leaf parsley

1. Cut off stalks from artichokes and, using scissors, trim off pointed ends from outer leaves. Rinse well. Cook in boiling salted water 15 minutes. Drain well and stand upside down on paper towels to dry.

2. To prepare sauce, combine all ingredients in a saucepan. Mix well and bring to a boil. Cover and gently simmer gently 10 minutes, stirring occasionally. Remove thyme sprigs. Add artichokes to sauce, cover and cook gently 30 minutes. Carefully lift artichokes onto a plate and cool. Boil sauce, uncovered, 5 minutes; cool.

3. When artichokes are cold, remove chokes by spreading top leaves apart and pulling out inside leaves to reveal hairy choke. Using a teaspoon, scrape away hairs to expose heart. Arrange artichokes on 4 individual serving plates and spoon sauce around the artichokes. Cover and chill until needed.

Garnish with lemon wedges and oregano to serve.

Makes 4 servings.

1. Cut off woody part at bottom of asparagus stems and, using a knife, scrape off white part of stems. Cut asparagus spears diagonally in 3 or 4 equal pieces. Place in a large saucepan and add enough boiling salted water to cover. Cook, covered, 8 to 10 minutes, until just tender, drain well.

2. In a large skillet, melt butter. Add green onions and sauté gently 1 minute. Add lemon peel and juice, then stir in asparagus. Toss lightly in sauce over low heat 2 to 3 minutes, until heated through.

3. Season with salt, pepper and red pepper. Turn onto a warmed serving platter and sprinkle with toasted sesame seeds and sesame oil. Garnish with lemon slices and parsley; serve hot.

Makes 4 servings.

Ham & Asparagus Bundles

16 asparagus spears
4 slices prosciutto, halved lengthwise
8 long chives
Lemon juice
Freshly ground black pepper
HOLLANDAISE SAUCE:
1/4 cup white wine vinegar
1 teaspoon black peppercorns
2 large egg yolks
8 tablespoons butter, room temperature
1 to 3 pinches red (cayenne) pepper
TO GARNISH:
Lemon twists

1. Cut off woody bottom of asparagus stems and, using a knife, scrape off white part of stems. Tie asparagus in bundles with heads together. Place in an asparagus steamer or saucepan and add enough boiling water to reach just below asparagus heads. Cover and boil 12 to 14 minutes or until tender. Lift asparagus from water, drain and set aside.
2. To prepare hollandaise sauce, place vinegar and peppercorns in a saucepan. Bring to a boil and boil until reduced by half. Place egg yolks in a bowl with 1 tablespoon of butter and beat well. Strain hot vinegar into egg yolks, beating well. Return to pan and place over very low heat. Gradu-

ally add remaining butter in small pieces, whisking constantly until sauce is thickened and smooth. (Keep removing pan from heat while whisking in butter to prevent curdling.) Add red pepper and pour into a serving dish.
3. Cut asparagus spears in half. Form 4 pieces in a stack, with spear ends on top. Wrap in a piece of prosciutto and tie with a chive. Repeat with remaining asparagus, prosciutto and chives. Sprinkle with lemon juice and pepper. Garnish with lemon twists and serve with Hollandaise sauce.

Makes 4 servings.

Filo-Wrapped Vegetables

3 green onions, finely chopped
1 cup finely chopped Chinese cabbage
1/2 red or green bell pepper, finely chopped
1 garlic clove, crushed
4 ounces peeled shrimp, thawed if frozen, chopped
1 tablespoon light soy sauce
1 tablespoon oyster sauce
1/2 teaspoon sugar
1 teaspoon cornstarch
4 sheets filo pastry
Vegetable oil for deep-frying
TO SERVE:
Green onion flowers, as illustrated
Chili sauce

1. In a small saucepan, mix green onions, Chinese cabbage, bell pepper, garlic and shrimp. Stir in soy sauce, oyster sauce, sugar and cornstarch. Cook over medium heat 3 minutes, stirring constantly. Remove from heat; set aside.
2. Cut sheets of filo pastry in 24 (5-inch) squares. Sandwich together in pairs to form 12 double-thickness squares. Place 1 teaspoon of prepared mixture in center of each square, then draw corners of pastry together. Twist and pinch firmly to seal.

3. Half-fill a large deep saucepan with oil and heat to 375F (190C) or until a cube of day-old bread browns in 40 seconds. Lower bundles into oil, a few at a time, and deep-fry 2 to 3 minutes, until golden-brown. Drain on paper towels and keep warm while cooking remainder. Arrange on a warm serving plate and garnish with green onion flowers. Serve hot with chili sauce for dipping.

Makes 4 to 6 servings.

Flounder & Watercress Bundles

2 flounder fillets, skinned and boned
1-1/2 bunches watercress
6 tablespoons butter
3 shallots, finely chopped
1 tablespoon fresh lime juice
Salt and pepper to taste
5 sheets filo pastry
TO SERVE:
Watercress sprigs
Lime twists
Tartar sauce

1. Preheat oven to 375F (190C). Cut flounder in thin strips and place in a bowl. Trim off watercress stalks and coarsely chop leaves. In a saucepan, melt 2 tablespoons of butter. Add watercress and shallots and sauté 2 minutes; transfer to bowl. Add lime juice and season with salt and pepper. Mix well and set aside.
2. Melt remaining butter in a pan. Cut filo sheets in half crosswise; brush lightly with butter. Fold each piece in 3 layers by folding top one-third section over center one-third and bottom one-third over top to form a long narrow strip. Brush lightly with butter. Divide filling in 10 portions; place one in a corner of each pastry strip.
3. Fold pastry and filling over at right angles to form a triangle. Continue folding in this way along strip of pastry to form triangles. Brush all over with remaining melted butter and place on a baking sheet. Bake in preheated oven 15 minutes, until golden-brown and cooked through.

Serve hot, garnished with watercress sprigs and lime twists. Accompany with tartar sauce.

Makes 10 bundles.

Japanese-Style Cucumber

1 large cucumber
1 bunch watercress, stalks trimmed
4 ounces white crabmeat, thawed if frozen
1 (1-inch) piece gingerroot, peeled and grated
Salt and pepper to taste
SAUCE:
2 tablespoons rice vinegar
2 tablespoons chicken stock
2 teaspoons sugar
2 teaspoons Japanese soy sauce
TO GARNISH:
Watercress sprigs

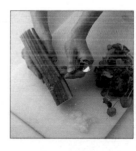

1. Trim ends of cucumber, then slit lengthwise along one side through to center, taking care not to cut through. Using a teaspoon, very carefully remove seedy flesh from center to form a channel.

Blanch watercress in boiling water 30 seconds; drain well and pat dry on paper towels.
2. In a bowl, finely flake crabmeat; add gingerroot and season with salt and pepper. Hold cut edges of cucumber open and carefully insert crab mixture into channel; top with blanched watercress. Press cucumber edges together and wrap tightly in plastic wrap. Chill at least 2 hours.
3. To prepare sauce, combine all ingredients in a small saucepan and bring to a boil, stirring constantly. Remove from heat and cool.

Just before serving, cut cucumber in 3/4-inch-thick slices and arrange on a flat serving platter. Pour a small amount of sauce over each slice and garnish with watercress.

Makes 4 to 6 servings.

Mussels with Pesto

4 pounds mussels in shells
1/2 cup dry white wine
PESTO:
2 ounces basil leaves
2 garlic cloves
1/4 cup pine nuts
Salt and pepper, to taste
1/4 cup grated Parmesan cheese
1/4 cup olive oil
TO FINISH:
1/4 cup dry bread crumbs

Oysters Rockefeller

8 ounces spinach leaves
4 bacon slices
1/2 cup butter
3 green onions, finely chopped
2 tablespoons chopped celery leaves
2 tablespoons chopped parsley
1/2 cup dry bread crumbs
1 tablespoon grated Parmesan cheese
1 tablespoon Pernod
24 large oysters, cleaned
Coarse sea salt

1. Preheat oven to 400F (205C). Put mussels and wine into a large saucepan, cover and cook over high heat, shaking pan, 4 to 6 minutes, until shells have opened. Drain, discarding any mussels that have not opened; discard the empty half shells. Set mussels aside.

2. To make Pesto, put basil, garlic, pine nuts, salt and pepper into a mortar, and pound until well blended. (This can be done in a food proces-

sor.) Blend in cheese, then add oil a little at a time, until the consistency is thick and creamy.

3. Arrange mussels in their half shells in 4 shallow ovenproof dishes. Spread a little pesto over each and sprinkle with bread crumbs. Bake 10 minutes, until piping hot. Serve immediately, as a starter.

Makes 4 to 6 servings.

1. Preheat oven to 425F (220C). Cook spinach with just the water clinging to the leaves after washing 3 to 4 minutes, until wilted; drain well and chop finely. Broil bacon until crisp, then chop finely. In a saucepan, melt butter; stir in green onions, celery leaves, parsley, spinach, bacon, bread crumbs and cheese. Stir in Pernod. Set aside.

2. To open each oyster, hold in paper towels on a work surface, flatter shell uppermost and hinged end towards you. Insert the point of an oyster knife into the gap in the hinge linking

the shells and twist the blade to snap shells apart.

Slide blade along the inside of the upper shell to sever the muscle. Remove any broken shell from the oyster with the point of the knife. Discard empty half shells.

3. Cover the centers of 4 ovenproof plates with sea salt. Set the oysters in their half shells in the salt. Spoon prepared stuffing over oysters and bake 6 to 8 minutes, until bubbling. Serve immediately, as a starter.

Makes 4 servings.

Shrimp Satay

1-1/2 pounds large raw shrimp in shells
1 teaspoon ground turmeric
1 teaspoon ground cumin
1/2 teaspoon ground fennel
1/2 teaspoon finely minced lemon peel
1 tablespoon light brown sugar
1/4 cup cream of coconut
DIP:
1 red chile
2 tablespoons honey
1/4 cup cider vinegar
6 thin cucumber slices
TO GARNISH:
Parsley sprigs

Singapore Lettuce Cups

1 red chile
3 ounces small green beans
3 ounces bean sprouts
1/4 cucumber, chopped
8 ounces peeled, cooked shrimp, thawed if frozen
3 tablespoons shredded green onion
1 tablespoon chopped cilantro
1 lettuce head
Cilantro leaves, to garnish
DRESSING:
1/3 cup shelled peanuts, roasted
1 teaspoon soy sauce
1 garlic clove, crushed
1 teaspoon light brown sugar
1/4 cup orange juice
1 tablespoon lemon juice

1. To peel shrimp, pull off tail and shell.
2. Using a small sharp knife, slit down center back and remove dark vein. Soak bamboo skewers in water.

In a bowl, mix together spices, lemon peel, sugar and cream of coconut. Add shrimp, cover and refrigerate 1 to 2 hours, stirring occasionally.

To prepare dip, wearing rubber gloves, cut chile in half lengthwise, carefully remove and discard seeds. Finely chop chile and mix with honey and vinegar. Cut cucumber slices in quarters and add to dip. Divide among 4 tiny serving dishes. Preheat broiler.
3. Thread shrimp onto bamboo skewers and cook under preheated broiler 5 to 6 minutes, turning occasionally. Arrange on 4 plates and garnish with parsley. Serve immediately, with the dip, as a starter.

Makes 4 servings.

1. Wear rubber gloves to prepare chile: cut in half, carefully discard stem and seeds; then chop finely. Cut beans in short lengths and blanch in boiling water 2 minutes. Blanch bean sprouts for a few seconds. Drain vegetables and refresh under cold running water. Mix together chile, beans, bean sprouts, cucumber, shrimp, green onion and cilantro.
2. To make dressing, in a food processor, coarsely grind peanuts, then mix with soy sauce, garlic, sugar, orange and lemon juices. Taste and add salt if necessary. Add to shrimp mixture and stir well.
3. Separate lettuce leaves. Place a spoonful of shrimp mixture on each leaf. Arrange on a serving platter and garnish with cilantro leaves. Serve as a starter.

Makes 6 to 8 servings.

Shrimp & Salmon Rolls

1 egg yolk
1/2 teaspoon Dijon-style mustard
Salt and pepper, to taste
2/3 cup olive oil and sunflower oil mixed
1 tablespoon lemon juice
1 ounce watercress, chopped
1 celery stalk, finely chopped
8 ounces peeled cooked shrimp, thawed if frozen
12 slices smoked salmon
TO GARNISH:
Chicory
Orange slices

1. In a bowl, blend egg yolk, mustard, salt and pepper; add oil drop by drop, beating thoroughly between each addition. As mayonnaise thickens, increase the flow of oil to a slow steady stream, beating constantly. Beat in lemon juice and check seasoning.
2. Stir in watercress, celery and shrimp. Lay smoked salmon slices on a work surface. Spoon equal amounts of filling onto each slice.
3. Roll up salmon carefully, enclosing the shrimp filling. Arrange 2 salmon rolls on each place and garnish with chicory and orange slices. Serve with brown bread and butter, as a starter or light lunch.

Makes 6 servings.

Langostinos & Pear Salad

24 to 32 cooked langostinos
1 beefsteak tomato, peeled and seeded
1 teaspoon chopped fresh basil
3 tablespoons plain yogurt
Salt and pepper, to taste
2 small pears
2 teaspoons lemon juice
Mache or lamb's lettuce
Radicchio
Chicory
Lettuce leaves
TO GARNISH:
Chervil sprigs

1. Remove shells: twist off the head, gently pull off the tail shell and remove body shell. Cut down the back and remove dark vein.
2. Finely chop tomato; set half aside for garnish. Put the other half in a blender or food processor with the basil, yogurt, salt and pepper; blend until smooth.

Peel, core and thinly slice pears.

Place half a sliced pear on each serving plate and brush with lemon juice. Arrange the langostinos alongside. Place a few salad leaves on each plate.
3. Pour a little tomato cream over the shellfish and top with a little chopped tomato. Garnish with chervil and serve as a starter or light lunch.

Makes 4 servings.

Fish & Seafood

Mussel-stuffed Crêpes

2/3 cup dry white wine
1 garlic clove, pressed or minced
2 shallots, finely chopped
2 pounds mussels, scrubbed
2 tablespoons butter
6 ounces wild mushrooms (see *Note*),
    chopped
6 tablespoons plain yogurt
2 teaspoons chopped parsley
8 crêpes (use your favorite recipe)

Tomato Sauce:
1 tablespoon olive oil
1 small onion, chopped
1 pound tomatoes, chopped
Pinch of sugar
2 teaspoons chopped parsley
Salt and pepper to taste

Preheat oven to 375F (190C).

In a large saucepan, combine wine, garlic, half the shallots and 1/3 cup water. Add mussels; cover and cook over high heat 3 to 5 minutes or until opened. Discard any unopened mussels. Drain, reserving cooking liquid. Remove mussels from shells (leave a few unshelled for garnish). Set aside.

Prepare Tomato Sauce: In a saucepan, heat oil. Add onion and sauté over low heat 4 to 5 minutes. Add tomatoes, mussel liquid and sugar; cover and cook 5 minutes. Remove from heat; add parsley. Puree in a food processor or blender; sieve, return to pan and cook until thick. Add salt and pepper.

Melt butter in a frying pan, add remaining shallots and sauté 2 minutes. Stir in mushrooms and cook 2 to 3 minutes or until tender. Remove from heat. Stir in mussels, yogurt and parsley; adjust seasoning.

Divide filling among crêpes; fold crêpes into quarters. Arrange in a single layer in a buttered baking dish; bake, uncovered, 15 minutes. Garnish crêpes with unshelled mussels; serve with heated Tomato Sauce.

Makes 4 servings.

Note: Use parasols, chanterelles, morels, fairy rings or cepes (porcini).

Prawn & Bacon Kabobs

12 cooked large prawns, shelled,
    deveined, halved crosswise
12 bacon slices, halved
Walnut oil

Mushroom & Rice Balls:
1 tablespoon butter
1 tablespoon walnut oil
1 shallot, finely chopped
1 garlic clove, pressed or minced
4 ounces button mushrooms, finely
    chopped
About 2 cups cooked long-grain rice
1-1/4 cups fresh white bread crumbs
1 tablespoon plus 1 teaspoon chopped
    fresh cilantro
1 egg, beaten
Salt and pepper to taste

To Garnish:
Assorted salad greens

First make Mushroom & Rice Balls:

In a saucepan, melt butter in oil. Add shallot and garlic and cook 1 minute or until softened. Stir in mushrooms, rice, crumbs, cilantro and egg; season with salt and pepper. Preheat broiler. Shape rice mixture into 16 walnut-size balls; place on a greased baking sheet. Broil about 3 minutes or until firm, turning once.

Wrap each prawn piece in half a bacon slice. Thread bacon-wrapped prawns alternately with Mushroom & Rice Balls on 8 short skewers. Place on a baking sheet; brush with oil. Broil 5 minutes or until bacon is crisp and browned, turning occasionally.

Garnish kabobs with salad greens.

Makes 4 servings.

Lemon Sole with Mushrooms

8 small skinless lemon sole fillets
1-1/4 cups fish or chicken stock
1-1/4 cups dry white wine
2 teaspoons cornstarch blended with
   1 teaspoon water
1/4 cup whipping cream
1 tablespoon chopped fresh fennel
   leaves
Salt and pepper to taste

Mushroom Stuffing:
1 tablespoon butter
1/4 cup finely chopped fennel bulb
8 ounces oyster mushrooms, chopped
1/3 cup pine nuts, toasted, chopped
1 cup fresh white bread crumbs
Juice and grated peel of 1/2 lemon

To Garnish:
Few oyster mushrooms, cooked
Fresh fennel leaves
2 teaspoons pine nuts, toasted

Preheat oven to 375F (190C).
   Prepare stuffing: In a large saucepan, melt butter. Add chopped fennel bulb and sauté 1 minute or until softened. Add mushrooms; cook 2 to 3 minutes or until tender. Stir in pine nuts, crumbs, lemon juice and lemon peel.
   Lay fish fillets flat, skinned side up. Top evenly with stuffing; roll up and place, seam side down, in a shallow baking dish. Mix stock and wine; pour over fish. Cover loosely with foil; bake 20 to 25 minutes or just until fish is opaque throughout. Carefully transfer fish rolls to a plate; keep warm. Strain cooking juices into a small saucepan, bring to a boil and reduce by half. Stir in cornstarch mixture; cook, stirring, until thickened. Remove from heat and stir in cream, chopped fennel leaves, salt and pepper.
   Arrange fish rolls on warmed serving plates; pour sauce over and around them. Garnish with whole mushrooms, fennel leaves and pine nuts. Serve with wild rice.

Makes 4 servings.

Salmon with Mushrooms & Dill

4 salmon steaks
1 tablespoon lemon juice
Salt and pepper to taste

Mushroom & Dill Butter:
5 ounces small mushrooms (see *Note*)
6 tablespoons unsalted butter, room
   temperature
1/2 teaspoon grated lemon peel
2 tablespoons chopped fresh dill

To Garnish:
Blanched snow peas
Dill sprigs

Preheat oven to 375F (190C).
   Place each salmon steak on a square of foil; sprinkle with lemon juice, salt and pepper. Wrap foil around salmon to enclose, then place packets on a baking sheet. Bake 10 to 15 minutes or just until fish is opaque throughout.
   Meanwhile, prepare Mushroom & Dill Butter. Leave a few mushrooms whole for garnish; finely chop the rest. In a small saucepan, melt 2 tablespoons butter; add whole mushrooms and sauté 1 minute or until just tender. Remove from pan and set aside. Add chopped mushrooms to pan and cook 2 to 3 minutes or until softened. Transfer to a small bowl and let cool 1 to 2 minutes; stir in lemon peel, chopped dill and remaining 1/4 cup butter.
   Remove skin and central bone from each salmon steak. Transfer salmon to warmed serving plates and top with Mushroom & Dill Butter. Garnish with snow peas, reserved whole mushrooms and dill sprigs. Serve immediately.

Makes 4 servings.

Note: Because of their small size, fairy rings and tiny button mushrooms are prettiest for this dish. You may also use a mixture of wild or cultivated mushrooms; if they are large, slice a few for garnish.

Leek & Mussel Omelette

3 tablespoons olive oil
1 shallot, finely chopped
Salt and pepper to taste
2/3 cup white wine
1 lb. mussels, cleaned
8 ozs. leeks, thinly sliced
8 eggs
1/4 cup butter
2 tablespoons chopped chervil

To Garnish:
Chervil sprigs

In a large saucepan, heat 1 tablespoon olive oil. Add shallot and 1/2 teaspoon salt and cook a few minutes to soften. Pour in wine and add mussels. Cover and cook about 5 minutes, until mussels open; discard any that do not. Remove mussels with a slotted spoon and shell; discard shells. Strain cooking liquid through muslin twice. Return liquid to pan and boil rapidly until reduced by half; set aside.

In a clean pan, heat remaining oil. Add leeks and cook gently 10 to 12 minutes, until soft. Add mussels and 2 teaspoons reduced cooking liquid. Check seasoning and heat through.

Meanwhile, prepare 4 (2-egg) omelettes. For each one: beat 2 eggs with salt and pepper. In a preheated omelette pan, melt 1 tablespoon butter until sizzling. Add eggs and cook until browned underneath but soft and creamy on top.

Spread 1/4 of filling on 1/2 of omelette. Sprinkle with 1/4 of chopped chervil and fold omelette over to cover. Serve immediately, garnished with sprigs of chervil.

Makes 4 servings.

Note: To clean mussels, scrub thoroughly under cold water, removing beards and discarding any with open or broken shells.

Scallop Seviche

1 lb. scallops
1/2 teaspoon salt
Juice 4 to 5 limes
1 small red bell pepper, seeded
1 fresh chili pepper, seeded, finely chopped
2 green onions, finely chopped
1 garlic clove, minced
1/2 oz. creamed coconut
1/4 cup whipping cream
2 tomatoes, sliced
2 avocados, sliced
2 tablespoons chopped cilantro

To Garnish:
Cilantro leaves

Put scallops into a bowl. Sprinkle with salt and pour over lime juice; scallops should be completely covered with juice. Cover bowl and chill 4 hours, turning scallops occasionally.

Slice bell pepper in fine strips; cut strips in 1-inch lengths. Add to scallops with chili, green onions and garlic. Return to refrigerator another hour.

In a small saucepan, break up creamed coconut with a wooden spoon until quite finely mashed. Add cream gradually and heat gently until smooth; cool.

Pour off lime juice, then add tomatoes and avocados to scallops. Pour over coconut cream and toss well. Check seasoning and add chopped cilantro.

Serve immediately, garnished with cilantro leaves.

Makes 4 servings.

Variation: Omit coconut cream sauce. Replace with a vinaigrette made from grapeseed oil and white wine vinegar.

Sole with Saffron & Chervil

2 tablespoons butter
4 lemon soles, filleted, skin and
   bones reserved

Fish Fumet:
2-1/2 cups water
1/2 onion, sliced
1 carrot, quartered
1 stalk celery
8 peppercorns
4 parsley sprigs
2 thyme sprigs
1 bay leaf

Saffron Sauce:
1 packet saffron
1 tablespoon boiling water
3 egg yolks
1/2 cup butter
2 tablespoons finely chopped
   chervil

To Garnish:
Salad leaves

To prepare fish fumet, in a large saucepan, put skin and bones from fish, water, onion, carrot, celery, peppercorns, parsley, thyme and bay leaf. Bring to a boil, then simmer gently 1 hour. Strain and reduce over high heat until about 1/4 remains. Set aside.

To make saffron sauce, infuse saffron in boiling water; strain and set liquid aside.

Combine egg yolks, fish fumet, butter and saffron liquid in top part of a double boiler or a bowl set over a pan of gently simmering water. Cook, whisking constantly, until thickened; do not allow water to get very hot. Just before serving, add chervil.

To cook fish, in a skillet, heat butter until almost smoking. Put in fish and fry several minutes on each side, until golden.

Serve immediately, garnished with salad leaves and accompanied by saffron sauce.

Makes 4 servings.

Trout with Watercress

4 (12-oz.) trout, cleaned, boned
Salt and pepper to taste
3 cups coarsely chopped
   watercress
1 grapefruit, segmented, chopped
1/4 cup dried bread crumbs
Butter

Sauce:
3 tablespoons white wine
2 tablespoons cold water
3 egg yolks
Pinch salt
1 cup butter
3 cups coarsely chopped
   watercress

To Garnish:
Watercress sprigs

To prepare sauce, in a small saucepan, combine wine and cold water. Boil until reduced to 1 tablespoon and cool.

In top part of a double boiler or a bowl set over a pan of simmering water, beat reduced liquor into egg yolks and salt. Keeping water in bottom pan to a slow simmer, gradually beat in butter, about 2 tablespoons at a time. Keep warm.

Put watercress in a bowl of boiling water; let stand 3 minutes then strain. Squeeze out all moisture and pound, then pass through a sieve—there should be 3 to 4 teaspoons puree. Set aside.

Preheat oven to 375F (190C). Season trout with salt and pepper. Fill each trout cavity with 1/4 of chopped watercress and grapefruit and 1 tablespoon bread crumbs. Place each trout on a square of foil, put a pat of butter on top and wrap up. Place in an ovenproof dish and bake in oven 25 minutes or until fish is cooked. Unwrap and place on warmed serving plates.

Stir watercress puree into warm sauce. Garnish fish with watercress and serve with sauce.

Makes 4 servings.

Fish Ragoût

**1 (2-1/2- to 3-lb) piece monkfish
or swordfish**
Salt and pepper to taste
3 tablespoons olive oil

Sauce:
1 tablespoon olive oil
1 onion, chopped
1-1/2 cups chopped parsley
1 teaspoon chopped rosemary
2 teaspoons chopped thyme
2 bay leaves
2 tablespoons capers
**2 tablespoons chopped black
olives**
**1 lb. tomatoes, skinned, seeded,
chopped**
2/3 cup finely chopped walnuts
1 cup red wine

Watercress Puree:
2 tablespoons butter
1 lb. watercress

To Garnish:
Lemon slices
Watercress sprigs

Preheat oven to 375F (190C).

Place fish in an ovenproof dish. Season with salt and pepper and pour over olive oil. Bake in oven about 40 minutes or until fish is cooked, basting occasionally.

To prepare sauce, in a large saucepan, heat olive oil. Add onion and saute until golden. Add herbs, capers, olives, tomatoes, walnuts and wine; simmer 30 minutes. Discard bay leaves. Puree in a blender or food processor; pour sauce over fish and return to oven 5 minutes.

To make watercress puree, in a small saucepan, melt butter. Add watercress and cook gently until softened. Puree in a blender or food processor, then season to taste.

Serve fish hot, garnished with lemon slices and watercress and accompanied by watercress puree.

Makes 6 servings.

Salmon with Dill & Mustard

4 (8-oz.) salmon steaks
Salt and pepper to taste
2 teaspoons olive oil

Sauce:
1 teaspoon salt
1 tablespoon sugar
1 teaspoon ground black pepper
1/2 teaspoon ground allspice
1/4 cup cognac
1/4 cup white wine
4 teaspoons Dijon-style mustard
2 tablespoons chopped dill weed

To Garnish:
Chicory
Curly endive

To prepare sauce, in a small saucepan, put salt, sugar, pepper, allspice, cognac and wine. Bring to a boil and boil vigorously until reduced by half. Strain and keep hot.
Preheat grill on high setting.

Season salmon steaks with salt and pepper. Place on lightly oiled foil and drizzle a little olive oil on top of each salmon steak. Fold foil to make a basket; do not close completely. Grill steaks 6 to 8 minutes, until cooked through and browned; there is no need to turn them over. Remove from foil and place on warmed serving plates.

Stir mustard and dill into hot sauce. Pour a spoonful over each steak. Garnish with chicory and curly endive to serve.

Makes 4 servings.

Note: Dill and mustard sauce can also be served with whole baked or grilled salmon. Increase sauce quantities according to weight of fish; note that amount of sauce per portion is quite small.

Asparagus & Salmon Quiches

Pastry:
3/4 cup all-purpose flour
3 tablespoons oatmeal
6 tablespoons butter, chilled
About 2 tablespoons cold water

Filling:
1/2 Camembert cheese
4 ounces smoked salmon
16 asparagus tips, blanched
1 egg
2/3 cup half and half
Salt and pepper, to taste
Red (cayenne) pepper

To Garnish:
Parsley sprigs

Preheat oven to 400F (205C).

To make pastry, place flour, oatmeal and butter in a food processor fitted with the metal blade and process 45 seconds. Add water and process 15 seconds or until pastry holds together. Divide pastry into 4 pieces, roll each out on a floured surface to a 5- or 6-inch circle. Line 4 individual flan pans with dough. Refrigerate while preparing filling.

Cut Camembert into 8 sections; cut each section in half horizontally. Cut salmon into 16 small strips; roll up. Place 4 sections of Camembert in each flan pan, rind side down, and arrange salmon rolls and asparagus tips on top.

Beat egg and half and half together; season with salt, pepper and a little cayenne. Pour into flan pans and bake 25 minutes or until a knife inserted off center comes out clean.

Serve warm, garnished with parsley, with a mixed salad.

Makes 4 servings.

Note: If you do not have a food processor, make pastry by cutting butter into oatmeal and flour.

Smoked Trout Gougère

Filling:
3 smoked trout
2 tablespoons butter
6 ounces celery hearts, thinly sliced
8 ounces asparagus, cut into 1-inch pieces
1 tablespoon all-purpose flour
2/3 cup half and half
2 tablespoons chopped parsley
2 tablespoons lemon juice

Choux Pastry:
1/4 cup butter
2/3 cup water
2/3 cup all-purpose flour, sifted
2 eggs plus 1 yolk, beaten
Pepper, to taste
3 ounces Austrian smoked cheese or Cheddar cheese, shredded (3/4 cup)

To Garnish:
1/4 cup (1 oz.) sliced almonds, toasted

Preheat oven to 400F (205C). Butter a large shallow baking dish or 4 individual ovenproof dishes.

First prepare filling. Remove skin and bones from trout; flake flesh into large pieces. Set aside.

In a large saucepan, melt butter. Add vegetables and sauté 1 minute. Stir in flour. Remove from heat and gradually stir in half and half; return to heat and bring to a boil, stirring, until thickened. Add trout, parsley and lemon juice to pan; remove from heat.

To make pastry, in a medium saucepan, melt butter in water over low heat; increase heat and bring to a boil. Remove from heat and add flour all at once; beat with a wooden spoon until dough is smooth and leaves side of pan. Beat in eggs and yolk a little at a time until dough is smooth and shiny. Season with pepper and stir in 2 ounces (1/2 cup) of the cheese.

Spoon choux mixture evenly around edge of prepared dish(es). Fill center with fish mixture; sprinkle with remaining cheese. Bake 30 minutes (20 minutes for individual gougères) until pastry is puffed and golden. Sprinkle with almonds and serve immediately.

Makes 4 servings.

Turbot with Pine Nuts

1 tablespoon vegetable oil
1 small onion, finely chopped
4 turbot cutlets, about 7 ounces each
1/2 cup white wine
1/4 cup water
Salt and pepper, to taste
1 tablespoon chopped dill
1/4 cup whipping cream
1/4 cup pine nuts, toasted
TO GARNISH:
Dill sprigs

1. In a large skillet, heat oil, add onion and cook until softened. Add fish, pour over wine and 1/4 cup water and sprinkle with salt and pepper. Cover and simmer 5 minutes, until the fish is opaque and just cooked. Remove with a spatula and arrange on a warmed serving dish; reserve cooking liquid.
2. Sieve liquid, pressing through onion. Return to saucepan and boil rapidly to reduce by half, then add dill and cream. Adjust seasoning if necessary.
3. Heat through gently, then pour over fish. Sprinkle with pine nuts and garnish with dill sprigs to serve.

Makes 4 servings.

Shrimp with Cashews

2 tablespoons vegetable oil
3 ounces cashew nuts (2/3 cup)
2 garlic cloves, sliced
1 (1/2-inch) piece gingerroot, peeled and chopped
1 red bell pepper, thinly sliced
4 ounces snow peas, topped and tailed
6 ounces shiitake mushrooms, stalks removed, halved
1 teaspoon cornstarch
1 tablespoon each soy sauce and sherry
12 ounces shrimp, thawed if frozen
4 green onions, sliced diagonally
1/2 teaspoon five-spice powder
6 ounces bean sprouts
1 teaspoon sesame oil
Salt and pepper, to taste

1. In a wok, heat half the oil, add cashews and stir-fry until golden-brown. Remove from wok and set aside.
2. Add remaining oil to wok, then add garlic, gingerroot, bell pepper, snow peas and mushrooms and stir-fry 4 minutes.
3. Blend cornstarch with soy sauce and sherry; add to wok with shrimp. Stir until thickened, then add green onions, five-spice powder, cashews and bean sprouts and stir-fry 1 to 2 minutes, to heat through. Add sesame oil, season with salt and pepper, and serve with cooked rice.

Makes 4 servings.

Shrimp with Lychees

1 pound lychees
3 tablespoons sunflower oil
1 bunch green onions, finely chopped
1 (2-inch) piece gingerroot, finely sliced
1-1/2 pounds uncooked peeled shrimp, thawed if frozen
8 ounces snow peas
1 tablespoon sesame oil
2 tablespoons saké or dry sherry
Salt and pepper to taste

Curried Fish in Pineapple

2 small pineapples
1-1/2 pounds monkfish or swordfish, skinned
1 tablespoon butter
1 tablespoon vegetable oil
6 green onions, finely chopped
1 small chile, seeded, finely chopped
4 teaspoons garam masala or curry powder
1/4 teaspoon saffron threads
1 teaspoon ground cumin
1 tablespoon lime juice
1-1/4 cups whipping cream
1 cup slivered almonds (4 oz.), toasted
Salt and pepper to taste

1. Peel all but 8 lychees; set aside. Make 4 long cuts through skin and pulp of each unpeeled lychee from top to bottom. Peel back skin and pulp to form petals, leaving seed exposed to form center of flower; set aside.
2. Heat a wok or large skillet; add sunflower oil. When hot, add green onions and gingerroot and stir-fry 30 seconds. Add shrimp and stir-fry 2 minutes. Stir in snow peas and cook 1 minute. Add sesame oil and peeled lychees and cook 30 seconds. Add saké or sherry and salt and pepper.
3. Transfer to warmed individual serving plates. Garnish with lychee flowers and serve at once.

Makes 4 to 6 servings.

1. Cut pineapples in half lengthwise through leaves. Cut out pineapple pulp, then cut in 1/2-inch cubes and set aside; reserve pineapple shells.
2. Cut fish in bite-size pieces. Melt butter and oil in a large skillet or wok over medium heat. Add green onions and chile and stir-fry 3 minutes. Stir in garam masala, saffron and cumin and cook 1 minute. Add fish and lime juice to pan and stir-fry 5 minutes. Pour in cream and bring to a boil. Lower heat and simmer 5 minutes, stirring frequently. Add pineapple cubes and 1/2 of almonds. Season with salt and pepper. Cook 2 minutes.
3. Spoon curried mixture into pineapple halves. Sprinkle with remaining almonds and serve at once.

Makes 4 servings.

Note: Chile flowers make an attractive garnish for this dish. To make, slice chile lengthwise, leaving stem end intact. Place in a bowl of iced water until open.

Spinach & Anchovy Soufflé

1 pound spinach, washed
4 tablespoons butter
1/2 cup all-purpose flour
1-1/4 cups milk
3 large egg yolks
1/2 cup shredded Cheddar cheese (2 oz.)
5 canned anchovy fillets, drained and finely chopped
Pepper to taste
Freshly grated nutmeg
4 large egg whites
TO GARNISH:
Cherry tomatoes

1. Discard tough stalks from spinach; shake off excess moisture. Pack into a saucepan (without additional water), cover and cook gently, turning occasionally, until volume decreases. Simmer 8 to 10 minutes, until tender. Place in a sieve and press with a saucer to extract moisture. Chop finely in a food processor.
2. Preheat oven to 350F (175C). Lightly grease a 5-cup soufflé dish. In a saucepan, melt butter, stir in flour and cook 1 minute. Add milk and bring to a boil, stirring constantly. Reduce heat and simmer 2 minutes, stirring constantly. Remove from heat and mix in spinach, egg yolks, cheese and anchovies. Season with pepper and nutmeg. Whisk egg whites until soft peaks form. Add 3 tablespoons to spinach mixture and stir to mix. Using a large metal spoon, lightly fold in remaining egg whites.
3. Pour mixture into prepared soufflé dish and smooth surface. Run back of a metal spoon around outer edge to form a central dome for a top hat effect. Bake in preheated oven 40 to 45 minutes, until well risen and golden-brown. Serve immediately, garnished with cherry tomatoes.

Makes 3 to 4 servings.

Scampi Mediterranean

4 ripe tomatoes
1 Spanish onion
2 medium-size zucchini
1 red bell pepper, cored and seeded
1/4 cup olive oil
1 garlic clove, crushed
2 tablespoons all-purpose flour
1/4 cup dry white wine
1 tablespoon tomato paste
1 cup water
Salt and pepper to taste
1 pound uncooked peeled shrimp
3/4 cup fresh white bread crumbs
1 tablespoon chopped fresh marjoram
4 ounces mozzarella cheese
TO GARNISH:
Sprigs of marjoram

1. Preheat oven to 375F (190C). Place tomatoes in a large bowl, cover with boiling water and let stand 30 seconds. Drain and peel, then chop coarsely. Quarter and thinly slice onion. Cut zucchini in 1/4-inch slices. Cut bell pepper in thin strips.
In a large saucepan, heat 3 tablespoons of oil. Add onion, zucchini, bell pepper and garlic and cook gently 3 minutes.
2. Stir in flour and cook 1 minute. Add wine, tomato paste and water. Season with salt and pepper and cook gently 5 minutes, stirring occasionally. Add tomatoes and mix well. Divide mixture between 4 individual ovenproof dishes. Top with shrimp.
3. Heat remaining oil in a saucepan. Remove from heat and stir in bread crumbs and marjoram; mix well. Sprinkle over mixture in dishes. Chop mozzarella cheese and sprinkle on top. Bake in preheated oven 30 minutes or until topping is golden and shrimp is cooked. Serve hot, garnished with sprigs of marjoram.

Makes 4 servings.

Tempura

1 zucchini
1 small eggplant
1 green bell pepper, cored and seeded
8 button mushrooms
2 small sweet potatoes, peeled
6 green onions
2 lemon sole or flounder fillets, skinned and boned
4 cooked jumbo shrimp in shell
1 egg yolk
2 cups all-purpose flour
1/2 teaspoon baking soda
Vegetable oil for deep-frying
DIPPING SAUCE:
1 tablespoon mirin (Japanese rice wine)
1 tablespoon Japanese soy sauce
1-1/4 cups chicken stock

1. Cut zucchini and eggplant in 1/2-inch slices. Halve eggplant slices. Cut bell pepper in 1-inch pieces. Trim mushrooms. Cut sweet potatoes in 1/4-inch slices. Cut green onions and fish in bite-size pieces.
2. Peel shrimp, except for last section of tail shells.

To prepare batter, mix egg yolk and 1-3/4 cups ice cold water in a bowl. Sift flour and baking soda into another bowl and gradually add liquid, whisking until smooth. Let stand 15 minutes.

To prepare dipping sauce, combine mirin, soy sauce and stock in a saucepan and bring to a boil; cool.
3. Half-fill a wok or deep saucepan with vegetable oil and heat to 375F (190C) or until a cube of day-old bread browns in 40 seconds. Dip pieces of vegetable and fish, a few at a time, into batter. Deep-fry 1 to 2 minutes, until lightly golden. Drain well and keep warm while cooking remaining pieces.

Place a bowl of dipping sauce on each warmed serving plate and surround with vegetables and fish.

Makes 4 servings.

Pasta with Clam Sauce

1 red bell pepper
2 cups bread flour
Pinch of salt
2 eggs, beaten
1 tablespoon olive oil
SAUCE:
1/4 cup unsalted butter
1 onion, finely chopped
1 (14-oz.) can chopped tomatoes
Pinch of sugar
Salt and pepper, to taste
1 pound clams in shells, cooked
2 teaspoons chopped tarragon
3 tablespoons chopped parsley

1. Grill bell pepper until evenly charred. Wrap in foil until cool, then remove skin and discard seeds. Purée in a blender or food processor.

Sift flour and salt onto a work surface. Make a well in the center, add eggs, oil and bell pepper purée, then gradually mix in flour mixture to form a soft dough. Knead until smooth.
2. Put the dough through the thin setting of a pasta machine, or roll out as thinly as possible, then roll up like a jellyroll and cut into strips; set aside.

To make sauce, in a pan, melt butter, add onion and fry until softened. Add tomatoes, sugar, salt and pepper and simmer 20 minutes. Purée in a blender or food processor and return to pan.
3. Remove clams from shells and add to sauce with herbs; warm through briefly.

Cook pasta in plenty of boiling salted water 3 to 4 minutes; drain well. Serve the pasta topped with the sauce.

Makes 4 servings.

Note: Use a purchased fresh pasta, flavored with tomato, if preferred.

Variation: Substitute mussels for clams.

Clam Salad with Chile Dressing

1-1/2 pounds clams in shells
Salt and pepper, to taste
4 ounces small green beans
4 ounces button mushrooms
1/2 cup pine nuts
Salad greens
CHILE DRESSING:
1 red chile
1/2 teaspoon fennel seeds
1 tablespoon lemon juice
1/4 cup virgin olive oil
TO GARNISH:
Chervil sprigs

Mussel Soufflés

1-1/2 pounds mussels in shells
3/4 cup dry white wine
1 garlic clove, crushed
Few saffron strands
Few parsley sprigs
1 bay leaf
Salt and pepper, to taste
2 tablespoons butter
2 teaspoons all-purpose flour
1 tablespoon lemon juice
2 eggs, separated
1/4 cup shredded Gruyère cheese
1 tablespoon grated Parmesan cheese

1. Put clams into a saucepan with a little water, salt and pepper. Cover tightly and cook over high heat 2 to 3 minutes, until the shells have opened. Drain and discard any clams that have not opened. Remove clams from shells.
2. To make dressing, wearing rubber gloves, remove stem from chile, halve lengthwise and scrape out seeds; finely chop flesh. Crush fennel seeds and put in a small bowl with chile, lemon juice, oil, salt and pepper. Whisk until thickened.
Blanch beans in boiling salted water 2 minutes; drain and refresh under cold running water.
3. Thinly slice mushrooms. Lightly toast pine nuts. Arrange salad greens on 4 plates. Sprinkle with beans, mushrooms and clams. Drizzle dressing over salads and sprinkle with pine nuts. Garnish with chervil and serve as a light lunch or starter.

Makes 4 servings.

Variation: Substitute mussels for clams.

1. Preheat oven to 350F (175C). Scrub mussels thoroughly under cold running water. Scrape off any barnacles and pull off the beard that protrudes between the shells. Discard any that are open or cracked. Rinse the mussels in a colander.
Put mussels and wine into a saucepan, cover and cook over high heat, shaking pan, about 3 minutes, until shells have opened. Strain, reserving cooking liquid; discard any mussels that have not opened. Remove mussels from shells and set aside.
2. Put cooking liquid, garlic, saffron, parsley, bay leaf, salt and pepper into a pan; boil until reduced to 3/4 cup; strain into a cup. In the same pan, melt butter, add flour and cook 1 minute. Add strained cooking liquid and cook, stirring, until thickened and smooth; stir in lemon juice. Remove from heat and stir some hot mixture into egg yolks; return to pan with cheeses. In a bowl, whisk egg whites until stiff; fold into sauce. Check seasoning.
3. Divide mussels among 4 buttered ramekin dishes. Spoon soufflé mixture over mussels and bake 20 minutes, until puffed and golden-brown. Serve immediately, as a light lunch or starter.

Makes 4 servings.

Mussels with Two Sauces

4 pounds mussels in shells
1/2 cup dry white wine
TOMATO BASIL SAUCE:
1 (14-oz.) can chopped tomatoes
1 tablespoon tomato paste
2 teaspoons torn basil leaves
1 teaspoon chopped fresh oregano
Pinch of sugar
Salt and pepper, to taste
FENNEL SAUCE:
2 tablespoons butter
1 leek, finely chopped
1 fennel bulb, finely chopped
1/4 cup whipping cream

1. Put mussels and wine into a large saucepan, cover and cook over high heat, shaking pan, 4 to 6 minutes, until shells have opened. Drain, discarding any mussels that have not opened; discard the empty half shells. Arrange mussels in their half shells in an ovenproof dish and keep warm.
2. To make Tomato Basil Sauce, put all the ingredients into a saucepan and simmer 15 minutes, until thickened and smooth.

To make Fennel Sauce, in a pan melt butter, add leek and fennel, cover and cook about 5 minutes, until softened. Add cream, season to taste and simmer 2 minutes. Purée in a blender or food processor.
3. Arrange mussels on 4 to 6 plates and fill shells alternately with the two sauces. Serve as a starter or light lunch.

Makes 4 to 6 servings.

Mussels in Wine & Cream Sauce

2 cups Muscadet wine
Bouquet garni
6 pounds mussels in shells
2 tablespoons butter
2 shallots, finely chopped
Pinch of turmeric
1/2 cup whipping cream
2 egg yolks
Salt and pepper, to taste
Dash of Tabasco sauce
2 teaspoons chopped fresh tarragon

1. Put wine and bouquet garni into a large saucepan. Add mussels, cover and cook over high heat, shaking pan, 5 to 6 minutes, until shells open. Remove mussels with a slotted spoon and discard any that have not opened. Remove mussels from shells and set aside. Boil cooking liquid until reduced by half.
2. In another pan, melt butter; add shallots and fry gently until softened. Stir in reduced liquid and boil until reduced again by one-third. Strain and return to pan with turmeric and all but 1 tablespoon cream; simmer 1 minute.
3. Blend egg yolks with remaining cream and whisk in a little of the hot liquid. Whisk this slowly into pan and heat gently, without boiling, until thickened and smooth. Season with salt, pepper and Tabasco sauce. Add mussels and warm through. Sprinkle with tarragon to serve.

Makes 4 servings.

Scallops with Saffron Sauce

12 to 16 sea scallops in shells
3 tablespoons butter
1 small onion, finely chopped
2 tablespoons dry vermouth
1/2 cup dry white wine
2 tomatoes, peeled, seeded and chopped
1/4 teaspoon powdered saffron
4 ounces small asparagus tips
3 tablespoons crème fraîche
Salt and pepper, to taste

1. First open scallop shells. Holding scallop in a cloth with flat shell uppermost, insert small knife into the small opening between shells. Work blade across inside of flat shell to sever internal muscle. Pry shells apart.
2. Carefully loosen scallops from shells, rinse, removing any dark strands, and pat dry on paper towels.
3. In a skillet, melt half the butter and quickly fry scallops 2 to 3 minutes, until they turn opaque. Remove from pan with any juices and keep warm.

In the same pan, melt remaining butter, add onion and fry about 5 minutes, until softened. Add vermouth, wine, tomatoes and saffron;

bring to a boil, then simmer until liquid has reduced by half.

Meanwhile, lightly steam asparagus 3 to 4 minutes until crisptender; add to pan with scallops, crème fraîche, salt and pepper. Simmer 2 minutes; check seasoning. Serve with steamed new potatoes or pasta.

Makes 4 servings.

Note: If buying shelled scallops, use 1-1/2 pounds.

Variation: Serve in the cleaned shells, with toast, as a starter for 6 to 8.

Scallops & Spinach Chardonnay

6 ounces young spinach leaves
Salt, to taste
6 tablespoons butter
1 small onion, finely chopped
2 parsley sprigs
1/2 cup white Chardonnay wine
1/2 cup fish stock
6 black peppercorns
1/4 cup whipping cream
1 to 1-1/2 pounds shelled bay scallops

1. Put spinach into a pan with just the water clinging to the leaves after washing and add a pinch of salt. Cover and cook 3 to 4 minutes, until the leaves have just wilted. Drain and refresh under cold running water. Press out as much water as possible from the leaves. Set aside.
2. In a saucepan, melt 2 tablespoons butter, add onion and fry until softened but not browned. Add parsley, wine, stock and peppercorns. Bring to a boil, reduce heat, then simmer until reduced by two-thirds. Strain

and return to pan with cream. Keeping sauce at a gentle simmer, add remaining butter a small piece at a time, stirring with each addition, until sauce is smooth and shiny.
3. Rinse scallops, removing any dark strands, and pat dry with paper towels. Add to pan, cover and cook about 4 minutes, until just cooked. Stir in spinach and heat through. Taste and add salt if necessary. Serve with saffron rice and a crisp salad.

Makes 4 servings.

Spicy Stir-Fried Abalone

2 abalone in shells or 12 ounces abalone meat
2 tablespoons sunflower oil
1 garlic clove, chopped
1 teaspoon chopped gingerroot
1 dried red chile
2 tablespoons soy sauce
2 tablespoons rice wine or dry sherry
1 teaspoon sugar
1 teaspoon tomato paste
1 tablespoon shredded green onion

1. First shell abalone. Push the tip of an oyster knife (or other strong small knife) into the thin end of the shell underneath the flesh. Work the blade until the muscle is free. Take out the white meat; rinse thoroughly, discarding the intestine. Pat dry with paper towels.
2. Cut abalone into very thin slices, then pound with a mallet until limp and velvety to tenderize.
3. In a wok or frying pan, heat oil and briefly fry garlic, gingerroot and

chile. Add abalone and stir-fry 30 seconds. Remove abalone with a slotted spoon.

Add soy sauce, rice wine, sugar and tomato paste to pan. Bring to a boil, then simmer 2 minutes. Return abalone to pan and heat through.

Remove chile and sprinkle with shredded green onion to serve. Serve as a light lunch.

Makes 4 servings.

Shrimp & Spinach Soufflé

1 pound spinach leaves
Grated nutmeg, salt and pepper, to taste
3 tablespoons butter
1/4 cup all-purpose flour
2/3 cup milk
1 tablespoon lemon juice
1/2 cup shredded Cheddar cheese
6 ounces peeled small shrimp
3 eggs, separated
4 teaspoons sesame seeds

1. Preheat oven to 375F (190C). Put spinach into a large saucepan with just the water clinging to leaves after washing; season with nutmeg, salt and pepper. Bring to a boil, then cover and cook 5 minutes, until softened. Drain in a sieve, pressing out as much water as possible. Turn onto a board and chop finely. Drain again, then set aside.
2. In a saucepan, melt butter, add flour and cook 1 minute. Gradually stir in milk, cooking until thickened and smooth.

Remove from heat and stir in

lemon juice, cheese, shrimp, spinach, egg yolks, salt and pepper; stir well. In a bowl, whisk egg whites until stiff, then fold carefully into mixture.
3. Butter a 5-cup soufflé dish and sprinkle with half the sesame seeds. Spoon mixture into dish and sprinkle with remaining sesame seeds. Put on a baking sheet and bake 35 minutes, until puffed and golden-brown. Serve immediately, with a salad, as a starter or light lunch.

Makes 4 servings.

Shrimp Fettuccine

1 ounce prosc tto
12 basil leaves
6 tablespoons unsalted butter
2 garlic cloves, crushed
4 ounces peeled shrimp
12 ounces fresh spinach fettuccine
1/4 cup grated Parmesan cheese
Salt and pepper, to taste

1. Cut prosc tto in julienne strips. Tear basil leaves in half. In a large skillet, melt butter, add garlic and fry gently 1 minute. Add prosc tto, shrimp and basil and cook 2 minutes. Keep warm while cooking pasta.
2. Bring a large saucepan of salted water to a boil, add fettuccine and cook 3 minutes, or until *al dente;* drain thoroughly.
3. Add half the Parmesan cheese and salt and pepper to the sauce, stir well.

Add the fettuccine and toss thoroughly to coat with the sauce.

Divide among 4 plates and sprinkle with remaining Parmesan cheese. Serve piping hot, with a green side salad.

Makes 4 servings.

Note: Substitute 8 ounces dried fettuccine for fresh and cook 10 to 12 minutes.

Shrimp Risotto

1 pound cooked shrimp in shells
1 bay leaf
Few celery leaves
6 peppercorns
Salt, to taste
Few saffron threads
6 tablespoons butter
1 onion, chopped
1 garlic clove, crushed
2 cups Italian Arborio rice
1-1/4 cups dry white wine
2 zucchini, cut into strips
6 ounces oyster mushrooms, cut into pieces
2 tablespoons chopped parsley
4 tablespoons grated Parmesan cheese

1. Peel shrimp; set aside. Wash shells, then put in a saucepan with bay leaf, celery leaves, peppercorns, salt, saffron and 3-3/4 cups water. Bring to a boil, then simmer 20 minutes. Strain and reserve stock.
2. In a heavy saucepan, melt half the butter, add onion and garlic and cook about 5 minutes, until softened but not colored. Add rice and stir to coat all the grains with butter. Add one-third of the reserved stock and bring to a boil, then simmer, uncovered, until stock is absorbed. Gradually add

more stock and wine until it has all been absorbed and the rice is cooked; this will take about 20 minutes.
3. In a separate pan, melt remaining butter, add shrimp, zucchini and mushrooms and cook 2 to 3 minutes. Fold into rice, with parsley and half the Parmesan cheese; taste and add salt, if needed.

Serve piping hot, sprinkled with remaining Parmesan cheese.

Makes 4 servings.

Langostinos & Rice

16 to 24 cooked small langostinos
1-1/4 cups long-grain rice
1/4 cup wild rice
1/4 cup butter, softened
2 teaspoons chopped fresh tarragon
2 teaspoons snipped chives
1 garlic clove, crushed
2 tablespoons sunflower oil
1 zucchini, cut in thin strips
1 carrot, cut in thin strips
1/2 teaspoon cumin seeds
4 ounces oyster mushrooms, cut in pieces
1/2 cup fish stock
Salt and pepper, to taste

Seafood Kabobs & Mango Sauce

1-1/2 pounds cooked small langostinos
1 tablespoon olive oil
1 tablespoon lemon juice
1 tablespoon chopped fennel
1 tablespoon chopped parsley
Salt and pepper, to taste
1 ripe mango
8 bacon slices
8 green onions
1 tablespoon honey
Dash Tabasco sauce
1 garlic clove, crushed
1/4 cup orange juice
1 teaspoon soy sauce

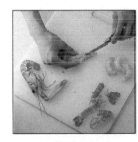  

1. Rinse langostinos, then remove shells: twist off the head, then gently pull off the tail shell and remove the body shell. Cut down the back and remove dark vein. Dry well with paper towels; set aside.
2. Cook both rices in 3 cups of boiling salted water 10 to 12 minutes, until tender and water is absorbed.

In a small bowl, blend butter, tarragon, chives and garlic together; set aside.
3. In a frying pan, heat half the oil, add langostinos and stir-fry quickly, until pink. Remove from pan and keep warm. Heat remaining oil in pan, add zucchini and carrot and stir-fry 1 to 2 minutes. Add cumin seeds and mushrooms and stir well.

Add rice, langostinos, stock and salt and pepper, bring to a boil, cover and cook gently 2 to 3 minutes.

Just before serving, stir in the herb butter; alternatively, serve mixture on individual plates, topped with a lump of herb butter.

Makes 4 servings.

Note: Langostinos are also called Dublin Bay prawns in Britain and scampi in Italy.

1. Peel langostinos, leaving tail section intact: twist off the head and carefully remove the body shell. Cut down the center back and remove dark vein. Soak bamboo skewers.

In a bowl, mix together oil, lemon juice, fennel, parsley, salt and pepper. Add langostinos and stir well. Cover and refrigerate while preparing remaining ingredients.
2. Peel mango and cut in half, along one side of seed; remove seed. Cut one half in 16 cubes. Cut each bacon slice in half and wrap around a mango cube. Halve green onions. Preheat broiler.
3. Thread marinated langostinos, bacon-wrapped mango and green onions onto 8 skewers.

Roughly chop remaining mango and put into a blender or food processor with honey, Tabasco sauce, garlic, orange juice and soy sauce. Blend until smooth; transfer to a saucepan and heat through gently.

Put the seafood kabobs under preheated broiler and cook 6 to 8 minutes, turning occasionally, until bacon is crisp. Serve hot with mango sauce.

Makes 4 servings.

Note: Langostinos are the same species as Dublin Bay prawns and scampi.

Lobster Salad

4 (1-lb.) live lobsters
Salt and pepper, to taste
DRESSING:
1 tablespoon sesame oil
2 tablespoons olive oil
1/2 teaspoon Dijon-style mustard
2 teaspoons white wine vinegar
Salt and pepper, to taste
2 tablespoons toasted sesame seeds
TO SERVE:
2 carrots
1 small celery root
Snipped chives

Lobster Filo Bundles

1/4 cup butter
2 tablespoons chopped watercress
Salt and pepper, to taste
6 ounces cooked lobster meat
8 sheets filo pastry
Melted butter for brushing
TOMATO SAUCE:
1 pound tomatoes, peeled, seeded and chopped
1 teaspoon tomato paste
Pinch of sugar
8 to 10 basil leaves, chopped
TO GARNISH:
Snipped chives and lemon twists

1. Secure lobster claws with rubber bands. Put lobsters, head down, in a large pan of fast boiling salted water. Cover, bring to a boil and simmer 12 minutes until shells are bright red. Remove from pan; cool under running water until lobsters are cool enough to handle.

Snap off legs and break each apart at the central joint; remove flesh with a skewer. Snap each claw free near the body, then crack the claw shells with a mallet and remove flesh in one piece if possible.
2. With the lobster on its back, cut down either side of the shell, then pull away the bony covering which protects the underside. Pry the flesh

free in one piece, starting at the tail. Discard the stomach sac near the eyes and the dark intestinal thread which runs the length of the body. Take out the grey-green liver, and coral if any; these can be used in sauces.
3. Rinse and dry lobster shells and place on 4 individual serving plates. Slice tail meat in medallions and arrange in the shells with remaining meat. Mix together dressing ingredients and pour over lobster. Shred carrots and celery root; place a little on each plate and sprinkle with chives. Serve as a starter or a light meal.

Makes 4 servings.

1. Preheat oven to 400F (205C). Make sauce as in step 3. In a bowl, blend together butter, watercress and salt and pepper. Roughly chop lobster meat. Brush one sheet of filo pastry with melted butter; fold in half and brush again with butter. Put a little lobster meat near one short edge and spread with watercress butter.
2. Roll up pastry to enclose lobster, tucking in the ends to form a bundle. Repeat with remaining filo pastry, lobster and watercress butter. Place the bundles on a greased baking sheet and brush again with melted butter.

Bake 15 minutes, until golden-brown.
3. To make sauce, put tomatoes in a saucepan with tomato paste, sugar and salt and pepper; simmer gently about 15 to 20 minutes, until thickened. Stir basil leaves into sauce.

Arrange 2 lobster bundles and a little tomato sauce on each serving plate and sprinkle chives over sauce. Garnish with lemon twists and serve as a light meal.

Makes 4 servings.

Lobster & Spinach Roulade

1 pound fresh spinach
Pinch of grated nutmeg
1/4 cup grated Parmesan cheese
4 eggs, separated
Salt and pepper, to taste
FILLING:
2 tablespoons butter
1/4 cup all-purpose flour
1 cup milk
2 tomatoes, peeled and seeded
6 ounces cooked lobster meat
2 teaspoons chopped dill
2 tablespoons lime juice

Lobster with Hollandaise

2 carrots, sliced
2 onions, sliced
Bouquet garni
1-3/4 cups white wine
Few fennel stalks
Few black peppercorns
2 (1-1/2-lb.) live lobsters
HOLLANDAISE SAUCE:
2 eggs
2 tablespoons lemon juice
Salt, to taste
2 teaspoons pink peppercorns, crushed
3/4 cup unsalted butter

1. Preheat oven to 375F (190C). Grease and line an 11 x 7-inch jelly-roll pan.

Put spinach into a saucepan with just the water clinging to the leaves after washing. Cover and cook 5 minutes, until softened. Drain well, pressing out as much water as possible. Chop finely, then place in a bowl with nutmeg, Parmesan cheese, egg yolks and salt and pepper; mix well.

In a bowl, whisk egg whites until stiff, then fold into spinach mixture. Pour into prepared pan; spread to level mixture. Bake 15 minutes, until firm.

2. Meanwhile, make filling. In a saucepan, melt butter, add flour and cook 1 minute. Gradually add milk, stirring until thickened and smooth. Simmer 2 minutes. Chop tomatoes and lobster; stir into sauce with dill, lime juice and salt and pepper to taste; heat through.

3. Invert the roulade onto a sheet of waxed paper and carefully remove lining paper. Cover with filling and roll up from a short edge, using the waxed paper to lift the roulade.

Cut in slices and serve warm, as a light meal or starter.

Makes 4 to 6 servings.

1. In a large saucepan, put carrots, onions, bouquet garni, wine, fennel, peppercorns and 2 cups cold water. Bring to a fast boil, add lobsters, cover and bring back to a boil. Cook 18 minutes, or until shells are bright red. Cool under running water.

2. Meanwhile, make sauce. Put eggs, lemon juice, salt and peppercorns into a blender or food processor and blend for a few seconds. Heat butter until foaming; pour half into blender or food processor and blend for a few seconds. Pour in remaining butter and blend 5 to 7 seconds, until thick and creamy. Pour into a heatproof bowl set over a saucepan of hot water and leave until thickened, stirring occasionally.

3. To prepare each lobster, first kill as on page 62 (left). Lay it on its back and, using a heavy sharp knife, cut through firmly from head to tail to split lobster in half; separate lobster halves. Discard the stomach sac near the eyes and the dark intestinal thread running the length of the body. Take out the liver and any coral.

Arrange the lobster halves on 4 plates and spoon the sauce over the meat. Serve, as a light meal, with salad.

Makes 4 servings.

Crab Mousse with Cucumber

8 ounces crabmeat (white and brown)
1 tablespoon lemon juice
1/4 teaspoon finely grated lemon peel
5 teaspoons unflavored gelatin powder
1/4 cup fish stock or water
4 (3-oz.) packages cream cheese, softened
1 tablespoon dry sherry
Salt and pepper, to taste
2 egg whites
1 cucumber
1 tablespoon chopped dill
1 tablespoon white wine vinegar
1 teaspoon Dijon-style mustard
2 tablespoons vegetable oil
TO GARNISH:
Dill sprigs and red lumpfish roe

Deviled Crab

4 (1-lb.) crab, freshly boiled
1 small onion
2 ounces button mushrooms
1 celery stalk
4 tablespoons butter
1 teaspoon prepared horseradish
2 teaspoons Dijon-style mustard
1 tablespoon Worcestershire sauce
2 tablespoons all-purpose flour
2 tablespoons dry white wine
2 tablespoons whipping cream
Salt and pepper, to taste
1/2 cup bread crumbs, toasted
1 tablespoon grated Parmesan cheese
TO GARNISH:
Snipped chives

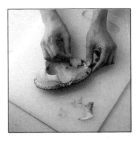  

1. In a bowl, mix together brown and white crabmeat, with lemon juice and peel. Sprinkle gelatin over stock in a small saucepan. Let stand until softened. Heat until dissolved.
2. Put crab, dissolved gelatin, cream cheese, sherry and pepper into a blender or food processor and blend until smooth. Taste and add salt if necessary. Turn into a bowl. Whisk egg whites until stiff, then fold into crab mixture.

Turn mixture into a dampened 3-3/4-cup mold and smooth the top. Cover and refrigerate mousse about 4 hours, until set.
3. Cut grooves along the cucumber skin with a zester, then slice thinly. In a small bowl, whisk dill, vinegar, mustard, oil, salt and pepper together until smooth.

Turn crab mousse out onto a serving plate and arrange overlapping slices of cucumber around the edge. Drizzle the dressing over the cucumber and garnish with dill sprigs and lumpfish roe. Serve as a starter or light meal.

Makes 4 to 6 servings.

1. Remove crabmeat from shells. When all the meat has been removed, break away the shell edge along the natural dark rim of the shell. Scrub shells.
2. Finely chop onion, mushrooms and celery. In a frying pan, melt half the butter, add the vegetables and fry gently about 5 minutes, until softened. Add horseradish, mustard and Worcestershire sauce and stir well.

Stir in the flour and cook 1 minute, stirring. Stir in wine and cream and cook, stirring, until thickened and smooth. Remove from heat and fold in crabmeat; season with salt and pepper.
3. Preheat broiler. Spoon mixture into crab shells and sprinkle with bread crumbs and cheese. Place under preheated broiler 3 to 4 minutes, until golden-brown.

Serve warm, topped with chives and accompanied by a salad.

Makes 4 servings.

Crab Ravioli with Baby Corn

RAVIOLI DOUGH:
2 cups bread flour
1/2 teaspoon salt
2 eggs, beaten
1 tablespoon olive oil
FILLING:
10 ounces crabmeat (white and brown)
2 tablespoons butter
Few drops of chili sauce
SAUCE:
6 tablespoons butter
6 ounces baby corn
2 tablespoons lemon juice
12 small basil leaves
TO SERVE:
Grated Parmesan cheese

Crab Burritos

1 tablespoon vegetable oil
1 small onion, finely chopped
1 pound tomatoes, peeled and chopped
1 tablespoon tomato paste
1/4 teaspoon red (cayenne) pepper
1 teaspoon paprika
2 teaspoons Worcestershire sauce
Salt and pepper, to taste
8 tortillas or crepes
6 ounces white crabmeat
2 ounces mozzarella cheese, shredded (1/2 cup)
Shredded lettuce
1 avocado
1 tablespoon lemon juice
4 tablespoons dairy sour cream

1. To make dough, sift flour and salt onto a work surface; make a well in the center and add eggs and oil. Gradually mix in flour to form a soft dough; knead 10 minutes. Wrap in foil and leave 1 hour.
2. Meanwhile, prepare filling. Flake crabmeat into a bowl. Melt butter and add to crab with chili sauce and salt and pepper to taste.

On a floured surface, roll out half the dough to a 16-inch square. Using a knife, mark the dough in 2-inch squares; do not cut. Put a little crab mixture into the center of each square. Brush along the edges of each square with water.

Roll out remaining dough to the same size and place over the filling. Press down between the filling to seal the squares, then cut in pockets. Cook in a large saucepan of boiling salted water 3 to 4 minutes; drain and keep warm.
3. To make sauce, in a saucepan, melt butter, add corn and cook, stirring, 2 to 3 minutes. Stir in lemon juice, basil, salt and pepper.

Arrange the ravioli on 4 warmed plates and pour the sauce over the top. Sprinkle with Parmesan cheese and serve immediately.

Makes 4 servings.

1. Preheat oven to 350F (175C). Grease an ovenproof dish.

In a saucepan, heat oil, add onion and fry until softened. Add tomatoes, tomato paste, cayenne, paprika, Worcestershire sauce, salt and pepper. Bring to a boil, then simmer, uncovered, about 20 minutes, until thick.
2. Spread a little sauce over each tortilla, sprinkle with crabmeat and mozzarella, then roll up, tucking in the ends. Put into prepared dish, cover and bake 20 minutes.
3. Place lettuce on individual serving plates. Peel and slice avocado, brush with lemon juice and arrange on the lettuce. Place 2 burritos on each plate and top with the tomato sauce and a spoonful of sour cream. Serve any remaining tomato sauce separately.

Makes 4 servings.

Seafood Treasure Chest

6 ounces puff pastry, thawed if frozen
Beaten egg, to glaze
1/2 cup dry vermouth
3 egg yolks
3/4 cup butter, melted and cooled
1 tablespoon chopped cilantro
Salt and pepper, to taste
12 ounces shelled bay scallops
4 ounces peeled cooked small shrimp, thawed if frozen
TO GARNISH:
8 cooked shrimp in shells (optional)

1. Preheat oven to 425F (220C). On a lightly floured surface, roll out pastry and cut in 4 (5" x 3") rectangles. Put on a dampened baking sheet and slash across top diagonally several times; brush with beaten egg. Bake 12 to 15 minutes, until puffed, crisp and golden-brown. Keep warm.
2. In a small saucepan, boil vermouth until reduced by half; cool slightly, then put into a heatproof bowl with egg yolks. Set over a pan of simmering water and whisk together about 10 minutes, until mixture thickens. Slowly whisk in melted butter to form

a sauce. Add cilantro, salt and pepper and keep warm over the water.

Steam scallops 3 to 4 minutes, until just firm. Add shrimp and steam 1 minute to heat through. Add to the sauce.
3. Split the pastry boxes in half horizontally. Put the bottoms on 4 warmed plates, spoon over the sauce and cover with the pastry lids. Garnish with whole shrimp and serve immediately, as a starter or light meal.

Makes 4 servings.

Seafood Terrine

4 ounces spinach leaves
1 (1-1/2-lb.) lobster, cooked
1 (1/4-oz.) package unflavored gelatin
1 (8-oz.) package cream cheese, softened
1/4 cup brandy
2 tablespoons lemon juice
2 cups whipping cream
Salt and pepper, to taste
8 ounces crabmeat (white and brown)
1 tablespoon chopped dill
YOGURT SAUCE:
1/2 cup plain yogurt
2 teaspoons chopped dill
2 teaspoons chopped fresh mint
TO GARNISH:
Dill sprigs and lemon twists

1. Blanch spinach in boiling water 1 minute; drain thoroughly and pat dry. Use spinach leaves to line a 9" x 5" loaf pan or mold, overlapping the edges. Remove lobster meat from shell.

Break up shell and put into a saucepan with 3/4 cup water. Simmer 15 minutes; strain. Sprinkle gelatin over hot liquid; stir until dissolved.
2. Put lobster meat and half of the cream cheese, the brandy, the lemon juice and the gelatin mixture into a blender or food processor and blend until smooth; turn into a bowl. Whip cream until soft peaks form and fold half into the mixture. Season with salt and pepper. Turn

into prepared mold and smooth the top; refrigerate.

Blend crabmeat with remaining cheese, brandy, lemon juice and gelatin mixture. Turn into a bowl and fold in remaining whipped cream, with dill, salt and pepper.
3. Pour crab mixture carefully over lobster mixture and smooth. Fold spinach leaves over top to enclose and cover and refrigerate about 3 hours, until set.

To make sauce, mix together yogurt, dill, mint, salt and pepper. Turn out terrine and cut into thick slices. Garnish with dill and lemon. Serve with yogurt sauce.

Makes 6 to 8 servings.

Marinated Seafood Kabobs

12 sea scallops
12 small shrimp, peeled
12 large shrimp, peeled
2 garlic cloves
2 tablespoons chopped parsley
1 tablespoon chopped basil leaves
2 tablespoons lime juice
1/4 cup olive oil
Salt and pepper, to taste
1 cup bread crumbs, toasted
TO SERVE:
Lime wedges

Fritto Misto di Mare

8 large shrimp
16 small shrimp
8 ounces small squid, cleaned
Seasoned flour for coating
1/2 cup *each* self-rising flour and cornstarch
1/2 teaspoon baking powder
Salt and pepper, to taste
1 egg, beaten
1 cup iced water
1 head radicchio
1 small fennel bulb
1 tablespoon pine nuts
2 tablespoons French dressing
Vegetable oil for deep-frying
Lime slices to garnish

     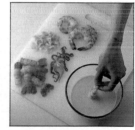

1. Rinse scallops, removing any dark strands, and pat dry; detach corals. Cut white part of each scallop in 2 circles. Put into a bowl with small and large shrimp. Soak bamboo skewers in water.

2. Finely chop garlic and put into a pestle and mortar with herbs. Pound together to form a paste, add lime juice and pound again. Gradually work in oil to form a thick sauce; season with salt and pepper. Pour over seafood and mix well. Cover and re-frigerate at least 1 hour. Preheat broiler.

3. Thread scallops and shrimp alternately onto 4 skewers and sprinkle with bread crumbs. Cook under pre-heated broiler 6 to 8 minutes, until bread crumbs are golden and seafood is firm; turn several times during cooking. Serve hot, with lime wedges and rice pilaf.

Makes 4 servings.

1. Peel shrimp, leaving tail sections intact. Cut down the back to remove dark vein. Cut squid pouch and tentacles in thin rings and fins in strips. Toss all seafood lightly in seasoned flour; shake off the excess.

Sift flour, cornstarch and baking powder into a bowl; add salt and pepper. Make a well in the center and add egg and a little iced water. Beat to incorporate dry ingredients; gradually add more water, beating well, until a smooth light batter is formed.

2. Separate radicchio leaves. Shred fennel and radicchio finely. Arrange on the side of 4 plates.

Sprinkle with pine nuts and drizzle over a little French dressing.

3. Heat oil to 350F (175C) or until a 1-inch bread cube turns golden-brown in 65 seconds. Dip seafood into batter and deep-fry in batches 2 to 3 minutes, until crisp and golden. Drain well on paper towels and keep hot, while cooking the remaining seafood.

Arrange seafood on the plates and garnish with lime slices. Serve immediately, as a starter or light meal.

Makes 4 servings.

Spanish Seafood Stew

1 pound mussels in shells, cleaned
12 clams in shells, cleaned
1/2 cup dry white wine
Salt and pepper, to taste
1 pound small squid, cleaned
4 cooked langostinos
3 tablespoons olive oil
1 onion, chopped
2 garlic cloves, crushed
1 tablespoon lemon juice
8 ounces tomatoes, peeled and quartered
1/4 cup sherry
8 ounces peeled shrimp, thawed if frozen
1 tablespoon chopped parsley

1. Put mussels, clams, wine, salt and pepper into a large pan. Cover and cook over high heat about 4 minutes, until shells have opened; discard any that do not open. Strain, then return liquid to pan and boil until reduced by half. Remove the mussels and clams from their shells.
2. Slice squid in rings. Remove shells and dark veins from langostinos.

In a saucepan, heat oil, add onion and garlic and fry gently until softened. Add squid and fry gently 10 minutes. Add lemon juice, tomatoes, reduced cooking liquid, sherry, salt and pepper and bring to a boil. Reduce heat, cover and simmer 10 minutes, until squid is tender.
3. Add langostinos, mussels, clams and shrimp; stir and cook 5 minutes. Sprinkle with parsley to serve.

Makes 4 servings.

Seafood in Cider Sauce

2 cups dry cider
1 onion, chopped
1 carrot, chopped
Bouquet garni
Salt and pepper, to taste
3 pounds mussels in shells, cleaned
1-1/2 pounds large shrimp
12 live crayfish
2 egg yolks
1/2 cup whipping cream
6 tablespoons butter, in pieces
6 ounces button mushrooms
2 tablespoons lemon juice
TO GARNISH:
Chervil sprigs and croûtons

1. Combine cider, onion, carrot, bouquet garni, salt, pepper and 1 cup water in a large saucepan. Bring to a boil, then cover and simmer 10 minutes. Add mussels, cover and cook over high heat 4 to 5 minutes, until shells have opened. Remove with a slotted spoon and discard any unopened ones. Remove mussels from shells.

Add shrimp and crayfish to the pan and cook about 5 minutes, until shells are pink. Remove with a slotted spoon and cool in cold water. Peel crayfish and shrimp, leaving on tail shells. Devein shrimp.
2. Strain cooking juices into a pan and boil until reduced by three-quarters. Blend egg yolks and cream with a little of the cooking juices. Stir in pan and cook gently 5 minutes, or until thickened; stir constantly and do not boil. Remove from heat and whisk in butter a little at a time, until glossy.
3. Put mushrooms, lemon juice and 2 tablespoons water in a small saucepan and cook gently about 5 minutes, until softened.

Arrange seafood and mushrooms on a warmed serving plate and pour over the sauce. Garnish with chervil and croûtons to serve.

Makes 4 to 6 servings.

Meat, Poultry & Game

Spiced Roast Chicken

1 (3-1/2-lb.) chicken
1 tablespoon butter
2/3 cup marsala

Mushroom Stuffing:
3 tablespoons butter
1 onion, finely chopped
1 teaspoon garam masala
4 ounces button, brown or chestnut
   mushrooms, chopped
1 cup coarsely grated parsnips
1 cup coarsely grated carrots
1/4 cup minced walnuts
2 teaspoons chopped fresh thyme
1 cup fresh white bread crumbs
1 egg, beaten
Salt and pepper to taste

To Garnish:
Thyme and watercress sprigs

To Serve:
Seasonal vegetables

Preheat oven to 375F (190C).
   Prepare stuffing: In a large saucepan, melt butter; add onion and sauté
2 minutes or until softened. Stir in
garam masala and cook 1 minute.

Add mushrooms, parsnips and carrots; cook, stirring, 5 minutes. Remove from heat; stir in remaining
stuffing ingredients.
   Stuff and truss chicken. Place,
breast down, in a roasting pan; add
1/4 cup water. Roast 45 minutes; turn
chicken breast up and dot with butter.
Roast about 45 more minutes or until
a meat thermometer inserted in
thickest part of thigh (not touching
bone) registers 185F (85C). Transfer
to a platter; keep warm.
   Pour off and discard fat from roasting pan; add marsala to remaining
cooking juices, stirring to scrape up
any browned bits. Boil over high heat
1 minute to reduce slightly; adjust
seasoning.
   Carve chicken and garnish with
thyme and watercress sprigs. Serve
with stuffing, flavored meat juices
and seasonal vegetables.

Makes 4 servings.

Chicken in Black Bean Sauce

12 ounces skinned, boned chicken
   breast, cut into strips
About 2/3 cup chicken stock
1 tablespoon plus 1 teaspoon sesame
   oil
1 tablespoon plus 1 teaspoon corn or
   peanut oil
4 green onions, sliced diagonally
6 ounces fresh shiitake mushrooms
   (see *Note*), sliced
8 ounces broccoli flowerets
1/4 cup preserved black beans, rinsed
2 teaspoons cornstarch blended with
   1 teaspoon water

Soy Marinade:
2/3 cup dry sherry
2 tablespoons soy sauce
1 teaspoon light brown sugar
1 garlic clove, pressed or minced
1 (1-inch) piece fresh gingerroot,
   grated
1 fresh red chile, seeded, thinly sliced

To Serve:
Hot rice or thin noodles

Prepare marinade: Combine all marinade ingredients in a shallow bowl

and mix well. Stir in chicken, cover
and refrigerate at least 1 hour. Lift
from bowl with a slotted spoon;
measure marinade and add enough
stock to make 1-1/4 cups. Set aside.
   In a wok or large frying pan, heat
sesame and corn or peanut oils over
high heat. Add chicken and stir-fry
about 4 minutes or just until
browned. Add green onions, mushrooms, broccoli and black beans; stir-
fry about 5 minutes or just until broccoli is tender-crisp.
   Mix stock-marinade mixture with
cornstarch mixture. Pour into wok or
pan and cook, stirring constantly, until sauce is thickened. Serve immediately, with rice or noodles.

Makes 4 servings.

Note: If fresh shiitake are unavailable, substitute button mushrooms.

Duck with Raspberry Sauce

4 boneless duck breasts, halved
1 tablespoon honey
1 garlic clove, pressed or minced
1/2 cup Madeira or sweet sherry
2 tablespoons butter
4 very large (about 4-inch-diameter) cultivated mushrooms
4 ounces raspberries
3 tablespoons whipping cream
Salt and pepper to taste

To Garnish:
Chervil or cilantro sprigs

Using a fork, prick skin of each duck-breast half several times. Spread duck pieces with honey and garlic; place in a shallow bowl. Pour Madeira or sherry over duck, cover and refrigerate at least 1 hour.

Remove duck from bowl with a slotted spoon, reserving marinade. In a large frying pan, melt butter over high heat; add duck and cook 2 minutes or until browned, turning once.

Reduce heat and cook 10 to 12 more minutes or until skin is a deep, rich brown and meat in thickest part is firm, but still pink. Transfer to a plate and keep warm.

Increase heat and add mushrooms to pan, turning quickly in duck juices. Pour in reserved marinade and cook about 4 minutes or until mushrooms are tender; transfer mushrooms to plate and keep warm.

Add raspberries to pan and cook over high heat until liquid in pan is slightly syrupy. Remove from heat; stir in cream, salt and pepper.

To serve, slice each duck breast; arrange each on a warmed serving plate with one mushroom. Spoon sauce over and around mushrooms. Garnish with chervil or cilantro sprigs.

Makes 4 servings.

Lamb & Mushroom Blanquette

1/4 cup butter
1-1/2 pounds lean shoulder of lamb, cut into 1-1/2-inch pieces
2-1/2 cups lamb or chicken stock
1/2 cup dry white wine
1 onion, quartered
1/2 teaspoon saffron threads
2 egg yolks
2/3 cup whipping cream
2 teaspoons lemon juice
Salt and white pepper to taste
1 garlic clove, halved
6 ounces wild mushrooms (see *Note*)

To Garnish:
Small bundles of lightly cooked spring vegetables

In a large saucepan, melt 2 tablespoons butter. Add lamb and sauté 2 minutes, just to seal; do not brown. Pour in stock and wine; bring to a boil, then skim surface. Add onion and saffron; reduce heat, cover and simmer 1-1/2 to 2 hours or until lamb is tender, skimming occasionally.

Strain stock through a fine sieve.

Discard onion; set lamb aside and keep warm. Return stock to pan and boil over high heat until reduced by half. Reduce heat to low. Beat together egg yolks and cream, then whisk into stock; heat gently, but do not boil. Season with lemon juice, salt and white pepper. Keep warm.

In a small frying pan, melt remaining 2 tablespoons butter. Add garlic and mushrooms and sauté 2 to 3 minutes or until mushrooms are tender. Discard garlic.

To serve, arrange lamb on a warmed platter or individual plates. Spoon sauce over meat; arrange mushrooms alongside meat. Garnish with spring vegetables.

Makes 4 servings.

Note: Use whatever wild mushrooms are available; fairy rings, morels, oyster mushrooms and chanterelles are pretty and flavorful. Or use a combination of cultivated types.

Beef Casseroled in Stout

1/4 cup butter
1/4 cup olive oil
1-1/2 pounds chuck or round steak, cut into 1-inch cubes
2 tablespoons all-purpose flour
1-1/4 cups stout
2 garlic cloves, halved
1 tablespoon chopped fresh rosemary
12 pearl onions, peeled
5 ounces baby carrots
Beef stock or water, if needed
6 ounces small button mushrooms
Salt and pepper to taste

To Garnish:
Rosemary sprigs

To Serve:
New potatoes or hot rice
Crusty bread

Preheat oven to 325F (165C).

In a large saucepan, melt 2 table-spoons butter in 2 tablespoons oil. Add beef (in batches, if necessary); cook over high heat just to seal. Transfer to a casserole.

Add remaining 2 tablespoons oil to pan; stir in flour and cook, stirring, 2 minutes. Remove from heat; gradually stir in stout. Heat gently, stirring, to form a smooth sauce. Add to casserole with garlic and chopped rosemary. Cover and bake 1-1/2 hours, stirring occasionally.

In a small frying pan, melt remaining 2 tablespoons butter. Add onions and sauté 2 to 3 minutes or until browned. Stir into casserole with carrots. Check level of liquid; if needed, add a little stock or water to cover meat. Return to oven and bake 30 more minutes.

Stir in mushrooms; season with salt and pepper. Return to oven; bake 30 more minutes or until meat is very tender.

To serve, garnish with rosemary sprigs and accompany with potatoes or rice and crusty bread.

Makes 4 servings.

Filets de Boeuf en Croûtes

1/4 cup butter
4 tenderloin steaks, each about 1 inch thick
6 ounces fresh wild mushrooms (see *Note*), sliced if large
2 tablespoons brandy
12 ounces puff pastry
6 ounces goose liver pâté with truffles (see *Note*)
Salt and pepper to taste
1 egg, beaten

Preheat oven to 425F (220C).

In a large frying pan, melt butter. Add steaks and cook 1 minute on each side, just to seal. Transfer to a plate; let cool.

Add mushrooms to pan and sauté 1 minute. Pour in brandy; stir to scrape up browned bits in pan. Ignite; when flames subside, set aside.

On a lightly floured surface, roll out pastry to a 12-inch square; cut into 4 (3-inch) squares. Place a fourth of the pâté in center of each square.

Cover pâté with mushrooms and their cooking juices, then place steaks on top. Season with salt and pepper.

Brush pastry edges with water. Draw up all 4 corners of each square to center; twist to seal, then press seams together. Turn packets over, seam side down; with a sharp knife, mark top of each in a lattice pattern (don't cut all the way through). Place on a baking sheet; brush with egg. Bake 25 to 30 minutes or until pastry is well risen and golden brown.

Serve with new potatoes and a green vegetable, such as asparagus.

Makes 4 servings.

Note: Use parasols, chanterelles, horse mushrooms, or cepes (porcini) or other boletes for this recipe.

Goose liver pâté with truffles is available in cans or jars in gourmet shops and good delicatessens. Other pâtés can be substituted.

Pork with Oyster Mushrooms

1 pound pork tenderloin
3-2/3 cups white bread crumbs (from
    day-old bread)
Grated peel of 1/2 lemon
Salt and pepper to taste
1 egg, beaten with 2 tablespoons
    water
1/4 cup butter
6 ounces oyster mushrooms,
    quartered if large
1 garlic clove, pressed or minced
1/4 cup Madeira
2/3 cup whipping cream

To Garnish:
Lemon slices
Parsley sprigs

To Serve:
**Green vegetables or tossed green
    salad**

Cut pork tenderloin into 1/2-inch
slanting slices; pound with a flat-
surfaced mallet to flatten. Mix
crumbs, lemon peel, salt and pepper.
Dip pork pieces into beaten egg to

coat, then roll in seasoned crumbs to
coat completely.

In a large frying pan, melt 3 tablespoons butter. Add pork, several
slices at a time; sauté slices 2 minutes
on each side or until meat is no longer
pink in center. Transfer to a warmed
dish and keep warm. Wipe out pan
with paper towels.

Melt remaining 1 tablespoon butter in same pan. Add mushrooms and
garlic and sauté 2 to 3 minutes or
until tender. Remove mushrooms
from pan; keep warm. Add Madeira
to pan and boil over high heat until
liquid is reduced by half; reduce heat,
stir in cream and heat through. Season with salt and pepper.

Arrange pork and mushrooms on
warmed serving plates. Spoon sauce
over mushrooms and garnish with
lemon slices and parsley sprigs. Serve
with green vegetables or a salad.

Makes 4 servings.

Pork Tenderloin with Truffles

4 ounces fresh or 3/4 ounce dried
    horn of plenty mushrooms
2 (12-oz.) pork tenderloins
2 garlic cloves, cut into slivers
1/2 ounce black truffles, cut into
    slivers
5 tablespoons butter
Pepper to taste
1 cup dry white wine
1 teaspoon all-purpose flour
Salt to taste

To Garnish:
Thyme or chervil sprigs

Preheat oven to 375F (190C). If using
dried mushrooms, place them in a
small bowl, cover with warm water
and let soak 20 minutes. Drain; rinse
well. Chop soaked or fresh mushrooms; set aside.

Trim pork tenderloins to the same
length. Slit each lengthwise down
center, being careful not to cut all the
way through. Lay pork out flat; make
2 more lengthwise cuts down each
piece to flatten meat further.

Arrange garlic slivers over one tenderloin; cover with mushrooms and
truffles. Dot with 2 tablespoons but-

ter and sprinkle with pepper. Cover
with second tenderloin; securely tie
pieces together with string at 1-inch
intervals.

In a large frying pan, melt 2 tablespoons butter; add pork and brown
on all sides. Transfer pork and its
cooking juices to a small roasting pan.
Pour in wine; roast 20 to 30 minutes
or until meat is no longer pink in
center. Transfer meat to a plate; keep
warm. Boil cooking juices over high
heat 1 minute to reduce slightly. Mix
remaining 1 tablespoon butter and
flour; add to juices and cook, stirring,
until thickened. Season with salt and
pepper.

Cut tenderloin into slices; spoon
sauce around meat and garnish with
thyme or chervil sprigs.

Makes 4 servings.

Note: Black horn of plenty mushrooms are used here to extend a tiny
quantity of the rarer black truffle.

Ham & Mushroom Pasta

3/4 cup dried cepes (porcini)
2 tablespoons butter
1 shallot, finely chopped
2 ounces small button mushrooms, quartered
2 (3-oz.) packages cream cheese with chives, cubed
2/3 cup whipping cream
1-1/2 ounces prosciutto, cut into strips
Pepper to taste
1 pound fresh tagliatelle

To Serve:
Tossed green salad
Cherry tomatoes

Place cepes in a small bowl; cover with warm water and let soak 20 minutes. Drain; rinse well to remove any grit.

Chop coarsely.

In a saucepan, melt butter; add shallot and sauté 2 minutes or until softened. Add cepes and button mushrooms and sauté 3 minutes or until button mushrooms are just beginning to brown. Stir in cream cheese, cream and prosciutto and cook over low heat, stirring constantly, until hot and well blended. Season with pepper.

Cook tagliatelle in plenty of boiling salted water about 3 minutes or just until al dente; drain thoroughly.

Add tagliatelle to sauce and toss well. Serve with a green salad and cherry tomatoes.

Makes 4 servings.

Saffron Chicken

1/4 cup plus 1 tablespoon boiling water
1 (3-inch) piece tamarind, shelled
1-1/2 teaspoons sugar
1-1/2 teaspoons salt
1 packet saffron
1 tablespoon boiling water
2 tablespoons vegetable oil
2 onions, sliced
4 (4-oz.) chicken breasts
1 (1-inch) piece gingerroot, finely chopped
4 garlic cloves, crushed
1 dried chili pepper, seeded, finely chopped
1-1/4 cups plain yogurt

To Garnish:
Few chives

Pour 1/4 cup boiling water over tamarind and soak 3 to 4 hours. Press tamarind liquid and pulp through a sieve; discard any fibrous residue. Mix tamarind with sugar and 1/2 teaspoon salt.

Soak saffron in boiling water about 30 minutes. Strain, reserving liquid.

In a large skillet, heat oil. Add onions and cook until browned. Add chicken breasts and cook until browned all over. Pour off oil from pan; add gingerroot, garlic, chili, yogurt and 1 teaspoon salt. Cover and cook at a slow simmer 20 minutes.

Add prepared tamarind and saffron to chicken. Cook, uncovered, over moderate heat 10 minutes, until sauce has reduced a little, stirring occasionally. Garnish chicken with chives and serve with saffron rice.

Make 4 servings.

Note: Tamarind imparts a sour flavor; if it is unavailable, substitute juice of 1/2 lemon.

Stuffed Veal Rolls

1 lb. veal scallops
2 tablespoons butter
1 tablespoon olive oil
1/2 cup white wine
2 tablespoons finely chopped
  parsley

Stuffing:
1 cup dried bread crumbs
1/2 cup grated Parmesan cheese
2 teaspoons salt
1/2 cup finely chopped walnuts
6 tablespoons finely chopped
  parsley
Water

To Garnish:
Lemon wedges
Salad leaves

Pound veal until thin. Cut in small pieces, about 1-1/2 inches square.

To prepare stuffing, mix together bread crumbs, cheese, salt, walnuts and 6 tablespoons parsley; add a little water to moisten.

Place a little stuffing on each veal square and roll up tightly. Thread 3 rolls each onto 4 wooden skewers.

In a skillet, heat butter and oil. Cook veal rolls, turning occasionally, until golden and cooked through. Remove from skillet and keep warm.

Pour off any fat from skillet. Add wine and stir into pan sediment. Let sauce bubble 3 to 4 minutes. Just before serving, add 2 tablespoons parsley.

Pour sauce over veal rolls and serve immediately, garnished with lemon wedges and salad leaves.

Makes 4 servings.

Variation: Use stuffing for larger rolls. Allow 1 to 2 scallops per person and increase quantity of stuffing by half. Pound each scallop thinly, top with stuffing, roll up and secure with wooden picks. Cook as above.

Pork with Clams

2 tablespoons olive oil
1-1/2 lbs. boneless pork, cubed
2 onions, sliced
4 garlic cloves, crushed
1 tablespoon paprika
1 teaspoon salt
1 bay leaf
1-2/3 cups white wine
1 lb. tomatoes, peeled, seeded,
  chopped
1 lb. clams, cleaned
1 onion, finely chopped
1 tablespoon chopped parsley
Salt and pepper to taste
3 tablespoon chopped cilantro

To Garnish:
Cilantro sprigs

In a flameproof casserole, heat oil. Add pork and cook until evenly browned. Add sliced onions and garlic and cook until softened. Add paprika, salt, bay leaf, wine and tomatoes. Cover and simmer gently about 1-1/2 hours or until meat is tender.

Meanwhile, in a large saucepan, put clams, chopped onion and parsley. Cover with water. Bring to a boil, then simmer gently until clams are cooked. They will open and rise to surface—discard any that do not open. Drain and set aside.

Just before serving, add clams to pork and heat through 5 minutes. Add salt and pepper and discard bay leaf.

Sprinkle with chopped cilantro and garnish with sprigs of cilantro to serve.

Makes 4 servings.

Variation: For a simple, tasty alternative, omit clams and increase pork to 2 pounds.

Beef with Oregano

2 tablespoons olive oil
4 strips bacon
2 lbs. boneless beef round steak,
    cut in 10 to 12 pieces
2 onions, quartered
2 tablespoons finely chopped
    oregano
2 tablespoons finely chopped
    parsley
1 bay leaf
1 large garlic clove, crushed
1/2 cup red wine
1/3 cup water
1 cup chopped green olives
2 tablespoons fresh bread crumbs
Grated peel 1 lemon
Salt and pepper to taste

To Garnish:
Oregano sprigs

To Serve:
Fresh bread
Green salad

In a flameproof casserole large enough to place beef in 1 layer, heat oil. Add bacon and sauté until crisp; remove with a slotted spoon and set aside. Add beef and cook until evenly browned. Add onions and toss in oil for 1 minute.

Add 1/2 of oregano and parsley, bay leaf, garlic, wine and water. Cover and simmer 2 hours. Add bacon and olives and continue cooking 45 minutes—the stew should be fairly liquid.

Mix together bread crumbs, lemon peel and remaining herbs and add to stew. Cook, uncovered, 10 to 15 minutes more. Season with salt and pepper. Discard bay leaf.

Garnish with oregano sprigs and serve with fresh bread and green salad.

Makes 4 servings.

Variation: Thyme can be added to this casserole for a stronger, more aromatic flavor. Substitute 1 tablespoon finely chopped thyme for 1/2 of oregano.

Lamb with Mustard & Tarragon

1 (4-lb.) boneless lamb shoulder
2 garlic cloves, slivered
4 teaspoons dry mustard
2 teaspoons salt
3 to 4 tarragon sprigs
Black pepper to taste
1 tablespoon olive oil
2 tablespoons butter
1 onion, finely sliced
3/4 cup white wine
1 tablespoon chopped tarragon

To Garnish:
Sprigs of tarragon

Preheat oven to 350F (175C).

Make several slits in lamb and insert garlic. Mix together mustard and salt and smear 1/2 of mixture on inside of lamb. Lay tarragon sprigs on lamb and season with black pepper. Roll up and secure with string. Rub outside of lamb with remaining mustard and salt mixture.

In a flameproof dish, heat oil and butter. Add lamb and brown on all sides. Add onion and cook for a few minutes to soften, then pour in wine. Stir and scrape up all juices and sediment. Cover and bake in oven 2-/12 to 3 hours, to desired doneness. Remove lamb from dish and let stand 10 minutes before serving.

Pour fat off cooking juices, then simmer several minutes, stirring constantly. Just before serving, remove string from lamb and carve. Add chopped tarragon to sauce. Serve garnished with tarragon sprigs.

Makes 6 to 8 servings.

Note: Lamb shoulder is one of the best cuts to use for casseroles; it is lean and full of flavor. Ask the butcher to bone it for you—add bones to soup for extra flavor.

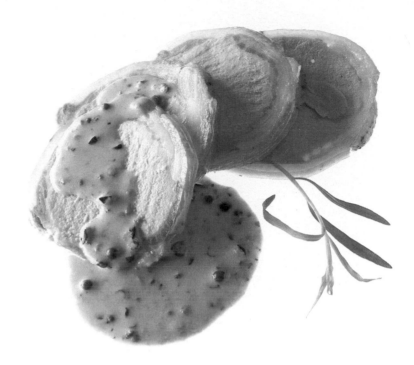

Spiced Lamb with Fruit

2 tablespoons olive oil
2 lbs. boneless lean lamb, cubed
1 onion, sliced
1 teaspoon each chopped sage,
 rosemary, thyme and marjoram
2 teaspoons fennel seeds
1/2 teaspoon fenugreek seeds,
 crushed
1 teaspoon ground coriander
1 teaspoon ground ginger
1 teaspoon ground turmeric
1 teaspoon ground mace
3 garlic cloves, crushed
1 lemon
1 orange
2 apples, peeled, cored, sliced
1 tablespoon honey
1/2 cup red wine
Salt and pepper to taste

To Garnish:
**Orange and lemon slices
Rosemary sprigs**

In a flameproof casserole, heat oil.
Add lamb a litttle at a time and
cook until evenly browned; remove with a slotted spoon and set
aside. Add onion to casserole and
cook a few minutes to soften. Return lamb and add all herbs, spices
and garlic.

Grate lemon and orange peel;
cut away pith from fruit. Divide in
segments and add to casserole
with grated peels, apples and honey. Pour over wine and season with
salt and pepper. Cover and cook
gently about 2 hours or until lamb
is very tender.

Serve lamb garnished with
orange and lemon slices and rosemary sprigs.

Makes 4 servings.

Note: This dish is particulary good
served with a fennel and watercress salad and a dish of rice mixed
with ground almonds, garlic and
parsley. It is an excellent choice
for a dinner party, as it can be prepared well ahead of time and
seems more flavorful if left for a
few hours before reheating.

Pork with Juniper Sauce

1 (3-lb.) boneless pork loin
3 garlic cloves, slivered
Salt and pepper to taste

Sauce:
18 juniper berries, crushed
1 teaspoon green peppercorns,
 crushed
2 tablespoons brandy
2 tablespoons whipping cream
1/3 cup plain yogurt

Preheat oven to 375F (190C).
Remove skin and most of fat
from pork. Make several slits in
pork and insert garlic. Season
pork with salt and pepper. Roll up
and secure with string. Rub outside of pork with salt and pepper.

Place pork in a roasting pan and
add 2 inches of water. Roast, uncovered, in oven about 1-1/2 hours
or until pork is cooked. Remove
from pan and set aside to cool.

To make sauce, pour off fat
from pan juices. Add juniper berries, peppercorns and brandy to
pan and simmer over moderate
heat until reduced by half. Flame
to burn off any remaining alcohol,
then set aside to cool. Skim surface
and whisk in cream and yogurt.
Check seasoning.

Serve pork cold with juniper
sauce.

Makes 6 servings.

Note: Juniper sauce is also excellent served hot with grilled or
sautéed pork chops; once sauce
has been flamed, stir in cream and
yogurt and serve immediately.

Venison with Apples

2 (1-lb.) venison steaks
All-purpose flour
1 onion, chopped
3 strips bacon, cut in strips
2 tablespoons butter
3 apples, cored, sliced
2 green onions, chopped
4 teaspoons chopped mint

Marinade:
1/4 cup olive oil
1 onion, quartered
1 large carrot, sliced
1 stalk celery, sliced
2 garlic cloves
Bouquet garni
2 bay leaves
2 teaspoons salt
8 black peppercorns
1/3 cup red wine

To Garnish:
Shredded green onion

Lay venison steaks in a shallow dish.

To prepare marinade, in a large saucepan, heat oil. Add vegetables, garlic, herbs and seasoning and sauté until lightly browned. Add wine and let marinade bubble for 2 minutes. Pour over steaks and refrigerate 2 days.

Preheat oven to 325F (165C).

Strain marinade into a bowl; discard vegetables and herbs. Lift out steaks and dry well. Season both sides, roll up and secure with string. Dust with flour and place in an ovenproof dish. Cover with chopped onion and bacon strips; pour over marinade. Cover tightly and bake in oven 3-1/2 hours.

Remove steaks from dish and keep warm. Pour off fat from dish; strain remaining juices and reheat sauce.

Just before serving, in a skillet, melt butter. Add apple slices and sauté until golden. Sprinkle with green onions and mint.

To serve, cut steaks in thick slices and arrange on a serving dish with apple slices. Garnish with green onion and serve sauce separately.

Makes 4 servings.

Chicken & Brie Filo Bundles

3 cooked chicken breasts, skinned, boned and thinly sliced
10 ounces blue Brie cheese, rind removed, cut into small chunks
Grated peel of 1 lemon
Juice of 1/2 small lemon
1/2 teaspoon chopped fresh thyme
2 tablespoons chopped parsley
1/4 cup unsalted butter, melted
6 sheets filo pastry, halved

Preheat oven to 400F (205C).

Mix together chicken, Brie, lemon peel and juice, thyme and parsley.

Brush insides of 4 (3-1/2-inch diameter) round molds with melted butter.

Brush one half sheet of filo pastry with butter. Place another half sheet on top at a 45° angle; brush with butter. Top with another half sheet at a 90° angle. Make a fist and mold pastry, butter side in, around it. Push into a prepared mold, allowing surplus around top to stand above mold. Repeat with remaining filo sheets.

Divide chicken mixture into 4 portions and use to fill pastry cases. Bring edges of pastry into center one by one and seal together, but ensure points are sticking upright in a random way. Brush with any remaining butter. Place on a baking sheet and bake 25 minutes or until crisp and browned.

Carefully tip filo bundles out of molds, being very careful not to snap any of the fragile points. Place on baking sheet and return to oven 5 minutes, to brown bottom pastry.

Serve with buttered new potatoes and a mixed green salad.

Makes 4 servings.

Circassian Chicken

1 (3-lb.) chicken
1 onion, quartered
1 carrot, quartered
1 celery stalk, sliced
Bouquet garni
SAUCE:
2 white bread slices, crusts removed, chopped
1/4 cup milk
12 ounces walnut pieces (about 2-2/3 cups)
1 teaspoon lemon juice
1 garlic clove, crushed
Salt and pepper, to taste
TO GARNISH:
1 tablespoon walnut oil
1 teaspoon paprika
1 tablespoon chopped fresh parsley

Chicken Satay with Peanut Sauce

4 chicken breasts, skinned and boned
MARINADE:
2 tablespoons soy sauce
2 garlic cloves, crushed
1 tablespoon lemon juice
PEANUT SAUCE:
1/3 cup peanuts, toasted and skinned
2 tablespoons vegetable oil
1 small onion, chopped
2 garlic cloves, crushed
1/4 teaspoon chili powder
1 teaspoon ground coriander
1 teaspoon ground cumin
1/3 cup tomato juice
Water
1 teaspoon soy sauce
1 teaspoon lemon juice

1. Put chicken, onion, carrot, celery and bouquet garni in a large saucepan. Cover with cold water, bring to a boil, then cover and simmer gently about 1 hour, until cooked. Remove chicken from pan; strain stock and reserve. When cool enough to handle, remove chicken flesh from bone, cut into large pieces and keep warm.
2. To make sauce, put bread into a medium-size bowl. Add milk and soak 5 minutes. Put nuts in a food processor fitted with the metal blade and process until finely ground. Add bread and milk, lemon juice, garlic, seasoning and 1-1/4 cups reserved stock; process until smooth and about the consistency of whipping cream. Pour into a saucepan to reheat, adding a little more stock and seasoning if necessary.
3. Arrange chicken on a warmed serving dish and pour over sauce. Mix oil and paprika together and drizzle over the surface, then sprinkle with parsley. Serve warm or cold, with rice.

Makes 4 servings.

1. Mix marinade ingredients together in a medium-size bowl. Cut chicken breasts into 1-inch cubes; add to marinade, stir to coat completely and marinate 2 hours.
2. To make peanut sauce, put peanuts in a food processor fitted with the metal blade and chop finely. In a pan, heat oil, add onion and fry until softened. Add garlic, spices and peanuts and cook 1 minute. Mix in tomato juice, cook 1 minute, then gradually blend in enough water to make a good consistency. Bring to a boil, stirring; cook, stirring, until thickened. Add soy sauce and lemon juice; keep warm.
3. Thread chicken pieces onto 4 skewers. Cook under a preheated hot broiler 4 to 5 minutes on each side, basting frequently with the marinade. Serve with cooked rice and peanut sauce.

Makes 4 servings.

Note: To make green onion flowers for a garnish, trim, then shred the top leaving the bottom intact. Place in iced water to open.

Chicken & Filo Roulade

4 skinned chicken breasts, about 3 ounces each
4 lean smoked ham slices
2/3 cup walnut halves
2 ounces Stilton cheese
2 sheets filo pastry
1 tablespoon butter, melted
SAUCE:
1/3 cup walnut pieces
1 ounce Stilton cheese
1 garlic clove, chopped
1/3 cup half and half
2 tablespoons snipped chives
Salt and pepper, to taste
TO GARNISH:
Salad leaves

Chicken & Asparagus in Baskets

2 sheets filo pastry
6 ounces asparagus tips
2 tablespoons vegetable oil
1 onion, sliced
1 garlic clove, chopped
4 ounces button mushrooms
2 tablespoons all-purpose flour
1 cup chicken stock
1 tablespoon chopped fresh tarragon
2 tablespoons half and half
8 ounces cooked chicken, cut into fingers
1/2 cup pistachios (2 ounces), halved
Salt and pepper, to taste

1. Slice horizontally three-quarters of the way through chicken breasts; open them out, cover with plastic wrap and beat with a rolling pin to flatten. Cover each with a slice of ham; trim to fit. Chop walnuts in a food processor fitted with the metal blade; add Stilton and blend to a paste. Spread over the ham, roll up loosely like a jellyroll, and set aside. Preheat oven to 375F (190C).
2. Cut filo pastry in half lengthwise to make 4 (13" x 9") rectangles; pile on top of each other and cover with a clean towel to prevent pastry drying out. Take 1 rectangle and brush with butter; put a chicken roulade at the

lower end. Roll up from the short side folding in pastry at sides. Repeat with remaining chicken and pastry. Place on a baking sheet. Brush all over with butter, and bake 30 minutes, until crisp and golden.
3. To make sauce, chop walnuts in a food processor fitted with the metal blade; add Stilton, garlic and half and half and process until smooth. Turn into a small saucepan, add chives and seasoning and heat gently. Serve roulades sliced, on warmed individual plates, with sauce to one side. Garnish with salad leaves.

Makes 4 servings.

1. Preheat oven to 375F (190C). Cut filo pastry into 6-inch squares; pile on top of each other and cover with a clean towel to prevent pastry drying out. Drape 3 squares of pastry each over 4 inverted individual 6 ounce bombe molds (or similar ovenproof molds) and place on a baking sheet.
2. Bake 6 to 8 minutes, until golden-brown. Leave to cool, then gently ease off the molds with the help of a knife. If the filo baskets stick, cook them a few minutes longer.
3. Cut the asparagus into 1-1/2-inch lengths and cook in boiling salted

water 5 minutes; drain and set aside. In a pan, heat oil, add onion and fry until softened. Add garlic and mushrooms and cook 2 minutes, stirring occasionally. Remove from heat, stir in flour, then gradually add stock and tarragon. Bring to a boil, stirring, and cook 2 minutes. Add half and half, asparagus, chicken, nuts and seasoning.

Spoon filling into filo baskets. Serve on warmed individual plates, accompanied by broccoli.

Makes 4 servings.

Pheasant with Chestnuts

12 ounces chestnuts
1 tablespoon olive oil
1 (2-1/2- to 3-lb.) pheasant, cleaned
8 ounces pearl onions
2 tablespoons all-purpose flour
1-1/4 cups stock (made from pheasant giblets)
Grated peel and juice of 1/2 orange
1 tablespoon red currant jelly
2/3 cup red wine
Bouquet garni
Salt and pepper, to taste
CROUTES:
2 slices bread, crusts removed
Vegetable oil
2 tablespoons chopped fresh parsley

Stuffed Beef Rolls

4 smoked ham slices
8 thin beef slices, about 4 ounces each
2 tablespoons vegetable oil
2 garlic cloves, chopped
2 tablespoons all-purpose flour
1/2 cup beef stock
1 cup red wine
Bouquet garni
2 tomatoes, peeled, seeded and cut into strips
12 ripe olives, halved and pitted
STUFFING:
2/3 cup pitted prunes
1 cup fresh bread crumbs
1/4 cup grated parmesan cheese
3 tablespoons chopped fresh parsley
2 tablespoons pine nuts

1. Preheat oven to 350F (175C). Plunge the chestnuts into boiling water 2 minutes, then peel away skins. In a flameproof casserole dish, heat oil and brown pheasant all over until golden; remove. Add chestnuts and onions to casserole dish and cook 5 to 8 minutes, stirring, until beginning to turn golden-brown; remove from casserole dish.
2. Stir in flour, then gradually mix in stock and bring to a boil. Add orange peel and juice, red currant jelly, wine, bouquet garni and seasoning. Return pheasant, onions and chestnuts to casserole dish, cover and cook in the oven 1-1/2 hours, or until pheasant is tender.

3. Remove pheasant from casserole and arrange on a warmed shallow serving dish with onions and chestnuts; keep warm. Discard bouquet garni. Boil cooking liquid rapidly until reduced to a syrupy consistency.
To make croûtes, cut each bread slice into 4 triangles. Shallow-fry in hot oil until golden-brown. Dip one side of each croûte into the sauce, then into chopped parsley. Arrange around the pheasant. Spoon remaining sauce over pheasant and serve with braised red cabbage or brussels sprouts.

Makes 4 servings.

1. Preheat oven to 350F (175C). Cut ham slices in half lengthwise and put a piece on each slice of beef.
2. To make stuffing, chop prunes and put in a bowl with bread crumbs, Parmesan cheese, 2 tablespoons parsley and pine nuts; mix well. Divide equally between meat, roll up and tie with fine string.
3. In a flameproof casserole dish, heat oil and cook beef rolls, two at a time, turning to brown all over; remove and set aside.
Add garlic and cook 1 minute; stir in flour. Pour in stock and wine, add bouquet garni and bring to a boil, stirring. Return rolls to casserole dish, cover and cook in the oven 1-1/4 hours. Add tomatoes and olives and cook 15 minutes. Turn into a serving dish, sprinkle with remaining parsley and serve with cooked tagliatelle.

Makes 4 servings.

Pork with Prunes

2 pork tenderloins, about 1-1/2 pounds total
1 cup pitted prunes
1/4 cup pistachios (1 ounce)
2 tablespoons olive oil
8 ounces pearl onions, peeled
1 tablespoon all-purpose flour
1-1/4 cups veal or chicken stock
1 cup red wine
Salt and pepper, to taste
2 teaspoons cornstarch, blended with a little water
1 tablespoon chopped fresh parsley

Calves' Liver with Apple

1 cup dried apple rings, soaked 2 hours
4 tablespoons butter
1 teaspoon honey
1 pound calves' liver
2 tablespoons seasoned flour
1 tablespoon olive oil
1/2 cup veal or chicken stock
1/2 cup red wine
1 teaspoon chopped sage
1/4 cup pine nuts, toasted
TO GARNISH:
Sage leaves

1. Make a horizontal cut along the length of each tenderloin, three-quarters of the way through the meat; open it out flat.
2. Lay 10 to 12 prunes down the center of one tenderloin, sprinkle with pistachios, and cover with second tenderloin. Tie tenderloins together securely with string. In an oval flameproof casserole dish, heat oil and brown meat and onions thoroughly all over. Stir in flour, then gradually mix in stock and wine. Bring to a boil, season, cover and simmer gently 35 to 40 minutes.
3. Add remaining prunes to the cas-

serole; cook another 15 to 20 minutes. Lift meat from casserole with a slotted spoon. Carve into slices, remove string and arrange on a warm serving dish; keep hot. Remove onions and prunes with a slotted spoon; set aside. Strain cooking liquid, return to casserole dish and stir in blended cornstarch. Bring to a boil and cook, stirring, until thickened. Add prunes, onions and parsley, heat through, then spoon around the meat. Serve with braised red cabbage or celery.

Makes 6 servings.

1. Drain apple rings and pat dry with paper towels. In a medium-size skillet, melt half the butter and add honey. Fry apple rings in a single layer 4 to 5 minutes, turning once. Remove from pan and keep warm. Wipe out pan.
2. Coat liver slices completely with seasoned flour. Heat remaining butter and oil in pan. Add liver and fry 1 to 2 minutes on each side, depending on thickness. Add stock, wine and

sage and cook 2 minutes. Remove liver with a slotted spoon; reserve cooking liquid.
3. Arrange liver and apple rings on a warm serving dish; keep warm. Boil reserved liquid 2 minutes to reduce slightly, then spoon over the liver. Sprinkle with pine nuts and garnish with sage to serve.

Makes 4 servings.

Moroccan Lamb Stew

3 tablespoons olive oil
1-1/2 pounds lean lamb, cut into 1-inch cubes
2 onions, sliced
2 garlic cloves, chopped
2 teaspoons chopped gingerroot
1 teaspoon ground cinnamon
1/2 teaspoon ground cloves
3 cardamom pods, split open
1 tablespoon plus 1 teaspoon all-purpose flour
1-3/4 cups beef stock
Grated peel and juice of 1/2 orange
Salt and pepper, to taste
1 thyme sprig
1 teaspoon each wine vinegar and brown sugar
1 cup dried apricots, soaked overnight
1/4 cup pistachios (1 ounce)

Spiced Pilaf

2/3 cup chopped dried apricots
4 tablespoons olive oil
1 onion, chopped
1 teaspoon ground allspice
1 garlic clove, chopped
1-1/2 cups long-grain rice
2-1/2 cups beef stock or water
Salt and pepper, to taste
1 cup fresh bread crumbs
1 pound lean ground lamb
1 tablespoon tomato paste
1 teaspoon ground cumin
1 egg, beaten
1/2 cup pine nuts
2 tablespoons chopped parsley

1. In a flameproof casserole dish, heat 2 tablespoons oil and fry meat briskly in batches until browned; remove from casserole dish and set aside. Add onions to casserole dish and fry until softened, then add garlic, gingerroot and spices and fry 1 minute.
2. Stir in flour, then stir in stock, orange peel and juice, seasoning, thyme, vinegar and sugar; bring to a boil. Return meat to the casserole, cover and simmer gently 30 minutes.
3. Drain apricots, add to casserole and simmer 30 minutes, until meat is tender. Serve sprinkled with pistachios and accompanied by couscous.

Makes 4 servings.

1. Cover apricots with boiling water and let soak 1 hour; drain well.

In a large saucepan, heat 2 tablespoons oil, add onion and fry until softened. Add allspice, garlic and rice and fry, stirring, 1 to 2 minutes. Add stock, bring to a boil, add salt and pepper, reduce heat, cover and cook gently 15 minutes, until liquid has been absorbed.
2. Meanwhile, soak bread crumbs in 1/2 cup water 5 minutes; squeeze dry and place in a bowl. Add lamb, tomato paste, cumin, egg and seasoning and mix together thoroughly. With dampened hands, roll into balls, each the size of a large marble.
3. In a medium-size skillet, heat remaining oil, add pine nuts and fry, turning constantly, until golden-brown; remove from pan. Add meatballs to pan and fry quickly 5 to 8 minutes, until golden all over.

Meanwhile, add apricots to cooked rice mixture, cover and heat through. Fluff rice and arrange on warm plates. Spoon meatballs on top and sprinkle with pine nuts and parsley to serve.

Makes 4 servings.

Chicken & Pineapple Kabobs

3 skinned chicken breast fillets
1 large green bell pepper
1 small pineapple
6 bacon slices
3 bananas
MARINADE:
2 tablespoons soy sauce
1/3 cup pineapple juice
2 teaspoons finely chopped gingerroot
1 garlic clove, crushed
1 teaspoon dry mustard
2 tablespoons dry sherry
1 tablespoon olive oil
1 tablespoon lemon juice
TO GARNISH:
Salad leaves and chopped parsley

1. Cut each chicken fillet in 4 large chunks, then put into a bowl. Mix all marinade ingredients and pour over chicken. Refrigerate at least 2 hours.
2. Cut bell pepper in half, remove seeds and cut in 12 squares. Peel pineapple, cut in slices, then in chunks, discarding core.

Using scissors, cut each bacon slice in half crosswise. Cut each banana in 4 chunks. Wrap each banana chunk in a strip of bacon. Remove chicken from marinade, reserving marinade.
3. Preheat grill to medium. Thread prepared ingredients onto skewers in following order: pineapple, chicken, bacon-wrapped banana and bell pepper. Repeat twice more and finish with a pineapple chunk.

Brush with reserved marinade and grill about 20 minutes, until chicken is tender, turning and basting with marinade frequently. Serve immediately on a bed of salad leaves, sprinkled with chopped parsley.

Makes 4 servings.

Chicken with Cape Gooseberries

4 skinned chicken breast fillets
1 garlic clove, crushed
1 tablespoon finely chopped tarragon
Salt and pepper
1 tablespoon vegetable oil
1 tablespoon butter
6 shallots, finely chopped
SAUCE:
8 ounces cape gooseberries, peeled
3/4 cup dry vermouth
1 tablespoon sugar
2/3 cup dairy sour cream
TO GARNISH:
4 whole cape gooseberries
Sprigs of tarragon

1. To make sauce, put gooseberries in a small saucepan with vermouth and sugar. Cook over low heat, stirring occasionally, until sugar dissolves, then increase heat and bring to a boil. Cover and simmer 10 minutes, stirring occasionally. Remove from heat and strain gooseberries through a fine sieve into a bowl, pressing pulp through sieve with back of a wooden spoon; set aside.
2. Season chicken with garlic, tarragon, 1/4 teaspoon salt and a pinch of pepper; set aside. In a large skillet, heat oil and butter, add shallots and cook 2 minutes, stirring constantly. Add chicken breasts and cook 6 minutes each side.
3. Pour strained gooseberry pulp into a saucepan. Add 1/4 cup of sour cream and cook over low heat 2 minutes, stirring; check seasoning.

Place chicken breasts on warmed individual serving plates and spoon over sauce. Top with remaining sour cream.

Peel back petals of skin from whole gooseberries to reveal fruit. Garnish chicken with gooseberry flowers and tarragon sprigs. Serve immediately.

Makes 4 servings.

Duck with Kumquat Sauce

1 (4-lb.) oven-ready duck
Salt and pepper to taste
1/2 cup superfine sugar
1/2 cup water
4 ounces kumquats
1/2 cup wine vinegar
Juice of 1 orange
1-1/4 cups chicken stock
1 tablespoon arrowroot blended with 1 tablespoon water
1 tablespoon orange-flavored liqueur
TO GARNISH:
Sprigs of parsley or cilantro

1. Preheat oven to 400F (205C). Prick duck skin all over with a fork; season with salt and pepper. Place on a rack in a roasting pan containing 1/4 cup plus 2 tablespoons water. Cook 1-3/4 to 2 hours or until tender.

Meanwhile, in a heavy-bottom saucepan over low heat, dissolve 2 tablespoons of sugar in water. Cut kumquats in slices and add to pan. Cover and simmer 15 minutes or until tender; set aside.
2. In another saucepan, dissolve remaining sugar in vinegar, then boil rapidly until reduced to a light caramel. Carefully add orange juice and stock and simmer 10 minutes.

Stir in blended arrowroot and cook over low heat, stirring until sauce is thickened and shiny. Stir in drained kumquats and liqueur; heat through gently.
3. Cut duck in half down breast bone, then cut each half in 2 portions. Arrange on a warmed serving dish and pour over sauce. Serve immediately, garnished with parsley or cilantro sprigs.

Makes 4 servings.

Note: If duck has giblets, use to make stock. If not, use chicken stock.

Liver with Raspberries

12 ounces raspberries
2 tablespoons all-purpose flour
1 teaspoon dried leaf sage
Salt and pepper to taste
1 pound calves' liver, cut in thin strips
1/4 cup butter
1 tablespoon finely chopped sage leaves
1/4 cup raspberry vinegar
1/3 cup kirsch or framboise
2 teaspoons superfine sugar
Sage leaves to garnish

1. Set aside 12 raspberries for garnish. Puree remaining raspberries in a blender or food processor; strain and reserve.

Put flour in a flat dish and season with dried sage and salt and pepper. Coat liver strips with seasoned flour, shaking off excess.
2. Melt butter in a skillet. Add liver and fry 2 minutes, turning to brown on all sides. Add chopped sage and fry 1 minute. Transfer liver to a warmed plate with a slotted spoon and keep hot.

3. Skim off any excess fat from pan. Stir vinegar and kirsch or framboise into pan juices and cook 1 minute, stirring constantly. Add raspberry puree and simmer 1 minute. Stir in sugar and check seasoning.

Arrange liver on warmed individual plates and drizzle over raspberry sauce. Garnish with reserved raspberries and sage leaves. Serve at once.

Makes 4 servings.

Pork with Plums & Gin

1-1/2 pounds pork tenderloin
8 red plums
1/3 cup water
1 tablespoon superfine sugar
1 bay leaf
Salt and pepper to taste
1 tablespoon gin
MARINADE:
1 garlic clove, crushed
3 tablespoons olive oil
2 tablespoons gin
2 teaspoons lime juice
1 small onion, finely chopped
TO GARNISH:
1 or 2 plums, peeled, sliced
Sprigs of cilantro or parsley

Date & Lamb Pilaf

1 (2-lb.) lamb shoulder
3 tablespoons olive oil
1 large onion, finely chopped
3 garlic cloves, chopped
1 teaspoon ground cinnamon
1 teaspoon ground allspice
1/4 teaspoon ground ginger
5 cardamom pods, split open
12 ounces fresh dates
3 cups white long-grain rice
3 cups chicken stock
1 tablespoon grated orange peel
Pinch of saffron threads
Salt and pepper to taste
1/2 pomegranate
1/2 cup shelled pistachios

1. Put pork into a shallow dish. Mix all marinade ingredients in a small bowl and pour over pork. Cover and refrigerate 4 hours, turning pork occasionally. Transfer pork to an ovenproof dish; reserve marinade.
2. Preheat oven to 350F (175C). Put plums into a bowl, cover with boiling water and let stand 1 minute. Peel, halve and remove pits. Add plums to reserved marinade. Stir in water and sugar. Add bay leaf and season with salt and pepper. Pour plum mixture over pork. Cover and bake in oven 40 minutes, until juices run clear when pork is pierced with a skewer.
3. Transfer pork to a warmed dish; keep hot. Skim off fat from cooking juices and discard bay leaf, then puree in a blender or food processor. Transfer plum puree to a small saucepan, add gin and boil 2 minutes; check seasoning.

Carve pork in slices and arrange on individual serving plates. Drizzle over plum sauce. Garnish with plum slices and cilantro or parsley sprigs. Serve at once.

Makes 4 to 6 servings.

1. Cut lamb in 1-inch cubes. In a large flameproof casserole, heat olive oil, then add onion and garlic and fry 5 minutes or until softened. Stir in cinnamon, allspice, ginger and cardamom and fry, stirring constantly, 30 seconds.

Add lamb and cook 8 to 10 minutes, turning frequently to ensure lamb browns evenly.
2. Halve dates and remove pits. Reserve 1/2 of dates; chop remainder in small pieces and add to lamb. Add rice, stock, orange peel, saffron and salt and pepper; bring to a boil. Lower heat, cover and simmer 15 to 20 minutes or until liquid has been absorbed and rice is tender; stir occasionally during cooking.
3. Halve pomegranate and scoop out seeds, separating them; add seeds to casserole with pistachios and remaining dates. Cook 2 minutes to heat through. Check seasoning, adding more spice if necessary. Spoon onto a heated platter and serve at once.

Make 6 to 8 servings.

Chicken Szechuan

1 pound skinned chicken breast fillets
4 carrots
1 large red bell pepper, cored and seeded
6 green onions
1 (1-1/2-inch) piece gingerroot
2 large eggs, beaten
Salt and pepper to taste
1 cup cornstarch
Vegetable oil for frying
1 garlic clove, crushed
4 teaspoons sugar
2 tablespoons soy sauce
2 tablespoons malt vinegar
TO GARNISH:
Sprigs of chervil

Eastern-Style Hotpot

7-1/2 cups chicken stock
1 (1-inch) piece gingerroot, peeled and grated
1 garlic clove, crushed
1 skinned chicken breast fillet
6 ounces beef fillet
2 ounces snow peas
2 medium-size zucchini
1/2 Chinese cabbage
1 bunch green onions
DIPPING SAUCE:
1/2 teaspoon chili sauce
1 garlic clove, crushed
1/4 cup light soy sauce
2 tablespoons peanut oil
Good pinch of sugar
1 teaspoon cider vinegar

1. Slice chicken in thin strips. Cut carrots and bell pepper in matchstick strips. Cut green onions in slivers. Peel gingerroot and cut in slivers.

In a bowl, mix eggs with salt and pepper. Dip chicken strips into eggs, then into cornstarch to coat.
2. In a large saucepan, heat 2 inches of oil. Add 1/4 of chicken strips and fry 3 to 4 minutes, until cooked through and lightly golden. Drain on paper towels while cooking remainder in batches.

In a wok or skillet, heat 3 tablespoons oil. Add carrot and bell pepper strips and stir-fry 1-1/2 minutes.

Remove with a slotted spoon and set aside. Add garlic and gingerroot to pan and stir-fry 30 seconds.
3. Add sugar, soy sauce and vinegar to wok. Add vegetables and chicken and toss in sauce 2 to 3 minutes to heat through and glaze. Add green onion slivers and toss lightly. Serve immediately, garnished with chervil.

Makes 4 servings.

Note: This dish is delicious served with rice and accompanied by shrimp crackers.

1. In a large saucepan, combine stock, gingerroot and garlic. Cover and simmer 10 minutes. Meanwhile, cut chicken and beef in very thin strips.
2. Trim snow peas and remove strings. Slice zucchini thinly. Cut Chinese cabbage and green onions in short lengths. Arrange vegetables, chicken and steak on a platter.

To prepare dipping sauce, combine all ingredients. Pour into small serving bowls.

Transfer stock mixture to a Mongolian hotpot or large metal fondue pot over a burner in center of table; bring back to simmering.
3. Invite guests to cook their own meal. Place pieces of chicken or beef and 1 or 2 vegetables in small Chinese wire baskets and lower into simmering stock 1-1/2 to 2 minutes. Or hold food with wooden chopsticks in stock. Dip into dipping sauce before eating. Continue until ingredients are used. Serve remaining stock in soup bowls.

Makes 4 servings.

Stuffed Turnips

8 (4-oz.) turnips, peeled
10 tablespoons butter
1 onion, finely chopped
12 ounces veal scallops, minced
Finely grated peel of 1 large lemon
2 cups fresh bread crumbs
8 fresh sage leaves, finely chopped
1/4 cup chopped parsley
1 large egg, beaten
Salt and pepper to taste
1-1/4 cups chicken stock
1/2 cups whipping cream
8 slices large tomato, about 1/2 inch thick
TO GARNISH:
Sprigs of parsley and sage

Red Cabbage & Sausage

1 pound red cabbage
6 tablespoons butter
1 large Spanish onion, chopped
1 garlic clove, crushed
2 tablespoons light-brown sugar
2 tablespoons cider or wine vinegar
1-1/4 cups chicken stock
Salt and pepper to taste
1/4 to 1/2 teaspoon caraway seeds, if desired
4 frankfurters
4 ounces each chorizo and Zywiecka sausage
1 large baking apple
1-1/2 pounds new potatoes, cut in even pieces
TO GARNISH:
Watercress sprigs
Apple slices

1. In a saucepan of boiling salted water, cook turnips 15 to 20 minutes or until tender when pierced with a skewer. Drain and cool enough to handle. Hollow out turnips, using a melon baller or teaspoon, leaving 1/4-inch shells.
2. Preheat oven to 350F (175C). In a skillet, melt 8 tablespoons of butter. Add onion and veal and cook 5 minutes, stirring constantly. Remove from heat. Stir in lemon peel, bread crumbs, 1/2 of sage and parsley, beaten egg and salt and pepper; mix well. Spoon into hollowed-out turnips to cover top surface area completely; press in mounds. Place in a greased shallow ovenproof dish. Melt remaining butter and brush over stuffing and turnips. Add 1/2 cup of stock to dish. Bake in preheated oven 40 minutes, until stuffing is golden. Transfer turnips to a plate; keep warm.
3. Pour juices from dish into a pan. Add remaining stock and herbs and cream. Simmer 4 to 5 minutes, until slightly thickened. Place tomato slices on a warmed serving dish. Set a halved turnip on each and spoon sauce over turnip. Garnish with parsley and sage to serve.

Makes 4 servings.

1. Preheat oven to 300F (150C). Cut cabbage in quarters, dicarding stalk; shred finely. Heat 4 tablespoons of butter in a flameproof, enamel-lined casserole dish. Add onion, garlic and sugar and cook gently 5 minutes. Add cabbage and cook 5 minutes, stirring frequently. Add vinegar, stock, seasoning, and caraway seeds,if desired. Stir well, cover and bake in preheated oven 1-1/4 hours.
2. Meanwhile, cut frankfurters, chorizo and Zywiecka sausages in chunky slices. Peel, core and chop apple. Add sausages and apple to casserole, stir well. Cover and bake 30 minutes more.

3. Meanwhile, cook potatoes in boiling salted water 15 to 20 minutes, until tender. Drain, return to pan and place over a low heat a few seconds to dry. Mash with remaining butter and season; beat until smooth. Using a pastry bag fitted with a large star nozzle, pipe borders of mashed potatoes around edge of 4 individual serving dishes. Spoon cabbage mixture into center. Garnish with watercress and apple to serve.

Makes 4 servings.

Note: Zwyiecka is a smoked garlic spiced sausage available from delicatessens and supermarkets.

Vegetarian Dishes

Risotto con Funghi

1 ounce dried cepes (porcini)
1/2 cup butter
1 small onion, finely chopped
2 cups short-grain rice, such as pearl
4 ounces fresh mushrooms (see *Note*),
    quartered or sliced
2/3 cup dry white wine
5 cups hot chicken stock
3 tablespoons freshly grated
    Parmesan cheese
Salt and pepper to taste

To Garnish:
Chopped parsley
Parsley sprigs

To Serve:
Tomato salad

Place cepes in a small bowl; cover with warm water and let soak 20 minutes. Drain; rinse well to remove any grit. Chop coarsely.

In a saucepan, melt 1/4 cup butter. Add onion and sauté about 5 minutes or until golden. Stir in rice and fresh mushrooms and cook 2 to 3 minutes or until rice is translucent. Add wine and cepes; cook about 3 minutes or until wine is absorbed. Reduce heat, add 2-1/2 cups stock, cover and simmer about 10 minutes or until almost all stock has been absorbed.

Add 1-1/4 cups more stock to pan and continue to cook, checking periodically and adding more stock as needed, until rice is tender and all liquid has been absorbed. Total cooking time will range from 20 to 30 minutes. Stir in remaining 1/4 cup butter, cheese, salt and pepper.

Transfer risotto to warmed serving plates and garnish with chopped parsley and parsley sprigs. Serve with a tomato salad.

Makes 4 to 6 servings.

Note: Dried cepes give this dish an incomparable flavor; for visual appeal and texture, I like to add fresh mushrooms. Use sliced fresh cepes (if available) or quartered button mushrooms. Avoid brown mushrooms, since they tend to color the risotto gray.

Gruyère & Mushroom Tart

Egg Pastry:
1-1/2 cups all-purpose flour
Pinch of salt
1/2 cup butter, cut into pieces
1 egg yolk
2 to 3 tablespoons water

Tart Filling:
1 tablespoon butter
1 shallot, finely chopped
6 ounces mushrooms (see *Note*),
    chopped
4 ounces Gruyère cheese, grated
3 eggs, lightly beaten
1 cup whipping cream
Pepper to taste
Generous pinch of freshly grated
    nutmeg

To Serve:
Tossed green salad

To make pastry, sift flour and salt into a large bowl; cut in butter until mixture resembles fine crumbs. Add egg yolk and 2 to 3 tablespoons water; mix to form a firm but pliable dough. Roll out dough on a lightly floured surface and use to line an 8-inch tart pan; prick shell lightly and chill 15 minutes. Meanwhile, preheat oven to 425F (220C). Bake tart shell blind 15 minutes. Remove from oven; reduce temperature to 375F (190C).

Meanwhile, prepare filling. In a small saucepan, melt butter. Add shallot and sauté 4 to 5 minutes or until golden. Add mushrooms and cook 2 to 3 minutes or until tender. Spread mixture in prepared pastry shell.

In a bowl, mix cheese, eggs and cream; season with pepper. Pour into pastry shell and sprinkle with nutmeg. Bake about 35 minutes or until filling is just set. Serve warm, cut into wedges, with salad.

Makes 6 servings.

Note: Use any mushroom variety for this recipe, or combine several kinds.

Stuffed Mushrooms

3/4 cup Brazil nuts, toasted, very
 finely chopped
1 teaspoon olive oil
1/2 teaspoon salt
8 large (2- to 3-inch-diameter)
 mushrooms (see *Note*)
1/4 cup butter
2 onions, chopped
1 garlic clove, pressed or minced
1 tablespoon chopped fresh thyme
1 cup fresh white bread crumbs
Juice and grated peel of 1 lemon
1/2 cup grated sharp Cheddar or
 Gruyère cheese
Salt and pepper to taste

To Garnish:
Thyme sprigs
Lemon slices

To Serve:
Tossed green salad

Preheat broiler. Combine nuts, oil
and 1/2 teaspoon salt; set aside.

Remove stems from mushrooms;
chop stems and set aside.

In a large frying pan, melt butter;
brush half the melted butter over

mushroom caps. Place caps, stemmed
side down, on a baking sheet.

Reheat remaining butter. Add onions and garlic; sauté 5 to 7 minutes
or until onions are softened and gold-
en. Add chopped thyme and
chopped mushroom stems; cook 1
minute. Transfer to a bowl; stir in
nuts, crumbs, lemon juice, lemon
peel, cheese, salt and pepper. Set
aside.

Broil buttered mushroom caps 3
minutes, turning once. Spoon stuffing evenly onto stemmed sides of
caps; broil 4 to 6 minutes or until
stuffing is very hot.

Serve immediately, garnished with
thyme sprigs and lemon slices. Accompany with a green salad.

Makes 4 servings.

Note: Freshly picked wild meadow
mushrooms are preferable to cultivated mushrooms in this dish.

Mushroom & Herb Roulade

6 ounces mushrooms (see *Note*),
 finely chopped
1 bay leaf
1-1/4 cups milk
1/4 cup butter
1/2 cup all-purpose flour
1/2 cup grated Swiss cheese
1/2 teaspoon Dijon-style mustard
4 eggs, separated
1 hard-cooked egg yolk, sieved
2 tablespoons finely snipped chives,
 dill or parsley
2 tablespoons whipping cream
Salt and pepper to taste

To Garnish:
Herb sprigs

Preheat oven to 400F (205C). Grease
a 13" x 9" x 2" baking pan and line
with parchment paper.

In a saucepan, combine mushrooms, bay leaf and half the milk.
Bring to a boil; reduce heat and simmer 2 minutes. Remove from heat,
cover and let stand 10 to 15 minutes.
Strain, reserving mushrooms and
liquid; discard bay leaf. Add remaining milk to liquid.

In same pan, melt butter; stir in

flour and cook, stirring, 1 minute. Remove from heat; gradually stir in milk
mixture. Cook, stirring, until thick
and smooth. Stir in cheese and mustard. Transfer a third of the sauce to a
bowl; keep warm.

To sauce left in pan, add reserved
mushrooms; then add raw egg yolks,
one at a time, stirring well. In a clean
bowl, whisk egg whites until stiff; fold
into mushroom mixture. Pour into
prepared pan and bake 12 to 15 minutes or until golden and firm. Turn
out onto waxed paper; peel off parchment paper.

Stir sieved egg yolk, herbs, cream,
salt and pepper into reserved sauce.
Spread over roulade; roll up from a
short side. Slice, garnish with herb
sprigs and serve at once, with a green
salad.

Makes 4 servings.

Note: Use parasols or horse mushrooms if you can get them; otherwise,
use cultivated varieties.

Hot Mushroom Soufflé

1/4 cup butter
8 ounces mushrooms (see *Note*),
  chopped
1/2 cup all-purpose flour
1-1/4 cups milk
3/4 cup grated Swiss cheese
Salt and pepper to taste
3 eggs, separated

To Garnish:
Parsley sprigs

Preheat oven to 425F (220C). Grease a deep 4-cup soufflé dish.

In a saucepan, melt butter. Add mushrooms and sauté about 5 minutes or until quite tender. If mushrooms exude a lot of liquid, remove them with a slotted spoon and boil liquid over high heat until reduced, then return mushrooms to pan.

Add flour to pan; cook, stirring constantly, 2 minutes. Remove from heat and gradually stir in milk. Return to heat and cook, stirring, until smooth and very thick; stir in cheese. Remove from heat again and season with salt and pepper. Let cool slightly; then beat in egg yolks, one at a time.

In a clean bowl, whisk egg whites until stiff; carefully fold into mushroom mixture. Pour into prepared soufflé dish and bake on center rack of oven 40 to 45 minutes or until well risen, browned, and firm on top. Serve immediately, garnished with parsley sprigs.

Makes 4 servings.

Note: Horn of plenty, chanterelles, horse mushrooms and the anise-flavored *Agaricus silvicola* are particularly suitable for this recipe.

Baked Stuffed Avocados

1 tablespoon butter
8 ounces mushrooms (see *Note*),
  chopped
1 tablespoon plus 1 teaspoon
  all-purpose flour
Pinch of dry mustard
2/3 cup milk
1/2 cup grated sharp Cheddar cheese
Salt and pepper to taste
4 small ripe avocados
1 egg, separated

Herbed Crumbs:
2 tablespoons butter
1 cup fresh white bread crumbs
Pinch of celery salt
2 teaspoons chopped fresh dill
2 teaspoons chopped parsley

To Garnish:
Assorted salad greens

Preheat oven to 400F (205C). Prepare Herbed Crumbs: In a small saucepan, melt butter; add crumbs and cook, stirring, 3 to 4 minutes or until just beginning to color. Remove from heat and stir in celery salt, dill and parsley; set aside.

In another saucepan, melt 1 tablespoon butter. Add mushrooms and sauté 2 to 3 minutes or until tender. Stir in flour and mustard; cook, stirring, 1 minute. Remove from heat and gradually stir in milk; return to heat and cook, stirring, until thick and smooth. Stir in cheese. Remove from heat; add salt and pepper.

Halve and pit avocados. Scoop out some of flesh, leaving a 1/2-inch-thick shell; coarsely chop flesh and add to sauce. Stir in egg yolk.

In a clean bowl, whisk egg white until stiff; fold into sauce. Divide mixture among avocado shells; place shells on a baking sheet. Sprinkle with Herbed Crumbs and bake about 25 minutes or until hot. Serve immediately, garnished with salad greens.

Makes 4 servings.

Note: Parasols, chanterelles, hedgehog fungus and shaggy manes are ideal for this recipe. If you use cultivated mushrooms, try brown rather than white varieties.

Brie & Mushroom Tart

Tart Pastry:
2 cups all-purpose flour
Pinch of salt
1/2 cup butter

Spinach-Brie Filling:
2 tablespoons butter
**6 ounces mushrooms (see *Note*),
    sliced**
**8 ounces spinach leaves, rinsed,
    shredded**
**10 ounces Brie cheese, rind removed,
    diced**
3 eggs
2/3 cup half-and-half
Salt and pepper to taste

To Serve:
Tossed green salad

To make pastry, sift flour and salt into a large bowl; cut in butter until mixture resembles fine crumbs. Add about 3 tablespoons water and mix to form a firm dough.

Roll out dough on a lightly floured surface and use to line a greased 8-inch tart pan; prick shell lightly and chill 15 minutes. Meanwhile, preheat oven to 400F (205C). Bake tart shell blind 10 to 12 minutes. Remove from oven; reduce temperature to 350F (175C).

Prepare filling: In a large frying pan, melt butter. Add mushrooms and sauté 1 to 2 minutes. Add spinach and cook 1 to 2 minutes or until wilted. Turn out into a sieve and press out excess liquid; transfer spinach mixture to pastry shell. Tuck cheese cubes into spinach mixture. Beat together eggs, half-and-half, salt and pepper; pour over spinach mixture. Bake 30 to 35 minutes or until filling is set.

Serve warm or cold, with salad. (Tart tastes best warm.)

Makes 6 servings.

Note: Use button mushrooms or wild varieties such as chanterelles, horse mushrooms or parasols; or use a mixture.

Spinach & Feta in Filo

1/4 cup butter
1 shallot, finely chopped
1 garlic clove, pressed or minced
**12 ounces mushrooms (see *Note*),
    finely chopped**
1/3 cup white wine
**1 tablespoon plus 1 teaspoon tomato
    paste**
1 tablespoon chopped fresh dill
Salt and pepper to taste
**8 ounces spinach leaves, rinsed,
    chopped**
8 ounces feta cheese, crumbled
1 egg yolk
Pinch of freshly grated nutmeg
8 sheets filo pastry

Preheat oven to 400F (205C). In a saucepan, melt 2 tablespoons butter. Add shallot and garlic and sauté 2 minutes. Add mushrooms, wine and tomato paste; cook over high heat, stirring frequently, 8 to 10 minutes or until all liquid has evaporated. Stir in dill, salt and pepper; set aside.

In another pan, cook spinach, with just the water that clings to the leaves, 2 to 3 minutes or until wilted. Turn out into a sieve and press out excess liquid; transfer spinach to a bowl. Add cheese, egg yolk and nutmeg; mix well.

Melt remaining 2 tablespoons butter. Brush a baking sheet with some of butter; place a sheet of pastry on baking sheet. Brush lightly with butter, cover with a second sheet of pastry and brush again. Spread mushroom mixture over pastry, leaving a 1-inch border; cover with spinach mixture. Dampen pastry edges; cover fillings with remaining 6 pastry sheets, brushing each sheet with butter. Seal edges. With a sharp knife, score a deep cross on surface. Bake about 25 minutes or until pastry is crisp and golden brown.

Serve hot or warm, quartered or in slices, with salad and new potatoes.

Makes 4 servings.

Note: Use meadow mushrooms, horse mushrooms or parasols; or use cultivated button mushrooms.

Scrambled Eggs with Truffles

6 eggs
1/2 ounce fresh or canned white
    truffles
Salt and pepper to taste
6 to 8 fresh asparagus spears
2 slices whole wheat bread
3 tablespoons butter
2 tablespoons whipping cream

To Garnish:
Chervil sprigs

In a bowl, beat eggs until blended. Cut truffles into very fine slivers; set half aside. Add remaining slivers to eggs; if using canned truffles, add any juices as well. Season with salt and pepper, cover and refrigerate at least 2 hours.

When you are almost ready to cook eggs, prepare asparagus. Break off tough stalk ends; using a potato peeler, thinly peel stalks. Cook in boiling water 4 to 5 minutes or until just tender; drain and keep hot.

Meanwhile, toast bread and spread with 1-1/2 tablespoons butter; keep hot.

In a deep nonstick frying pan, melt remaining 1-1/2 tablespoons butter over low heat. Add egg-truffle mixture and cook, stirring lightly with a wooden spoon, about 3 minutes or until eggs begin to thicken and set. Take care not to overcook—eggs should be creamy and soft. Stir in cream.

Arrange asparagus and hot toast on 2 warmed serving plates and divide scrambled eggs between them. Sprinkle with reserved truffle slivers. Garnish with chervil sprigs and serve immediately.

Makes 2 servings.

Omelet with Chanterelles

5 eggs
2 tablespoons chopped fresh herbs,
    such as parsley, chervil, chives,
    tarragon or dill
3 tablespoons water
2 tablespoons butter

Chanterelle Filling:
1 tablespoon butter
1 garlic clove, halved
8 ounces chanterelles
2 tablespoons whipping cream
Salt and pepper to taste

To Garnish:
Herb sprigs

Prepare filling: In a small frying pan, melt butter. Add garlic and cook gently 1 minute, being careful not to burn butter. Discard garlic. Add chanterelles to pan and cook over high heat 5 minutes. If mushrooms exude a lot of liquid, remove them with a slotted spoon and boil liquid over high heat until reduced, then return mushrooms to pan.

Remove from heat, stir in cream and season with salt and pepper. Keep warm while preparing omelet.

In a bowl, beat together eggs, chopped herbs and 3 tablespoons water. In a nonstick frying pan, melt butter; pour in eggs. When edges begin to set, gently lift them with a spatula and push toward center, allowing uncooked eggs to flow underneath. Continue to cook in this way until omelet is almost set.

Spoon Chanterelle Filling over half the omelet, then fold other half over to enclose. Cut omelet in half and slide onto warmed serving plates. Garnish with herb sprigs and serve immediately.

Makes 2 servings.

Note: Eggs for omelets are exquisite when scented by truffles. Simply store a truffle with the eggs; its aroma will penetrate the shells.

Tagliatelle with Mushrooms

1/2 ounce dried cepes (porcini)
2 tablespoons butter
8 ounces small button mushrooms, quartered
1 garlic clove, pressed or minced
2/3 cup dry white wine
2 eggs
1/2 cup whipping cream
1 pound fresh tagliatelle
3 to 4 tablespoons freshly grated Parmesan cheese
Salt and pepper to taste

To Garnish:
Chopped parsley
Parsley sprigs

Place cepes in a small bowl; cover with warm water and let soak 20 minutes. Drain; rinse well to remove any grit. Chop coarsely.

In a saucepan, melt butter. Add button mushrooms and garlic; sauté 2 minutes. Add cepes and wine; cook over high heat 2 to 3 minutes or until mushrooms are tender and liquid is reduced by half. Keep hot.

Beat eggs and cream together; set aside.

Cook tagliatelle in plenty of boiling salted water about 3 minutes or just until *al dente;* drain well and return to pan. Add eggs and hot mushroom mixture to pasta and toss until eggs become creamy and start to set. Add cheese, salt and pepper and toss again. Serve immediately, garnished with chopped parsley and parsley sprigs.

Makes 4 servings.

Note: If you are fortunate enough to find fresh cepes or other boletes, use them in place of both dried cepes and fresh button mushrooms. You will need about 8 ounces; chop before using.

Pasta, Beans & Mushrooms

1 pound unshelled fava beans, shelled
8 ounces dried rigatoni
2 tablespoons butter or virgin olive oil
Salt to taste

Mushroom Sauce:
2 tablespoons virgin olive oil
2 shallots, finely chopped
1 garlic clove, pressed or minced
2 to 3 tablespoons chopped sun-dried tomatoes
12 ounces wild mushrooms (see *Note*), chopped if large
2 tablespoons finely chopped parsley
1 cup tomato puree
1/4 cup whipping cream
Salt and pepper to taste

To Garnish:
Freshly grated Parmesan cheese
Parsley sprigs

Prepare Mushroom Sauce: In a saucepan, heat oil. Add shallots and garlic and sauté 3 to 4 minutes or until softened and just beginning to color. Stir in sun-dried tomatoes, mushrooms and parsley; cook 2 minutes, stirring constantly. Stir in tomato puree and simmer 5 to 6 minutes or until mushrooms are tender. Stir in cream, salt and pepper; heat gently. Set aside.

Cook beans in boiling water 30 minutes or until tender. In another pan, cook rigatoni in plenty of boiling salted water 8 to 10 minutes or until *al dente*. Drain pasta and beans thoroughly and put in a large warmed serving bowl. Toss together with butter or oil and a little salt, if desired.

Gently reheat sauce; do not boil. Add half the sauce to bowl; toss lightly to mix, then spoon onto warmed plates and offer remaining sauce to spoon on top. Garnish with cheese and parsley sprigs.

Makes 4 servings.

Note: Use meadow or parasol mushrooms, morels, or cepes (porcini) or other large boletes.

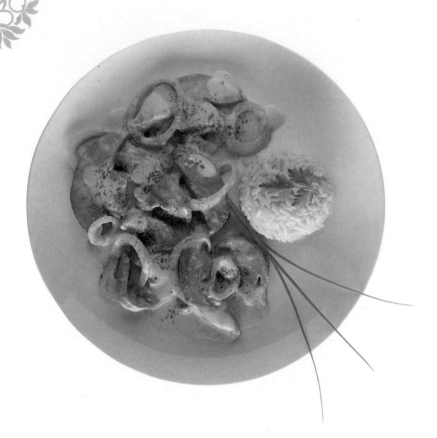

Mushroom Stroganoff

2 tablespoons butter
2 tablespoons virgin olive oil
2 onions, thinly sliced
1 or 2 garlic cloves, pressed or
    minced
1-1/2 pounds cepes (porcini) or large
    meadow mushrooms, sliced
1/4 cup brandy
1-1/4 cups dairy sour cream
Salt and pepper to taste
Paprika

To Garnish:
Whole chives

To Serve:
Saffron rice or crusty bread

In a large frying pan, melt butter in oil. Add onions and cook 5 to 7 minutes or until softened and golden. Add garlic and mushrooms; cook 2 minutes, stirring constantly.

Stir in brandy and cook, stirring frequently, 3 to 4 minutes or until mushrooms are tender. Reduce heat and stir in sour cream; heat gently, being careful not to boil. Season with salt and pepper.

Sprinkle with paprika and garnish with chives. Serve with saffron rice or warm crusty bread.

Makes 4 servings.

Note: Large, meaty-textured mushrooms are essential for this dish. For appearance as well as taste, your best choices are cepes or other boletes. Meadow mushrooms have a good flavor, but they'll color the sauce gray. Cultivated mushrooms aren't as flavorful as wild ones, but can give good results with the help of dried cepes or suillus.

Mushroom & Broccoli Stir-Fry

4 ounces firm tofu, cut into 3/4-inch
    cubes
2 tablespoons soy sauce
4 dried shiitake mushrooms
2 to 3 tablespoons peanut or olive oil
8 ounces broccoli flowerets
1 garlic clove, pressed or minced
2 teaspoons shredded fresh
    gingerroot
1 red onion, cut into thin wedges
1 (4-oz.) jar straw mushrooms,
    drained
3 tablespoons dry sherry
1 teaspoon cornstarch
Generous pinch of sugar
Black or Szechuan pepper to taste

To Garnish:
1 teaspoon sesame seeds, toasted
Cilantro sprigs

To Serve:
Hot rice or thin noodles

In a small bowl, toss tofu with soy sauce; set aside. Place shiitake in a another small bowl, cover with 1/2 cup hot water and let soak 20 minutes. Drain, adding soaking liquid to tofu. Rinse shiitake well; trim off tough stems and slice caps.

In a wok, heat oil over high heat. Using a slotted spoon, remove tofu from marinade; reserve marinade. Add tofu to wok and stir-fry 1 minute or until browned; remove and set aside.

Add broccoli, garlic and ginger to wok and stir-fry 2 minutes. Add onion, shiitake and straw mushrooms and stir-fry 1 minute. Pour in tofu marinade and bring to a boil; simmer 2 minutes or until broccoli is tender-crisp. Stir in tofu.

Blend sherry, cornstarch and sugar; pour into wok and cook, stirring, until thickened. Season with pepper; transfer to a warmed serving dish.

Garnish with sesame seeds and cilantro sprigs. Serve immediately, with rice or noodles.

Makes 4 servings.

Note: Dried wood ears may also be added for their pretty, frilly appearance and chewy texture. Reconstitute them with the shiitake.

Wild Rice Salad

1-1/4 cups quick-cooking cracked
   wheat
3 tablespoons wild rice, rinsed,
   drained
4 ounces Gruyère cheese, diced
4 ounces Pipo Crème or other creamy
   blue cheese, diced
10 cherry tomatoes, halved
2 green onions, shredded
1/4 cup virgin olive oil
8 ounces mixed chanterelles and
   oyster mushrooms, quartered if
   large
1 garlic clove, chopped
2 tablespoons white wine vinegar
2 tablespoons chopped fresh dill
Pinch of sugar (optional)
Salt and pepper to taste

To Garnish:
Dill sprigs

Place cracked wheat in a bowl; pour
1-1/4 cups cold water over it. Let
stand about 1 hour or until wheat is

tender, but still chewy.

Meanwhile, in a small saucepan,
combine wild rice and 1 cup water.
Bring to a boil; then reduce heat,
cover and simmer about 45 minutes
or until rice is tender. Drain; let cool.

Drain any unabsorbed water from
wheat. In a large salad bowl, combine
wheat, rice, cheeses, tomatoes and
green onions.

In a large frying pan, heat oil. Add
mushrooms and sauté 4 minutes. Remove from heat and add garlic, vinegar, chopped dill and sugar, if desired; season with salt and pepper.
Add to salad and toss lightly to mix.
Serve immediately; or chill and serve
cold. Garnish with dill sprigs before
serving.

Makes 4 to 6 servings.

Saffron Rice Pilaf

Generous pinch of saffron threads
1 tablespoon sesame or olive oil
1/2 cup slivered almonds
3 tablespoons butter
1 onion, chopped
1 garlic clove, pressed or minced
1 large carrot, cut into matchstick
   pieces
1 celery stalk, cut into matchstick
   pieces
1-1/2 cups brown rice
10 ounces mixed chanterelles and
   oyster mushrooms, quartered if
   large
1/3 cup golden raisins
2-1/2 cups mushroom or vegetable
   stock
4 ounces snow peas, halved
1 to 2 tablespoons chopped fresh
   cilantro
Salt and pepper to taste

To Garnish:
Fresh cilantro leaves
Marigold petals (optional)

Place saffron in a small bowl, cover
with 1/4 cup boiling water and let
soak 20 minutes.

In a saucepan, heat oil. Add
almonds and cook, stirring, 1 to 2
minutes or until browned. Transfer
to a plate and set aside.

Melt butter in pan over medium
heat. Add onion, garlic, carrot and
celery; cook 3 to 4 minutes or until
vegetables just begin to soften. Add
rice and cook 4 minutes, stirring
often. Stir in mushrooms, raisins,
stock and saffron with its soaking liquid. Bring to a boil; reduce heat,
cover and cook 25 to 30 minutes or
until rice is tender.

Stir in snow peas, chopped cilantro,
toasted almonds, salt and pepper.

To serve, garnish pilaf with cilantro
leaves and sprinkle with marigold
petals, if desired.

Makes 4 servings.

Sorrel Tart

Pastry:
1-3/4 cups all-purpose flour
1/2 teaspoon salt
**7 tablespoons butter, cut in small
 pieces**
1 egg yolk
About 1/3 cup chilled water

Filling:
2 tablespoons olive oil
2 large onions, sliced
2 teaspoons light-brown sugar
1 lb. sorrel
1 teaspoon salt
1/3 cup whipping cream
Pinch grated nutmeg

To Garnish:
Parsley sprigs

To prepare pastry: sift flour and salt into large bowl. Cut in butter until mixture resembles bread crumbs, then add egg yolk with water. Work together using finger tips until mixture forms a firm smooth dough. Wrap in plastic wrap and chill several hours.

Preheat oven to 400F (205C). On a lightly floured surface, roll out pastry thinly and line a 9-inch flan dish. Fill pastry with dried beans and bake blind in oven 10 to 15 minutes, until lightly colored. Lower temperature to 375F (190C).

To prepare filling, in a skillet, heat oil. Add onions and sugar and cook gently about 15 minutes to soften.

Meanwhile, in a large un-covered saucepan, cook sorrel, with water clinging to leaves after washing, and salt 10 minutes until reduced and moisture has evapo-rated. Drain well and chop coarsely.

Place onions in crust. Cover with sorrel, pour over cream and season with nutmeg. Bake in oven 30 minutes. Serve hot or cold, gar-nished with parsley.

Makes 6 first-course servings or 4 main-course servings.

Vegetables with Ricotta

6 tomatoes
6 small zucchini
1/2 cup ricotta cheese
1/4 cup sour cream
1 teaspoon chopped lemon thyme
1 teaspoon chopped marjoram
Salt and black pepper to taste
**2 tablespoons chopped green
 pitted olives**
**3 to 4 tablespoons chopped
 pistachio nuts**
2 teaspoons dried bread crumbs
2 tablespoons olive oil

To Garnish:
Lemon thyme sprigs
Marjoram sprigs

Preheat oven to 350F (175C). Cut tops off tomatoes. Scoop out flesh and invert tomatoes to drain. Cut zucchini in half length-wise and scoop out flesh.

Sieve ricotta cheese into a bowl; mix in sour cream, thyme, mar-joram and season with salt and pepper.

Fill tomatoes 3/4 full with ricotta mixture; top with chopped olives. Fill zucchini with ricotta mixture. Top with pistachio nuts, then bread crumbs.

Place vegetables in an oven-proof dish large enough to hold them in 1 layer. Drizzle olive oil over them. Put a little water in bot-tom of dish and bake, uncovered, in oven 20 to 25 minutes, until zucchini are tender.

Transfer vegetables to a serving dish and garnish with lemon thyme and marjoram sprigs. Serve hot.

Makes 6 servings.

Asparagus Gratin

1-1/2 lbs. asparagus

Sauce:
1 leek, finely chopped
2 teaspoons all-purpose flour
3/4 cup milk
4 teaspoons chopped tarragon
2 tablespoons whipping cream
Salt and black pepper to taste
1 egg

To Garnish:
Tarragon sprigs

Preheat oven to 375F (190C).

Trim and cook asparagus in usual way; drain off cooking water, reserving 1/3 cup. Set asparagus aside.

To prepare sauce, in a saucepan, melt 1/2 of butter. Add leek, cover and cook gently 5 minutes.

Stir in flour and cook gently 2 to 3 minutes.

In a separate pan, heat milk and reserved asparagus cooking liquid; do not allow to boil. Add to roux and stir over low heat until sauce has thickened. Remove from heat and stir in tarragon, cream and season with salt and pepper. Beat egg lightly and stir into sauce.

Lay asparagus in a gratin dish, tips facing alternate ends. Pour over sauce, dot with remaining butter and bake in oven 10 to 12 minutes, until golden and sauce is bubbling.

Serve from baking dish, garnished with tarragon sprigs.

Makes 4 to 6 servings.

Blue Brie & Broccoli Flan

Pastry:
2-1/4 cups all-purpose flour
Pinch of salt
5 tablespoons butter, chilled
1 egg yolk
3 to 4 tablespoons cold water

Filling:
6 to 8 ounces broccoli
6 ounces Lymeswold or blue Brie,
   white rind removed
2 tablespoons half and half
3 eggs, beaten
2 tablespoons chopped parsley
Salt and pepper, to taste

To make pastry, sift flour and salt into a bowl; add butter. Using a pastry blender or 2 knives, cut butter into flour until pea-size and well coated with flour. Beat egg yolk with 3 tablespoons water; add to bowl and mix to form a soft dough. Add more water if necessary. Form pastry into a ball and flatten slightly into a round with floured hands. Wrap in plastic wrap and refrigerate 15 minutes.

On a lightly floured surface, roll out pastry and use to line a 9-inch flan pan. Prick base with a fork; refrigerate 10 minutes.

Preheat oven to 375F (190C).

To make filling, cook broccoli in boiling salted water 5 to 6 minutes. Drain, rinse in cold water, drain thoroughly, then chop coarsely. Set aside.

Break cheese into pieces and put in the top section of a double boiler set over simmering water. Heat gently until melted. Remove from heat. Beat together half and half and eggs, then blend into melted cheese. Stir in parsley and season lightly with salt and pepper.

Arrange broccoli in pastry shell, pour cheese mixture over broccoli and bake in oven 30 to 40 minutes or until lightly browned and a knife inserted off center comes out clean. Serve warm, with a salad.

Makes 6 to 8 servings.

Spinakopitta

1/2 cup plus 2 tablespoons butter
8 ounces zucchini, thinly sliced
1 pound fresh spinach, shredded
4 green onions, thinly sliced
4 ounces marinated feta cheese (feta
  with oregano and olive oil),
  crumbled
2 eggs, beaten
Pepper, to taste
8 sheets filo pastry

Preheat oven to 350F (175C).

In a saucepan, melt 2 tablespoons of the butter; add zucchini. Sauté zucchini 4 minutes. Spoon into a large bowl; add spinach and onions and mix well. Add feta cheese, mix in eggs and season with pepper.

Melt remaining butter; liberally butter a deep 11" x 7" baking pan. Line bottom and sides with 4 sheets of filo pastry, brushing each sheet with melted butter. Spoon vegetable mixture evenly over pastry base; cover with remaining 4 sheets of filo, brushing each with melted butter. Trim; tuck trimmings down inside dish to prevent filling escaping.

With a sharp knife, score top two layers of pastry into squares or diamonds. Cover with waxed paper and bake about 45 minutes or until golden and crisp on top. Serve warm or cold, cut into shapes, with a mixed salad.

Makes 8 servings.

Note: If marinated feta cheese is unavailable, use plain feta and add 2 teaspoons olive oil and 1/2 teaspoon dried leaf oregano when preparing filling.

Cheese & Mushroom Nests

8 ounces purchased puff pastry
Milk to glaze
1 teaspoon sesame seeds

Sauce:
1-1/4 cups milk
1 onion slice
6 peppercorns
1 bay leaf
Pinch of ground mace
1 tablespoon butter
1 tablespoon all-purpose flour
1 teaspoon dry mustard
2 tablespoons half and half
2 ounces Leicester cheese, crumbled

Filling:
2 teaspoons butter
2 shallots, chopped
1 cup sliced mushrooms
2 tomatoes, peeled, seeded and sliced
1 tablespoon lemon juice
1 tablespoon snipped chives
8 quail's eggs, hard-cooked

Preheat oven to 400F (205C).

Roll out pastry and cut into 4 (4-inch) circles. Using a 2-inch-round cutter, mark centers and press halfway through pastry. Rough up edge of each circle with a knife. Brush with milk and sprinkle with sesame seeds. Put on a dampened baking sheet and bake 15 to 20 minutes or until puffed and golden brown, turning baking sheet around once. Cool on a wire rack. Using a sharp knife, remove center circles; discard.

Meanwhile, make sauce: in a saucepan, combine milk, onion, peppercorns, bay leaf and mace. Bring to scalding point, then set aside 10 minutes to infuse; strain.

In a clean pan, melt butter, stir in flour and gradually stir in strained milk. Bring to a boil and boil 1 to 2 minutes. Remove from heat. Add mustard, half and half and cheese, cover and set aside on a very low heat.

To make filling, in a skillet melt butter; add shallots and mushrooms and cook 2 minutes. Add tomatoes and lemon juice and cook 3 minutes; add chives. Immediately divide among pastry cases. Pour a little sauce over the top and arrange 2 quail's eggs on the sauce; one egg can be halved, if desired. Serve immediately with salad.

Makes 4 servings.

Goat's Cheese Soufflé

1/4 cup plus 1 tablespoon butter
1/2 cup all-purpose flour
1-1/4 cups milk
1/4 teaspoon freshly grated nutmeg
Salt and pepper, to taste
4 eggs, separated
5 ounces goat's cheese, crumbled

To Garnish:
Herbs
Salad leaves

Evenly butter an 8-inch soufflé dish and refrigerate to let the butter harden. Preheat oven to 375F (190C).

In a saucepan, melt 1/4 cup of the butter, stir in flour and cook 1 minute, stirring. Remove from heat and gradually blend in milk. Return to heat and cook, stirring or until sauce thickens. Remove from heat and stir in remaining butter, nutmeg, salt and pepper.

Cool a few minutes, then gradually beat in egg yolks. Stir in cheese; heat gently 30 seconds to melt and blend into sauce.

In a bowl, whisk egg whites with a pinch of salt until stiff peaks form. Fold about one-quarter into cheese mixture until thoroughly blended; fold in remaining egg whites.

Pour mixture into chilled dish. Put dish on a baking sheet and bake 30 to 40 minutes or until puffed and golden brown. Serve immediately, garnished with a few herbs and salad leaves.

Makes 4 to 5 servings.

Note: To make individual soufflés, divide the mixture among 4 or 5 individual soufflé dishes and bake 15 to 20 minutes or until puffed and golden brown.

Cheese & Chive Puffs

Choux Pastry:
2/3 cup all-purpose flour
Pinch each of salt and red (cayenne) pepper
1/4 cup (1 oz.) shredded sharp Cheddar cheese
1/4 cup butter
2/3 cup water
2 eggs, beaten

Filling:
2 ounces cream cheese with chives
6 ounces carrots, finely grated

Sauce:
1 bunch watercress
1/3 cup milk
2 tablespoons half and half
1 ounce cream cheese with chives
Salt and pepper, to taste

To Garnish:
Carrot flowers or strips
A few chives
Parsley sprigs

To make pastry, sift flour, salt and cayenne into a bowl. Mix in cheese. Put butter and water in a saucepan and bring to a boil. Remove from heat and immediately beat in flour mixture all at once. Return to low heat and beat vigorously until a soft ball forms and leaves the side of the pan. Cool slightly, then gradually add beaten eggs, beating between each addition. Continue beating until mixture is smooth and glossy; cover and leave until cold.

Preheat oven to 425F (220C). Grease a baking sheet. Pipe or spoon about 16 small mounds onto baking sheet. Bake 15 minutes. Reduce temperature to 375F (190C) and bake 10 to 15 minutes or until puffed and golden. Transfer to a wire rack and slit the side of each puff.

To make filling, blend cheese and carrots in a small bowl; spoon into choux puffs.

To make sauce, put watercress, milk, half and half and cheese in a blender or food processor fitted with the metal blade and process until smooth. Pour into a small saucepan and heat gently. Season to taste.

To serve, put 2 or 3 puffs on each plate with a little sauce. Garnish with carrot, chives and parsley.

Makes 16 puffs.

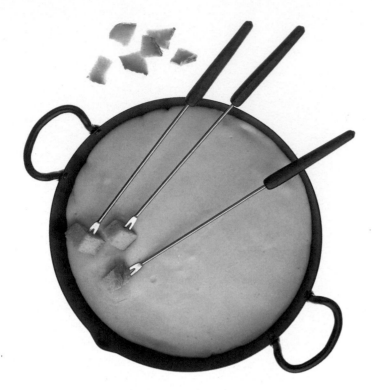

Fondue Suisse

1 garlic clove, halved
1 tablespoon cornstarch
1 cup dry white wine
8 ounces Gruyère cheese, diced
8 ounces Emmenthaler cheese, diced
Pepper, to taste
3 tablespoons kirsch
1 French bread loaf, cut into cubes

Rub cut garlic around the inside of an earthenware fondue dish or heavy pan; discard garlic.

Blend cornstarch with a little of the wine. Pour remaining wine into pan and bring to a boil. Add cheeses and stir until melted and blended.

Add blended cornstarch and pepper and cook about 2 minutes or until mixture combines and becomes creamy; do not boil or the fondue will become stringy. Stir in kirsch.

To serve, keep fondue warm at the table. Divide bread cubes among 4 side plates for the diners, who dip bread into fondue using long-handled forks. Accompany with a chilled dry white wine.

Makes 4 servings.

Garlic & Herb Fondue

1 garlic clove, halved
2/3 cup dry white wine
1 tablespoon cornstarch
1-1/4 cups dairy sour cream
2 (5-oz.) packages full-fat soft cheese
   with garlic and herbs
Pinch of freshly grated nutmeg
Salt and pepper, to taste

To Serve:
1 pound cauliflower, broken into
   flowerets
1 pound broccoli, broken into
   flowerets
Chopped parsley
1 French bread loaf, cut into cubes,
   toasted

Rub cut garlic clove around inside of an earthenware fondue dish or a heavy pan; discard garlic. Add 1/2 cup wine; bring to a boil. Blend cornstarch with remaining wine; add to pan and cook, stirring constantly, until thickened. Reduce heat. Add sour cream and cheese; stir until cheese has melted. Add nutmeg, salt and pepper. Keep warm.

Bring a pan of salted water to a boil, add cauliflower and broccoli and boil 5 to 6 minutes or until crisp-tender. Drain well and place in a warm serving dish.

Sprinkle fondue with parsley and serve immediately with the cauliflower and broccoli and bread cubes.

Makes 4 to 6 servings.

Brazil Nut & Cranberry Loaf

2 celery stalks
1 onion, chopped
3 tablespoons vegetable oil
1 garlic clove, crushed
2 tablespoons all-purpose flour
1 (7-oz.) can chopped tomatoes
3/4 cup Brazil nuts, chopped
2 cups whole-wheat bread crumbs
4 ounces cranberries
1 tablespoon plus 1 teaspoon soy sauce
2 tablespoons chopped parsley
1 egg, beaten
4 green onions
1 teaspoon red currant jelly
3/4 cup vegetable or chicken stock
1/4 cup port

1. Preheat oven to 350F (175C). Grease and line a 9" x 5" loaf pan. Chop celery and onion. In a medium saucepan, heat 2 tablespoons oil, add onion and fry until softened. Add celery and garlic and fry 3 minutes, stirring occasionally. Mix in 1 tablespoon flour, then add tomatoes and cook until thickened, stirring.

2. Add the nuts, bread crumbs, half the cranberries, 1 tablespoon soy sauce, the parsley and egg. Season with salt and pepper to taste, and mix well. Turn into prepared pan, cover with foil and bake 1 hour.

3. To make the sauce, chop the green onions diagonally, keeping green and white parts separate. In a small pan, heat remaining oil and fry white part of green onions 1 minute. Mix in remaining 1 tablespoon flour and red currant jelly, then gradually stir in the stock and port. Bring to a boil, stirring, then add remaining soy sauce, cranberries, green part of green onions and pepper to taste; cook 5 minutes.

Turn out nut loaf, cut into slices with a sharp knife and serve with the cranberry sauce. Accompany with snow peas.

Makes 4 servings.

Hazelnut Croquettes

6 large dried cloud ear mushrooms
6 tablespoons sunflower oil
1 onion, chopped
3 garlic cloves, chopped
1 celery stalk, chopped
2 teaspoons ground coriander
1/4 cup all-purpose flour
1 tablespoon soy sauce
Scant cup hazelnuts, ground
2 cups fresh bread crumbs
2 tablespoons chopped parsley

MUSHROOM SAUCE:
1 tablespoon butter
2 tablespoons sherry
1/4 cup whipping cream
1 teaspoon chopped fresh thyme
2 teaspoons cornstarch

1. Soak mushrooms in boiling water to cover 30 minutes; drain, reserving 2/3 cup liquid. Finely chop half the mushrooms; slice remaining mushrooms. Set all mushrooms aside.

2. In a medium-size saucepan, heat 2 tablespoons oil, add onion, 2 garlic cloves and celery; fry gently until softened. Add coriander and fry 1 minute, then stir in 2 tablespoons flour. Off the heat, stir in reserved mushroom liquid and soy sauce. Bring to a boil and cook 2 minutes, until thickened. Add chopped mushrooms, ground hazelnuts, bread crumbs, parsley and seasoning; mix thoroughly.

3. Season remaining flour. Divide nut mixture into 12 portions and, using dampened hands, shape into croquettes. Roll in seasoned flour to coat. Heat remaining oil in a medium-size skillet; add croquettes. Fry about 2 minutes on each side, until golden-brown and crisp. Keep warm while making sauce.

In a small saucepan, melt the butter and quickly fry remaining sliced mushrooms and garlic. Add sherry, 2 tablespoons water, cream and thyme; cover and simmer 5 minutes. Blend cornstarch with 1/2 cup water; stir into sauce. Bring to a boil, stirring, and cook 1 minute. Serve the croquettes with the sauce, and accompany with French beans.

Makes 4 servings.

Fennel Italiano

4 large fennel bulbs
2 tablespoons olive oil
2 garlic cloves, chopped
1 large onion, quartered and thinly sliced
1 (14-1/2-oz.) can peeled tomatoes, chopped
2 tablespoons tomato paste
1/3 cup dry white wine or dry vermouth
Salt and pepper to taste
6 ounces mozzarella cheese, thinly sliced
2 to 3 teaspoons chopped marjoram
TO GARNISH:
Ripe olives

1. Preheat oven to 350F (175C). Cut off and reserve fennel leaves for garnish. Cut fennel bulbs in quarters. Cook in boiling salted water to cover 15 minutes; drain well.

2. Meanwhile in a large saucepan, heat oil. Add garlic and onion and sauté 5 minutes. Add tomatoes and juice, tomato paste and wine or vermouth. Season with salt and pepper. Bring to a boil. Simmer, uncovered, 10 minutes. In a blender or food processor fitted with the metal blade, process until smooth.

3. Arrange fennel in 4 greased individual ovenproof dishes. Pour sauce over fennel and cover with mozzarella cheese. Sprinkle with chopped marjoram and pepper. Bake in preheated oven 30 to 40 minutes or until fennel is tender. Garnish with olives and reserved fennel fronds. Serve hot.

Makes 4 servings.

Note: Serve with warm crusty bread.

Gruyère & Tomato Jalousie

1 tablespoon olive oil
2 medium-size zucchini, chopped
1 small onion, chopped
1 large tomato, chopped
2 teaspoons chopped fresh oregano
1 garlic clove, crushed
Salt and pepper to taste
1/2 cup shredded Gruyère cheese (2 oz.)
1/4 cup unsalted cashews, ground
1 (17-1/2-oz.) package frozen puff pastry, thawed
Beaten egg to glaze
TO GARNISH:
Sprigs of oregano

1. In a large saucepan, heat oil. Add zucchini and onion and fry 3 minutes. Remove from heat. Add tomato, oregano, garlic and seasoning. Cool in a strainer, then stir in cheese and ground nuts.

2. On a lightly floured surface, roll out pastry thinly to a 12-inch square. Mark in 2 pieces, one 12" x 6-1/2" and the other 12" x 5-1/2". Place smaller piece on a dampened baking sheet. Cover with zucchini mixture to within 1/2-inch of edges. Brush border with beaten egg.

Sprinkle other pastry lightly with flour, then fold in half lengthwise. Lightly mark a margin about 3/4 inch from the 3 cut edges. Using a sharp knife, cut folded edge at 1/4-inch intervals within marked margin.

3. Lift pastry over 1/2 of filling; unfold to cover remaining area. Seal edges, then press together and flute. Chill 30 minutes. Preheat oven to 425F (220C).

Brush jalousie lightly with beaten egg. Bake in preheated oven 15 minutes. Reduce heat to 375F (190C) and bake 15 minutes more, until golden. Serve hot or cold, garnished with oregano sprigs.

Makes 4 to 6 servings.

Pepper Rings

2/3 cup green lentils
1 onion, chopped
2 garlic cloves, chopped
2 dried red chiles, chopped
1/4 teaspoon ground coriander
1/4 teaspoon ground cumin
4 ounces shelled fava beans
2 tablespoons olive oil
1 tablespoon lemon juice
Salt and pepper to taste
1 each large red and green bell pepper
4 ounces goat cheese
TO GARNISH:
Sprigs of flat-leaf parsley

Tofu & Corn Stir-Fry

1 large red or green bell pepper, cored and seeded
1 bunch green onions
3 ounces button mushrooms
8 ounces tofu
3 tablespoons corn oil
16 dwarf (baby) ears-of-corn
4 ounces snow peas, trimmed
1 garlic clove, crushed
2 teaspoons light soy sauce
1 teaspoon dry sherry
1 (1/2-inch) piece gingerroot,
peeled and cut in thin slivers
1 teaspoon sugar
1/4 cup pine nuts, toasted

1. Place lentils in a bowl. Cover with boiling water and soak 30 minutes. Drain and place in a saucepan with 1 cup cold water. Add onion, garlic, chiles, coriander and cumin. Bring to a boil. Cover and simmer about 45 minutes, until water is absorbed and lentils are tender.
2. Meanwhile, cook fava beans in boiling water 15 to 20 minutes, until tender; drain. Place lentil mixture in a blender or food processor. Add fava beans, 4 teaspoons of oil, lemon juice and salt and pepper. Blend until fairly smooth; cool. Cut stalk ends off bell peppers and remove core and seeds.

Press bean mixture into bell peppers and level surfaces. Wrap in plastic wrap and chill at least 2 hours.
3. Preheat broiler. Cut bell peppers in 1/2-inch thick slices. Place on a broiler pan and brush lightly with remaining oil.
Slice cheese thinly and cut in quarters. Arrange 2 overlapping pieces on each bell pepper slice. Broil 4 to 5 minutes or until cheese is lightly golden. Serve immediately, garnished with parsley.

Makes 6 servings.

1. Cut bell pepper in thin slivers. Cut green onions diagonally. Slice mushrooms. Drain and cut tofu in cubes.
2. In a wok or large skillet, heat oil. Add corn and bell pepper and stir-fry 4 minutes. Add snow peas, green onions, mushrooms, tofu and garlic and stir-fry 4 to 5 minutes.
3. In a small bowl, mix soy sauce, sherry, gingerroot and sugar. Stir

mixture into vegetables and heat through 1 minute, stirring gently. Spoon mixture into a warmed serving dish. Sprinkle with pine nuts and serve immediately.

Makes 4 servings.

Note: This dish is good served with rice or noodles.

Ratatouille Cheese Gougère

CHOUX PASTRY:
3-1/2 tablespoons butter
2/3 cup water
2/3 cup all-purpose flour, sifted
2 eggs, beaten
1/2 cup shredded Monterey Jack cheese (2 oz.)
FILLING:
1 small eggplant
1 large zucchini
Salt
3 tablespoons olive oil
2 red bell peppers, cored, seeded and cut in 1-inch pieces
1 Spanish onion, quartered and sliced
1 garlic clove, crushed
1 large tomato, peeled and chopped
Salt and pepper to taste

1. To prepare filling, quarter eggplant. Cut zucchini in 1/4-inch slices. Arrange in a colander, sprinkling each layer with salt. Let stand 30 minutes to drain.

2. Preheat oven to 400F (205C). To prepare pastry, in a saucepan, place butter and water. Heat gently until butter is melted. Bring to a boil, remove from heat and immediately add flour, all at once, and a pinch of salt, stirring quickly with a wooden spoon until smooth. Return pan to heat a few seconds and beat until mixture forms a ball and leaves side of pan clean. Remove from heat and gradually add eggs, beating after each addition until glossy. Stir in cheese. Spoon mixture around edge of 4 greased individual ovenproof dishes. Bake in preheated oven 30 minutes, or until well risen and golden.

3. Meanwhile, rinse eggplant and zucchini; drain and pat dry. In a pan, heat oil. Add all filling ingredients. Cover and cook gently 30 minutes. Spoon ratatouille into center of choux rings and serve immediately.

Makes 4 servings.

Broccoli Soufflé Tartlets

PASTRY:
1-1/2 cups all-purpose flour, sifted
1/2 cup whole-wheat flour
Pinch of salt
4 tablespoons margarine, chilled and diced
1/4 cup shortening, chilled and diced
1-1/4 cups finely shredded Cheddar cheese (5 oz.)
FILLING & TOPPING:
12 ounces broccoli spears, cut in even-sized spears
4 tablespoons butter
1/4 cup all-purpose flour
1-1/4 cups milk
2 eggs, separated
Salt and pepper to taste

1. Preheat oven to 400F (205C). To prepare pastry, place flour and salt in a bowl and cut in fats. Add 1/2 cup of cheese and mix well. Stir in 3 to 4 tablespoons cold water and mix to a firm dough. Knead gently and divide in 6 pieces. On a lightly floured surface, roll out dough and line 6 (4-inch) fluted flan pans. Prick bottoms with a fork. Line with foil and fill with dried beans. Bake 5 minutes; remove foil and beans and bake 5 minutes more. Remove from oven. Reduce heat to 375F (190C).

2. Cook broccoli in boiling salted water 6 to 8 minutes. Drain and cut in pieces. In a pan, melt butter. Stir in flour and cook 1 minute. Blend in milk. Bring to a boil, stirring. Cook 2 minutes.

3. Arrange 1/2 of broccoli in pastry shells. In a blender or food processor fitted with the metal blade, process remaining broccoli with sauce, egg yolks and 1/2 cup of remaining cheese. Season and transfer to a bowl. Whisk egg whites stiffly, then lightly fold into sauce. Spoon over broccoli and sprinkle with remaining cheese. Bake in oven 20 minutes, until golden. Serve hot.

Makes 6 servings.

Spinach & Ricotta Roulade

1-1/2 pounds spinach
2 tablespoons butter
3 shallots, very finely chopped
1/3 cup all-purpose flour
2/3 cup milk
2 tablespoons grated Parmesan cheese
4 large eggs, separated
Salt and pepper to taste
FILLING:
2 tablespoons dairy sour cream
1 cup ricotta cheese
3 green onions, chopped
2 tablespoons chopped fresh parsley
2 to 3 pinches red (cayenne) pepper
TO GARNISH:
Radish roses, as illustrated

Sorrel & Asparagus Crepes

24 young tender sorrel leaves
1/4 bunch watercress
4 tablespoons unsalted butter
1-1/4 cups all-purpose flour
Pinch of salt
2 eggs, beaten
1 cup milk
2/3 cup water
1 to 2 tablespoons corn oil
1 pound asparagus spears
2 tablespoons lemon juice
3/4 cup plain yogurt
Salt and pepper to taste
2 tomatoes, sliced
1/2 cup shredded Emmenthaler cheese (2 oz.)
TO GARNISH:
Lemon wedges

1. Lightly grease a jellyroll pan and line with lightly greased parchment paper. Preheat oven to 400F (205C).

Prepare and cook spinach as for Spinach & Anchovy Soufflé, page 54. In a saucepan, melt butter. Add shallots and sauté 3 minutes. Stir in flour and cook 1 minute, then gradually blend in milk. Bring to a boil, then cook 2 minutes, stirring constantly (the sauce will be very thick). Remove from heat and stir in spinach, Parmesan cheese and egg yolks. Add salt and pepper and beat well.

2. Whisk egg whites until stiff but not dry; using a metal spoon, lightly fold into mixture. Spread into prepared pan. Level surface and bake in preheated oven for 25 minutes or until set and firm to the touch.

Meanwhile, in a bowl, mix all filling ingredients; season with salt.

3. Turn roulade onto a sheet of lightly greased parchment paper. Loosen edges from lining paper and remove it in strips. Spread roulade with filling. Roll up, starting from a short side and using paper to help. Serve hot, garnished with radish roses.

Makes 6 servings.

1. Shred sorrel. Chop watercress. In a saucepan, melt 1 tablespoon of butter. Add sorrel and watercress; cook gently 2 minutes; cool.

Sift flour and salt into a bowl. Add eggs and gradually beat in milk and water. Stir in sorrel and watercress.

2. In an 8-inch skillet, heat a little oil, swirling it over bottom and side. Pour in enough batter to coat bottom of pan evenly. Cook over high heat 2 minutes; turn and cook other side until golden; set aside. Use remaining batter to prepare 7 more crepes.

3. Preheat oven to 350F (175C). Prepare and cook asparagus as for Ham & Asparagus Bundles, page 40. Cut in bite-size pieces. Melt remaining butter in a pan; remove from heat. Add lemon juice, yogurt and salt and pepper. Spoon over crepes; fold each in half, then in half again. Insert asparagus into folds.

Arrange crepes in a greased shallow ovenproof dish. Place tomato slices between them and sprinkle with cheese. Cover with foil and bake in preheated oven 15 minutes. Uncover and bake 7 minutes more. Garnish with lemon wedges.

Makes 4 servings.

Baked Mushrooms in Madeira

1/4 cup butter, room temperature
1 pound large meadow mushrooms,
  thickly sliced
1 large garlic clove, thinly slivered
Salt and pepper to taste
2/3 cup Madeira

To Garnish:
1 tablespoon chopped parsley

Preheat oven to 375F (190C). Spread butter over bottom of a large, shallow baking dish. Arrange mushrooms in a single layer in dish and dot evenly with garlic slivers. Season with salt and pepper; pour Madeira over top.

Bake, covered, 25 to 30 minutes or until mushrooms are very tender. Serve hot or cold, sprinkled with parsley.

Makes 4 servings.

Note: Fresh cepes (porcini) are delicious cooked this way. Cultivated brown mushrooms can also be used, but their flavor is not as rich as that of the wild variety.

Eggplant Gâteaux

1 large eggplant, thinly sliced
3 tablespoons garlic salt
1-1/4 cups tomato puree
3 to 4 tablespoons virgin olive oil
12 ounces mushrooms (see *Note*),
  finely chopped
1 garlic clove, pressed or minced
1 tablespoon chopped fresh basil
2 tablespoons brandy
Salt and pepper to taste
1/4 cup plain yogurt

To Garnish:
Flat-leaf parsley and basil sprigs

Preheat oven to 350F (175C). Rinse eggplant with cold water; place in a colander. Sprinkle with garlic salt and let stand 20 minutes. Rinse to remove salt; pat dry with a clean dishtowel.

Meanwhile, in a saucepan, boil tomato puree until reduced by half; set aside.

In a large frying pan, heat 2 to 3 tablespoons oil and sauté eggplant (in batches, if necessary) 4 to 5 minutes or just until softened. Use slices to line 4 (4-inch) ramekins, reserving enough slices to cover filling.

In same pan, heat remaining 1 to 2 tablespoons oil over high heat; add mushrooms, garlic and basil. Cook 10 to 12 minutes or until all liquid has evaporated. Add brandy and cook 2 minutes. Season with salt and pepper and divide among prepared ramekins. Top with yogurt, then with tomato puree. Overlap eggplant slices to enclose filling; press down lightly. Cover ramekins with foil; bake 20 minutes.

Turn out of ramekins and garnish with parsley and basil sprigs.

Makes 4 servings.

Note: Use meadow or horse mushrooms or cepes (porcini), or a mixture of wild varieties, rather than cultivated kinds.

Serve these gâteaux as a stylish accompaniment to lamb or chicken. They can be assembled in advance, then baked just before serving.

Salads

Italian Mushroom Salad

1 small head red oak leaf or lollo
   rosso lettuce
1/2 red onion, thinly sliced
8 ounces button mushrooms, thinly
   sliced
2 ounces Parmesan cheese
2 teaspoons finely chopped parsley

Lemon Dressing:
5 tablespoons virgin olive oil
Finely grated peel of 1/2 lemon
Juice of 1 small lemon
1/4 teaspoon coarse-grained mustard
Pinch of sugar
Salt and pepper to taste

Prepare Lemon Dressing: Stir all
dressing ingredients together in a
small bowl, or combine in a screw-top
jar and shake well. Set aside.

Tear lettuce into bite-size pieces;
arrange lettuce and onion on individual serving plates. Set aside.

Place mushrooms in a large bowl.
Pour dressing over them and toss well
to coat. Pare cheese into wafer-thin
slices and add to mushrooms, tossing
lightly to mix.

Arrange mushroom mixture atop
lettuce, sprinkle with parsley and
serve immediately.

Makes 4 servings.

Note: The mushrooms may be left to
marinate in the dressing up to 2
hours, but it's best to add the Parmesan to the salad just before serving.

Pepper & Mushroom Salad

1 each green, red and yellow bell
   pepper, halved, seeded
2 tablespoons virgin olive oil
1 shallot, finely chopped
1 garlic clove, pressed or minced
6 ounces wild mushrooms (see *Note*),
   cut into large pieces
1 to 2 tablespoons red wine vinegar
1/2 teaspoon Dijon-style mustard
Salt and pepper to taste
2 ounces feta cheese, crumbled

To Garnish:
Parsley sprigs

Preheat broiler. To prepare peppers,
place on a baking sheet, cut sides up;
broil 3 minutes. Turn and broil 5
more minutes or until skin blisters
and blackens. Peel off skin, cut peppers into 3/4-inch pieces and arrange
on individual serving plates. Set
aside.

In a frying pan, heat oil. Add shallot and garlic and sauté 2 minutes or
until softened. Add mushrooms and
cook 2 minutes. Using a slotted
spoon, arrange mushroom mixture
over peppers.

Add vinegar and mustard to pan
juices; boil over high heat until reduced to 1 to 2 tablespoons. Season
with salt and pepper, then drizzle
over peppers and mushrooms. Let
cool, then chill at least 30 minutes.
Before serving, adjust seasoning;
sprinkle with cheese and garnish with
parsley sprigs.

Makes 4 servings.

Note: A mixture of wild mushrooms
is ideal for this salad. If wild types are
unavailable, try a combination of
cultivated oyster mushrooms and
sliced button mushrooms.

Asparagus & Prawn Salad

4 ounces dried penne or other pasta
  shapes
1 pound asparagus
4 ounces button mushrooms, sliced
6 ounces shelled, deveined cooked
  prawns
1 green onion, shredded
1/2 cup dairy sour cream
Salt and pepper to taste

To Garnish:
Lemon slices
2 to 4 cooked prawns in shell

Following package directions, cook
pasta in boiling salted water until *al
dente*. Rinse under cold running water
and drain thoroughly. Transfer to a
large bowl.

Break off tough stalk ends from
asparagus. Cut off tips; set aside. Divide asparagus stalks into 2 equal portions; thinly slice one portion and set
the other aside. Cook asparagus tips
and sliced stalks in boiling water 1
minute. Rinse in cold water; add to
pasta with mushrooms, shelled
prawns and green onion.

Cook remaining asparagus stalks in
boiling salted water 6 to 7 minutes or
until soft. Drain well; transfer to a
food processor or blender, add sour
cream and puree until smooth. Add
to pasta salad and toss to mix; season
with salt and pepper.

Transfer to individual serving
plates and garnish with lemon slices
and unshelled prawns.

Makes 2 to 4 servings.

Mediterranean Lamb Salad

1 small (about 8-oz.) eggplant, diced
Salt
2 tablespoons virgin olive oil
1 small onion, thinly sliced
2 zucchini, thinly sliced
6 ounces wild mushrooms (see *Note*),
  sliced if large
4 tomatoes, peeled, seeded, quartered
12 pitted ripe olives
12 ounces rare roast lamb, cut into
  strips

Herb Dressing:
3 tablespoons virgin olive oil
2 tablespoons red wine vinegar
2 teaspoons Dijon-style mustard
1 tablespoon chopped fresh rosemary
1 tablespoon chopped fresh thyme
Pinch of sugar
Salt and pepper to taste

Prepare Herb Dressing: Stir all dressing ingredients together in a small
bowl, or combine in a screw-top jar
and shake well. Set aside.

Rinse eggplant with cold water and
place in a colander. Sprinkle with salt
and let stand 20 minutes. Rinse to
remove salt; pat dry with a clean dishtowel.

In a large frying pan or wok, heat 1
tablespoon oil. Add onion and sauté 3
minutes. Add eggplant and zucchini
and cook 4 to 5 minutes or until softened. Transfer to a large salad bowl.

In same pan, heat remaining 1
tablespoon oil. Add mushrooms and
sauté 2 to 3 minutes or until tender;
pour off any excess liquid. Add
mushrooms, tomatoes, olives and
lamb to salad bowl. Pour dressing
over salad and toss well to mix. Chill
at least 20 minutes before serving.

Makes 4 to 6 servings.

Note: Use a mixture of wild mushrooms, such as cauliflower fungus,
chanterelles, morels, hedgehog fungus and, if you are certain of their
identity, any of the russulas.

Cherry Tomato & Bacon Salad

1 pound cherry tomatoes
5 ounces brown or chestnut
   mushrooms, sliced
2 tablespoons olive oil
6 bacon slices, diced
1 tablespoon white wine vinegar
3 tablespoons dairy sour cream
Salt and pepper to taste

To Garnish:
4 pitted ripe olives, chopped
1 tablespoon snipped chives
Whole chives

Plunge half the tomatoes into a bowl of boiling water; leave for 30 seconds, then drain and peel. Repeat with remaining tomatoes. Transfer to a salad bowl and add mushrooms.

In a large frying pan, heat oil. Add bacon and cook about 3 minutes or until crisp; lift from pan with a slotted spoon and transfer to salad bowl. Deglaze pan with vinegar, stirring to scrape up browned bits; add pan drippings to salad with sour cream, salt and pepper. Toss lightly to mix and chill at least 15 minutes.

To serve, garnish with olives, snipped chives and whole chives.

Makes 4 to 6 servings.

Note: I like the earthy flavor of brown or chestnut mushrooms in this salad. If they aren't available, you can substitute button mushrooms.

Potato & Mushroom Salad

2 pounds small thin-skinned potatoes,
   peeled, boiled just until tender
   throughout, drained
1 small red onion
2 tablespoons virgin olive oil
6 ounces cepes (porcini, see *Note*),
   coarsely chopped
1 tablespoon white wine vinegar
2 tablespoons chopped fresh dill
Salt and pepper to taste
1/3 cup whipping cream
1 tablespoon coarse-grained mustard

To Garnish:
Dill sprigs

Let hot boiled potatoes stand until cool enough to handle, then thickly slice into a large bowl.

Cut onion into wedges and separate each wedge into layers.

In a large frying pan, heat oil. Add onion and cepes; sauté 2 minutes.

Add vinegar and cook 1 to 2 more minutes or until mushrooms are tender; remove onions and mushrooms from pan with a slotted spoon and add to potatoes.

If mushrooms have exuded a lot of liquid, boil liquid over high heat until reduced to 2 tablespoons. Add to salad with chopped dill, salt and pepper; toss lightly to mix, then transfer to a serving plate.

Mix cream and mustard and drizzle over salad. Serve warm or cold, garnished with dill sprigs.

Makes 6 servings.

Note: If cepes are not available, you can substitute meadow or button mushrooms, though the flavor won't be as good.

Lentil & Hazelnut Salad

2 cups small green lentils
2 carrots
1 small onion
5 garlic cloves
1 bay leaf
5 to 6 parsley sprigs
3 thyme sprigs
2-1/2 cups chicken stock
2 ozs. radishes, sliced
1 cup hazelnuts, sliced
4 ozs. mozzarella cheese, cubed
4 green onions, finely chopped
4 teaspoons finely chopped
  savory

Dressing:
3/4 cup hazelnut oil
1/3 cup white wine vinegar
Salt and black pepper to taste

To Garnish:
Thyme sprigs

Put lentils, carrots, onion and 4 garlic cloves in a large saucepan. Tie bay leaf, parsley and thyme in muslin and add to pan. Add chicken stock, cover and cook 15 to 20 minutes or until lentils are tender. Discard vegetables and herbs. Drain lentils thoroughly and put into a salad bowl.

To prepare dressing, crush remaining garlic clove. In a small bowl, blend together crushed garlic, oil and vinegar until creamy. Pour over lentils. Season with salt and pepper, cover and chill at least 30 minutes.

Just before serving, add radishes, hazelnuts, mozzarella cheese, green onions and savory to salad and toss well. Check seasoning. Garnish with thyme sprigs to serve.

Makes 6 servings.

Chicken & Dandelion Salad

1 (2-1/2-lb.) smoked chicken
40 dandelion leaves
4 stalks celery, cut in strips
1/2 cucumber, cut in strips
2 tablespoons olive oil
2 shallots, chopped
2 tablespoons chopped mint
1 tablespoon raisins
2 tablespoon pine nuts
1 garlic clove, crushed
2 teaspoons red wine vinegar
Salt and black pepper to taste
2 tablespoons crème fraîche

Skin chicken and cut flesh in serving pieces.

In a large saucepan of boiling salted water, plunge dandelion leaves 20 seconds to blanch. Drain and refresh with cold water. Drain and dry leaves carefully with paper towels.

In a large salad bowl, arrange chicken, dandelion leaves, celery and cucumber.

Heat oil in a skillet. Add shallots and sauté until softened. Add mint, raisins, pine nuts and garlic. Sauté gently 5 minutes more, taking care that garlic does not burn. Cool, then stir in vinegar.

Season dressing with salt and pepper. Add crème fraîche and pour dressing over chicken salad. Serve immediately.

Makes 4 servings.

Pine Nut, Pasta & Feta Salad

1-2/3 cups pasta bows
6 bacon slices
1/2 cup (2 oz.) pine nuts
4 tomatoes, peeled, seeded and chopped
8 ounces feta cheese, cut into 1/2-inch cubes
2 tablespoons torn basil leaves

Dressing:
2 garlic cloves, crushed
2 tablespoons grated Parmesan cheese
2 tablespoons lemon or lime juice
1/4 cup virgin olive oil
1/2 teaspoon Dijon-style mustard
Salt and pepper, to taste

To Garnish:
Basil sprigs

Cook pasta in boiling salted water 10 minutes or until *al dente;* drain under cold water and set aside.

Meanwhile, in a skillet, cook bacon in its own fat until crispy; drain on paper towels, crumble and set aside. Remove all but 1 teaspoon of the bacon fat from skillet. Add pine nuts to pan and cook until golden. Remove from pan and set aside.

To make dressing, combine all ingredients in a jar with a lid and shake until well blended.

Put tomatoes and cheese into a salad bowl; add bacon, pine nuts and basil and mix thoroughly. Add dressing and mix again. Garnish with basil sprigs.

Makes 4 main-dish servings or 6 side-dish servings.

Note: This salad is best tossed in dressing about 20 minutes before serving, to allow flavors to develop.

Haloumi & Sesame Seed Salad

1/2 head radicchio
1/2 head chicory
1/2 bunch watercress
6 ounces haloumi cheese
1 egg, beaten
3/4 cup fresh bread crumbs
Vegetable oil for deep-frying
2 tablespoons sesame seeds, toasted

Dressing:
3 tablespoons virgin olive oil
1 tablespoon wine vinegar
1/2 teaspoon honey
1 teaspoon Dijon-style mustard
1 garlic clove, crushed
Salt and pepper, to taste

To Garnish (Optional):
Nasturtium flowers

Break radicchio, chicory and watercress into bite-size pieces and put into a salad bowl.

To make dressing, mix all ingredients together with a small whisk until blended.

Cut cheese into 1/2-inch cubes and dip into beaten egg; drain thoroughly. Put bread crumbs in a plastic bag, add cheese cubes and toss to coat completely.

Heat oil in a deep-fryer to 360F (180C) or until a 1-inch bread cube turns golden brown in 1 minute and deep-fry cheese in batches until bread crumbs turn golden brown; drain thoroughly on paper towels.

Pour dressing over salad and toss until well coated. Top with fried haloumi and sprinkle with toasted sesame seeds. Serve immediately, garnished with nasturtium flowers, if desired.

Makes 4 servings.

Grape & Gorgonzola Salad

1/2 small melon
8 Romaine lettuce leaves
4 ounces seedless green grapes
3 ounces black grapes, seeded
9 ounces seedless red grapes

Dressing:
6 ounces Gorgonzola cheese,
   crumbled
3 tablespoons mayonnaise
1/4 cup chutney
1/4 teaspoon chili sauce
Squeeze of lemon juice

To Garnish:
Parsley sprigs
Few endive and radicchio leaves
A little paprika

First make dressing: combine all ingredients in a bowl; set aside. Cut
melon into 4 slices; remove rind and
seeds.

Place 2 lettuce leaves on each of 4
individual plates. Arrange melon and
grapes among the leaves.

Put a spoonful of dressing on top of
each salad and garnish with parsley,
chicory and radicchio leaves. Sprinkle
a little paprika over dressing just before serving.

Makes 4 servings.

Note: If a thinner dressing is desired,
add half and half or milk until the
correct consistency is reached.

Rainbow Salad

1 small red bell pepper
1 small green bell pepper
1 small yellow bell pepper
8 ounces snow peas

Dressing:
3 ounces full-fat soft cheese with
   garlic and herbs
3 tablespoons crème fraîche or dairy
   sour cream
1 tablespoon chopped mixed herbs
Pinch of grated nutmeg
1/4 teaspoon paprika (optional)
Salt and pepper, to taste

To Garnish:
1 tablespoon chopped parsley
1/2 cup (2 oz.) chopped walnuts
A little paprika (optional)

Cut all the peppers into julienne
strips. Add the peppers and snow
peas to a large pan of boiling water
and boil 2 minutes to blanch; drain
and refresh in cold water. Arrange
the vegetables attractively on a large
salad platter, or in individual servings.

To make dressing: in a bowl, mix
together cheese and crème fraîche
until evenly combined. Stir in herbs,
nutmeg, and paprika if using. Add
salt and pepper to taste. Spoon dressing on top of salad.

Mix together parsley and walnuts
for the garnish and sprinkle on top of
the salad. Sprinkle with a little paprika, if desired. Serve immediately as an
accompaniment, or with crusty bread
as a light meal.

Makes 4 to 6 servings.

Broccoli & Blue Cheese Salad

12 ounces broccoli
1 red apple, quartered and cored
1/2 cup slivered almonds, toasted
DRESSING:
2 ounces blue cheese, softened
2/3 cup plain yogurt
1 tablespoon chopped parsley
1 tablespoon snipped chives
Salt and pepper, to taste

Bacon & Watercress Salad

2 red-skinned apples, quartered and cored
1 bunch of watercress
2 heads of Belgian endive
LEMON DRESSING:
3 tablespoons olive oil
1 tablespoon lemon juice
1/2 teaspoon honey
Salt and pepper, to taste
TO GARNISH:
4 bacon slices
1/2 cup macadamia nuts, toasted

1. Divide broccoli into flowerets. Bring a large saucepan of water to a boil, add broccoli and cook 4 minutes. Drain, rinse in cold water and drain again thoroughly.
2. To make dressing, put blue cheese on a plate and mash it with a fork. Scrape into a bowl and gradually beat in yogurt to make a smooth paste. Add parsley, chives and seasoning. Mix thoroughly.

3. Turn dressing into a bowl and thinly slice the apple into it. Mix together until well coated, then mix into broccoli with three-quarters of the nuts. Turn into individual dishes and sprinkle with remaining nuts. Serve as a delicious accompaniment to cold meats.

Makes 4 servings.

1. First, make dressing: put all ingredients in a jar with a tight-fitting lid and shake thoroughly until blended; pour into a large bowl.

Slice apples thinly into dressing; toss thoroughly to coat and prevent discoloration.
2. Break watercress into sprigs; cut Belgian endive into diagonal slices; add both to bowl and toss again. Turn into a salad bowl.
3. To prepare garnish, cut bacon into

strips and cook in a nonstick skillet until crisp. Sprinkle bacon and nuts over salad.

Serve immediately, as a light starter or delicious salad accompaniment.

Makes 4 servings.

Variation: Replace Belgian endive with 1 head of radicchio, torn into bite-size pieces.

Cauliflower & Avocado Salad

8 ounces shelled broad beans or fresh lima beans
12 ounces cauliflowerets
1 avocado
DRESSING:
2 ounces blue cheese
5 tablespoons half and half
1/4 cup chopped walnuts
Salt and pepper, to taste
Little milk (optional)
TO GARNISH:
1/4 cup chopped walnuts
Parsley sprigs

1. Bring a large saucepan of salted water to a boil, add broad beans and cook 6 minutes. Add cauliflower, bring back to a boil, and cook 2 minutes. Drain thoroughly and let cool.
2. To make dressing, put cheese, half and half, nuts and seasoning in a blender or food processor fitted with the metal blade and process until smooth. Turn into a bowl and thin with a little milk if necessary.
   Halve, pit and peel avocado, then slice, adding to the dressing; mix gently to coat.
3. Add to beans and cauliflower, mix again gently, then turn into individual serving dishes. Garnish with walnuts and parsley to serve, as an accompaniment.

Makes 4 servings.

Variation: Sprinkle with crisply fried chopped bacon as well as, or instead of, chopped walnuts.

Salade Tiède

1/4 head chicory
1/4 head oak leaf lettuce
Few radicchio leaves
Handful of arugula leaves or corn salad (lamb's lettuce)
1 head of Belgian endive
2 tablespoons walnut oil
8 ounces duck livers, cut into slices
2 tablespoons sherry vinegar or raspberry vinegar
Salt and pepper, to taste
TO GARNISH:
1/2 cup pecans
Edible flowers (optional)

1. Tear chicory, lettuce and radicchio into bite-size pieces and put into 4 individual salad bowls with the arugula leaves. Slice Belgian endive into diagonal slices and add to bowls.
2. In a medium-size skillet, heat oil and fry livers 2 to 3 minutes, turning occasionally to cook evenly. Add to the salads with the oil and juices from the pan.
3. Add vinegar to saucepan and stir to deglaze. Pour a little over each salad, season with salt and pepper and toss well. Sprinkle nuts and flowers, if desired, over each bowl.
   Serve as a delicious starter, or light lunch with crusty bread.

Makes 4 servings.

Variation: Use chicken livers instead of duck livers.

Apple Coleslaw

6 tablespoons plain yogurt
1 tablespoon lemon juice
1 teaspoon Dijon-style mustard
Salt and pepper, to taste
2 red-skinned apples, quartered, cored and chopped
8 ounces white cabbage
1/2 cup raisins
3/4 cup coarsely chopped hazelnuts, toasted
2 celery stalks, chopped
2 tablespoons chopped parsley

Oriental Chicken Salad

9 ounces cooked skinned chicken breast halves
1 red bell pepper, thinly sliced
6 ounces snow peas, trimmed
1 (7-oz.) can water chestnuts, drained
1/2 cup slivered almonds, toasted
4 ounces mushrooms, sliced
DRESSING:
2 tablespoons tahini
2 tablespoons rice vinegar or wine vinegar
2 tablespoons medium-dry sherry
1 teaspoon sesame oil
1 tablespoon soy sauce
1 garlic clove, crushed

1. In a medium-size bowl, mix together yogurt, lemon juice, mustard and seasoning; add apples and mix until thoroughly coated with the dressing.
2. Remove any core from cabbage and shred finely with a mandolin or in a food processor.
3. Add raisins, hazelnuts, celery, parsley and shredded cabbage to the apples. Toss the salad thoroughly un-til all the ingredients are coated with dressing. Turn into a salad bowl to serve.

Makes 6 servings.

Variations: Use snipped chives instead of chopped parsley. Chopped dates make a good substitute for raisins. Walnuts can be used instead of hazelnuts.

1. First, make dressing: put tahini in a small bowl and gradually mix in rice vinegar and sherry. Add oil, soy sauce and garlic and mix together thoroughly.
2. Cut chicken into 1/4-inch-wide strips and put in a medium-size bowl with bell pepper.
3. Cut snow peas in half diagonally if large. Blanch in boiling water 3 minutes; drain and rinse under cold running water to preserve color.

Slice water chestnuts thinly and add to chicken with snow peas, almonds and mushrooms. Pour over dressing and toss well.

Spoon the salad into a shallow serving dish and serve, as a main course salad, with crusty bread.

Makes 4 servings.

Date & Apple Crunch

4 Pippin apples, quartered and cored
3/4 cup chopped dates
1 red bell pepper, diced
4 celery stalks, chopped
3/4 cup coarsely chopped hazelnuts, toasted
DRESSING:
2 tablespoons olive oil
2 teaspoons lemon juice
2 teaspoons Dijon-style mustard
Salt and pepper, to taste
TO GARNISH:
2 heads of Belgian endive, separated into leaves

Apricot Rice Salad

3/4 cup chopped dried apricots
2 tablespoons wild rice
1/2 cup brown rice
4 ounces button mushrooms, sliced
2 celery stalks, sliced
1 cup pistachios (4 ounces)
DRESSING:
1 tablespoon hazelnut oil
3 tablespoons sunflower oil
1 tablespoon raspberry wine vinegar
1/2 teaspoon ground coriander
Salt and pepper, to taste
1/2 teaspoon honey

1. First, make dressing: put all ingredients in a jar with a tight-fitting lid and shake thoroughly until emulsified; pour into a medium-size bowl.
2. Chop apples and add to dressing; mix well to prevent discoloration.
3. Add remaining ingredients to bowl and toss well. Pile salad into the center of a flat serving plate. Tuck Belgian endive under the edge of the salad all the way around, to make a sunflower design.

Makes 6 to 8 servings.

Note: This salad is ideal to serve in the winter, especially at Christmas time. If you prefer, serve the salad on individual plates—you will need an extra head or two of Belgian endive for the "sunflower" pattern.

Variation: Toss the salad ingredients with a lemon-flavored mayonnaise: mix together 5 tablespoons mayonnaise, 4 tablespoons plain yogurt and 1 tablespoon lemon juice with seasoning to taste, and use instead of the above dressing.

1. Cover apricots with boiling water, soak 1 hour, then drain well; set aside.
  Bring a large saucepan of salted water to a boil, add wild rice and cook 10 minutes; add brown rice and cook 30 to 40 minutes, until tender. Rinse and drain thoroughly; set aside.
2. Put all dressing ingredients into a jar with a tight-fitting lid and shake vigorously to mix. Pour into a

medium-size bowl.
3. Add mushrooms to bowl and toss until thoroughly coated with dressing. Add celery, pistachios, apricots and rice; mix well. Turn into a salad bowl and serve as an accompaniment. This delicious salad goes particularly well with cold duck or game.

Makes 4 servings.

Crayfish Salad

20 live crayfish
1 pink grapefruit
4 ounces small green beans, halved
8 ounces thin asparagus spears
1 beefsteak tomato
1 avocado
8 oyster mushrooms
4 large lettuce leaves
1 orange
1/2 cup unsalted butter
1 teaspoon Dijon-style mustard
Salt and pepper, to taste

Crab & Orange Salad

2 (1-1/2 lb.) crab, freshly boiled
1 Belgium endive
2 oranges
3 ounces alfalfa sprouts
Few leaves chicory
ORANGE DRESSING:
2 tablespoons orange juice
2 teaspoons Japanese soy sauce
2 tablespoons sunflower oil
1 tablespoon lemon juice
1 tablespoon walnut oil
Salt and pepper, to taste
TO GARNISH:
Shredded green onion tops

1. Put crayfish into a large saucepan of boiling water. Bring to a boil, then simmer about 5 minutes, until they turn red. Drain and rinse with cold water to cool. Set aside 4 crayfish for garnish. Peel the rest, twisting off the heads and peeling away the tail shells; set aside.
2. Remove peel and white pith from grapefruit; cut between membrane into sections, over a bowl.

Blanch beans and asparagus in boiling water 4 minutes, then cool quickly under cold running water. Peel, seed and finely chop tomato. Peel, quarter and thinly slice avocado. Blanch mushrooms.

3. Place lettuce on 4 plates. Arrange vegetables on plates, alternating colors and placing a few grapefruit sections in center.

Squeeze the juice from the orange and put in a small saucepan with butter, mustard, salt and pepper. Heat gently until butter has melted, whisking constantly. Add crayfish and heat through briefly. Remove crayfish with a slotted spoon and arrange on the lettuce. Pour over the sauce, garnish with reserved whole crayfish and serve immediately.

Makes 4 servings.

1. Place crab shell-down on a work surface. Twist off claws and legs. Crack shell of each claw and extract meat. Break apart the legs and remove meat with a skewer. Twist free the apron on underside of crab and discard.
2. Insert a strong knife between main shell and underside and pry upwards to detach the underside. Scoop out and reserve meat from main shell, discarding the small greyish-white stomach sac and its appendages, just behind the crab's mouth.
3. Pull away the soft grey feather gills along the edges of the underside and

discard. Using a heavy knife, split the underside down the middle; remove flesh from the crevices using a skewer.

Separate endive leaves; peel and section oranges, discarding all white pith. Arrange endive and orange sections alternately in fan shapes on 4 plates. Place the alfalfa and chicory at the base; pile crab meat on top.

Put dressing ingredients into a jar with a lid, shake well and pour over the salad. Sprinkle crab with green onion and serve as a starter.

Makes 4 servings.

Antipasto Salad

1 pound taro root
2 tablespoons snipped chives
1 tablespoon chopped fresh parsley
2 heads Belgian endive
1 large fennel bulb
1 green bell pepper, cored and seeded
1 large tomato
1/2 head chicory
1/2 ripe Ogen melon
DRESSING:
3 tablespoons walnut oil
3 tablespoons sunflower oil
2 tablespoons white wine vinegar or lemon juice
1 garlic clove, crushed
Salt and pepper to taste

1. Peel taro root. Cut in even-size pieces and cook in boiling salted water 10 to 15 minutes, until just tender; do not overcook. Drain and cool enough to handle. Dice and place in a bowl. In a small bowl, whisk all dressing ingredients. Pour 1/4 cup of dressing over warm taro root. Add herbs and mix gently to avoid breaking up taro root; cool.
2. Separate Belgian endive in leaves. Cut fennel in quarters and separate layers. Slice bell pepper in rings. Thinly slice tomato. Divide chicory in leaves. Cut melon in thin slices, dis-card seeds, then cut pulp away from peel.
3. Arrange chicory on individual serving platters. Spoon taro root salad in center. Arrange other prepared vegetables and melon around salad. Whisk remaining dressing until thoroughly combined and drizzle over salad.

Makes 4 to 6 servings.

Variation: Use new potatoes or parboiled celery root instead of taro root.

Ribbon & Rose Salad

2 medium-size zucchini
2 large carrots
1 daikon
DRESSING:
2/3 cup mayonnaise
2 tablespoons snipped chives
1 garlic clove, crushed
1 tablespoon lemon juice
1 teaspoon tomato paste
1 tablespoon half and half
1/2 teaspoon sugar
Salt and pepper to taste
TO GARNISH:
12 small round radishes

1. Fill a large bowl of cold water with 24 ice cubes. Using a potato peeler, cut very thin lengthwise slices from zucchini. Drop into iced water. Peel carrots and daikon and drop into iced water.
2. To prepare radish roses for garnish, trim away root ends and larger leaves—leave on small leaves. Using a small sharp pointed knife, cut 3 petals from root to leaf end of radish, taking care not to cut through. Place in iced water. Push all vegetables down into water and refrigerate several hours to crisp and slightly curl ribbons and open roses.
3. To prepare dressing, combine all ingredients in a small bowl and mix well. Spoon into 4 small dishes and place on individual serving plates.

Drain vegetables and pat dry. Arrange ribbons of vegetables around bowls of dressing and garnish each salad with radish roses.

Makes 4 servings.

Spinach & Bacon Salad

8 ounces tender young spinach
8 bacon slices
2 slices white bread
2 shallots
1/2 cup olive oil
1 garlic clove, crushed
1/3 cup dark raisins
2 egg yolks
1/2 teaspoon dry mustard powder
4 anchovy fillets, mashed finely
2 tablespoons lemon juice
2 tablespoons grated Parmesan cheese
1 teaspoon sugar
Pepper to taste

1. Remove stalks from rinsed and dried spinach. Tear leaves in bite-size pieces and place in a serving bowl. Cut bacon in smaller pieces. Remove crusts and cut bread in cubes. Thinly slice shallots and separate in rings.
2. In a medium-size skillet, fry bacon until crisp and golden. Drain and cool. Mix oil with garlic and 2 tablespoons of bacon fat in skillet. Add bread cubes and fry until golden-brown, turning frequently. Drain and cool. Add bacon, raisins and shallots to spinach and mix lightly. Chill until

needed.
3. In a small bowl, mix egg yolks, dry mustard, anchovies, lemon juice, Parmesan cheese and sugar. Season with pepper, then gradually whisk in remaining garlic-flavored oil in a thin stream, whisking well to yield a smooth sauce. Just before serving, add dressing to salad and toss lightly until all ingredients are evenly coated. Sprinkle croutons over salad and serve immediately.

Makes 4 servings.

Chicken & Shrimp Salad

8 ounces skinned chicken breast fillet
8 ounces peeled shrimp, thawed if frozen
2 teaspoons sesame oil
1 garlic clove, crushed
1 (1-inch) piece gingerroot, peeled and grated
3 tablespoons light soy sauce
4 small firm tomatoes
1/4 head Chinese cabbage
4 ounces bean sprouts
1/2 head lollo rosso
Generous handful lamb's lettuce
1 bunch watercress
2 tablespoons corn or peanut oil
1 onion, quartered and cut in thin slivers
2 teaspoons sugar

1. Cut chicken in fine slivers and place in a bowl. Add shrimp, then stir in sesame oil, garlic, gingerroot and soy sauce. Mix well and refrigerate 30 minutes.
2. Meanwhile, prepare tomato roses for garnish. Using a small sharp knife and starting at smooth end of each tomato, remove peel in an even continuous strip about 1/2 inch wide. Start to curl peel from bottom end, with pulp-side inside, to form a bud-shape. Continue winding peel around bud-shape to form a rose. Cover loosely with plastic wrap and chill until needed.
    Finely shred Chinese cabbage.

Blanch bean sprouts in boiling water 15 seconds. Drain and refresh with cold water; drain again. Shred lollo rosso. Place prepared vegetables in a bowl and add lamb's lettuce and watercress, reserving a few sprigs for garnish. Toss well, then transfer salad to a shallow serving dish.
3. In a wok or skillet, heat oil. Add onion and stir-fry 2 minutes. Add shrimp mixture and stir-fry 3 to 4 minutes. Stir in sugar. Spoon hot mixture over salad. Garnish with tomato roses and watercress. Serve immediately.

Makes 4 servings.

Belgian Endive Salad

8 ounces fresh green beans, trimmed
2 heads Belgian endive, separated in leaves
1/2 head chicory, torn in bite-size pieces
1/2 cup pecan halves
1 green bell pepper, cored, seeded and sliced in rings
2 tomatoes, cut in wedges
5 ounces Roquefort cheese
ROQUEFORT DRESSING:
2 egg yolks
1 teaspoon sugar
1/2 teaspoon each salt and pepper
1/2 teaspoon Dijon-style mustard
2 tablespoons lemon juice or white wine vinegar
1-1/4 cups olive oil
2 tablespoons half and half
1 tablespoon snipped chives

Italian Salad Cups

1 green bell pepper
16 cherry tomatoes, halved
8 pitted ripe olives
8 stuffed green olives
4 green onions
4 ounces mozzarella cheese
1 head radicchio
DRESSING:
3 tablespoons olive oil
1 tablespoon red wine vinegar
1 garlic clove, crushed
Salt and pepper to taste
1/2 teaspoon wholegrain mustard
1/2 teaspoon sugar
TO GARNISH:
Sprigs of oregano

1. Cook green beans in a little boiling salted water 6 to 8 minutes, until just tender. Drain and refresh under cold running water; drain again. Arrange Belgian endive in a border around a serving bowl. Fill center with chicory. Arrange pecans, bell pepper rings and tomato wedges on top, allowing chicory to show around edge as a border. Dice 3 ounces of Roquefort cheese and place in center of salad. Cover with plastic wrap and chill.
2. To prepare dressing, in a small bowl, combine egg yolks, sugar, salt, pepper and mustard and whisk well. Gradually blend in lemon juice or vinegar. Set bowl on a damp towel to keep it steady. Add oil, drop by drop, beating well after each addition, until about 1/4 of oil has been added. Gradually increase amount of oil being added to a thin steady stream and continue beating to a thick consistency.
3. Stir half and half into dressing. Finely crumble in remaining Roquefort and beat until smooth. Stir in chives and transfer to a serving bowl. Serve with salad.

Makes 4 servings.

1. Skewer bell pepper firmly on a fork and hold over a flame until skin blisters and blackens. Or cut bell pepper in half and place skin-side up, on a broiler pan. Preheat broiler and broil bell pepper until skin blisters and blackens. Cool, then peel. Discard stalk end, core and seeds. Cut bell pepper in thin slivers and place in a bowl with cherry tomatoes.
2. Slice olives; thinly slice green onions. Cut cheese in small cubes. Add olives, green onions and cheese to bowl and toss gently.
Cut stem end off radicchio and carefully separate leaves. Select 8 cup-shaped leaves, rinse in cold water and pat dry. Wash and finely shred 4 more radicchio leaves and add to bowl.
3. Place all dressing ingredients in a screw-top jar and shake vigorously until well blended. Add to salad ingredients and toss lightly. Fill radicchio cups with salad mixture and arrange on a serving plate. Garnish with oregano.

Makes 4 servings.

Lettuce & Avocado Salad

2 heads cos or romaine lettuce
1 large ripe avocado
1 teaspoon lemon juice
DRESSING:
4 ounces raspberries
2 teaspoons sugar
5 teaspoons distilled malt vinegar
3 tablespoons sunflower oil
Salt and pepper to taste
TO GARNISH:
Chives

1. To prepare dressing, place 3 ounces of raspberries in a bowl; add sugar. Reserve remaining raspberries for garnish. Heat vinegar in a small saucepan until hot; pour over raspberries and cool. Strain through a fine sieve into a bowl, pressing raspberries with back of a wooden spoon to extract all juice and pulp. Add oil to raspberry mixture and season with salt and pepper. Whisk until blended.
2. Cut lettuce in quarters and arrange on a serving platter. Halve avocado, remove seed and peel. Cut pulp lengthwise in slices and brush with lemon juice.
3. Arrange avocado slices and lettuce on individual serving dishes. Just before serving, whisk dressing again and spoon a small amount over salad. Serve remainder separately. Garnish salad with remaining raspberries and chives.

Makes 4 servings.

Cucumber & Strawberry Salad

18 snow peas
1/2 cucumber
12 large strawberries
DRESSING:
3 tablespoons sunflower oil
1 tablespoon white wine vinegar
1/2 teaspoon sugar
Salt and pepper to taste
2 teaspoons finely chopped mint
TO GARNISH:
6 sprigs of mint
Beaten egg white
Sugar

 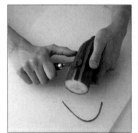 

1. To prepare mint sprigs for garnish, gently rinse and pat dry. Brush lightly with beaten egg white, then coat with sugar, shaking off excess. Set on waxed paper at least 1 hour to dry. Trim snow peas and blanch in boiling water 1 minute. Drain and refresh in cold water. Drain again and pat dry. Set aside.
2. Using notch of a canelle knife, remove lengthwise strips of skin from cucumber at regular intervals. Slice cucumber thinly. Cut strawberries in thin slices.
3. Arrange snow peas in a border on a serving plate. Arrange cucumber slices in overlapping circles inside. Arrange strawberries in center. Place all dressing ingredients in a screw-top jar and shake vigorously until well blended. Spoon over salad just before serving. Garnish with frosted mint sprigs.

Makes 4 servings.

Variation: Omit dressing and spoon chilled white or rosé wine over salad just before serving.

Accompaniments

Orange & Tarragon Mushrooms

3 tablespoons olive oil
1 shallot, finely chopped
1 pound small button mushrooms
1 (1-inch) piece fresh gingerroot, grated
1 garlic clove, pressed or minced
1 tablespoon sesame oil
2 tablespoons balsamic vinegar
1 teaspoon grated orange peel
Juice of 1 orange
Salt and pepper to taste

To Serve:
2 celery stalks, cut into thin julienne strips
1 tablespoon chopped fresh tarragon

In a large frying pan, heat 2 tablespoons olive oil. Add shallot and sauté 3 to 4 minutes or until lightly browned. Add mushrooms, ginger and garlic; cook, stirring frequently, 4 to 5 minutes or until mushrooms are tender. Using a slotted spoon, transfer vegetables to a bowl.

To liquid in pan, add sesame oil, vinegar, orange peel and orange juice. Boil over high heat until reduced by half. Pour mixture over mushrooms and let cool. Add salt and pepper; then chill at least 30 minutes.

To serve, arrange mushrooms on a serving plate. Surround with celery and sprinkle with tarragon.

Makes 4 servings.

Scented Garlic Mushrooms

12 ounces button mushrooms
2/3 cup white wine
1 bay leaf
Seeds of 2 white cardamom pods
2 garlic cloves, pressed or minced
3 to 4 tablespoons dairy sour cream
Salt and pepper to taste

To Serve:
Young spinach leaves

In a large saucepan, combine mushrooms, wine, bay leaf, cardamom seeds and half the garlic. Bring to a boil, then reduce heat and simmer, uncovered, about 10 minutes or until mushrooms are tender and liquid is reduced by about half.

Let cool slightly, then discard bay leaf and stir in sour cream and remaining garlic. Season with salt and pepper. Chill at least 30 minutes before serving.

Serve mushrooms with young spinach leaves.

Makes 4 servings.

Creamy Mushroom Potatoes

1/4 oz dried ceps (porcini)
reconstituted and chopped (see note)
4 oz button mushrooms,
chopped
1/3 cup light cream
1-1/2 oz butter
1-1/2 lb potatoes, cut into 1-1/2 in dice
salt and pepper, to taste
TO GARNISH:
sprigs of parsley or mixed herbs

Put ceps, mushrooms, cream and butter in a small saucepan and bring to the boil; remove from the heat, cover and leave to infuse for 15 minutes.

Meanwhile, cook potatoes in boiling water for 15 minute, or until soft. Drain well, then return to the pan for a few seconds to dry off. Transfer to a warmed mixing bowl and break up the pieces using a potato masher. Add mushroom mixture and beat with a wooden spoon until smooth and creamy. Season well with salt and pepper.

Transfer to a warmed serving dish and serve immediately, garnished with sprigs of parsley or other herbs.

Serves 4-6.

Note: To reconstitute porcini, put in a small bowl and cover with warm water. Leave to stand for 20 minutes, then rinse to remove any grit. This small amount gives a superb flavor.

If field or flat mushrooms are used instead of button mushrooms the potatoes will be colored an unappetizing grey.

Potato & Mushroom Cake

2 oz butter
1-1/2 lb old potatoes, thinly sliced
1 onion, thinly sliced
6 oz mushrooms, sliced (see note)
salt and pepper, to taste
freshly grated nutmeg
1/3 cup thick cream
TO GARNISH:
sprigs of herbs

Preheat oven to 375F (190C). Line a loose-bottomed 9 in cake pan with foil, then grease with a little butter.

Layer potato, onion and mushroom slices in the pan, seasoning layers with salt, pepper and nutmeg and dotting each layer with butter.

Finish with a layer of potato.

Pour over cream, cover with foil and bake in the oven for 1 hour. Remove foil and cook for 30 minutes, to crisp the top. Transfer to a warmed serving plate, garnish with herbs and serve hot.

Serves 4-6.

Note: Use chestnut, button or small cup mushrooms. Use ceps, if you are able to obtain them, for their superior flavor; cut into thin, bite-sized pieces.

Mushroom & Garlic Ragoût

**3 garlic heads, separated in
 cloves, unpeeled**
1 oz. dried porcini mushrooms
1 tablespoon olive oil
1 thyme sprig
1/2 cup red wine
1/2 teaspoon salt
1/2 cup beef stock
1 lb. button mushrooms
2 tablespoons whipping cream

To Garnish:
Thyme sprigs

In a small saucepan, simmer garlic cloves in water to cover 2 to 3 minutes. Drain, peel and trim root end.

In a small dish, cover porcini mushrooms with boiling water and soak 10 minutes. Drain, reserving soaking liquid.

Put garlic cloves, porcini mushrooms, oil, thyme, wine, salt, beef stock and 3 tablespoons reserved mushroom liquid in a saucepan.

Simmer, uncovered, 25 minutes.

If button mushrooms are large, cut in half. Add to saucepan, cover and cook 5 to 7 minutes, until mushrooms are cooked but still firm. Strain liquid into a small pan and reduce quickly to 2 tablespoons. Stir in 1/2 of cream. Discard thyme sprig.

Transfer mushrooms and garlic to individual serving dishes and pour over sauce. Spoon over remaining cream, garnish with thyme and serve immediately.

Makes 4 servings.

Note: If serving with roasted meat, poultry or game, 1 tablespoon meat juices can replace some of mushroom cooking liquid. Porcini mushrooms are available from Italian delicatessens; they are the same mushrooms as French *cèpes*.

Braised Endive

3 tablespoons butter
1 small onion, finely chopped
2 strips bacon, chopped
1-1/2 lbs. Belgian endive
3/4 cup chicken stock
1/2 teaspoon salt
Black pepper to taste
**1 tablespoon finely chopped
 lemon balm**

To Garnish:
Lemon balm sprigs

Preheat oven to 325F (165C).

In a skillet, melt butter. Sauté onion and bacon 5 minutes; remove with a slotted spoon and put into a flameproof baking dish.

Add endive to skillet and cook, turning in butter, until lightly browned on all sides. Remove with a slotted spoon and lay on top of onion and bacon. Pour over chicken stock; add salt and pepper. Cover and bake in oven 1-1/2 hours or until endive is tender. Transfer endive to a serving dish and keep warm.

Place baking dish over high heat and reduce cooking juices. Add lemon balm and pour over endive. Serve immediately, garnished with lemon balm sprigs.

Makes 4 servings.

Variations: Braising is also an excellent way of cooking celery hearts. Follow same method as above, but flavor with chopped fresh dill or parsley rather than lemon balm.

Fragrant Pilaf

3 tablespoons honey
2-1/2 cups boiling water
3 cups basmati rice
2 teaspoons salt
1/2 teaspoon ground cinnamon
6 tablespoons butter
3/4 cup blanched almonds
1 teaspoon pink peppercorns
3/4 cup chopped dried apricots
1/2 cup currants
1 tablespoon rose water

To Garnish:
Cilantro sprigs

In a bowl, place honey and boiling water; stir until dissolved. Pour into a large saucepan. Add rice, salt, cinnamon and 2/3 of butter. Bring to a rapid boil. Boil 3 minutes, then cover tightly and simmer over low heat 30 minutes.

Meanwhile, in a skillet, melt remaining butter. Add almonds and fry until lightly toasted. Add peppercorns, apricots and currants; fry 5 minutes, stirring frequently.

Add almond mixture to rice, burying it. Cover tightly and simmer over low heat 15 to 20 minutes or until all liquid is absorbed and grains of rice are separated and tender but firm. Add rose water. Let stand before serving, garnished with cilantro sprigs.

Makes 4 to 6 servings.

Note: This pilaf is excellent served with grilled kebabs and a bowl of creamy yogurt.

Variation: Use orange flower water in place of rose water.

Potatoes & Rosemary

2 lbs. potatoes
1/4 cup butter
2 onions, thinly sliced
1 (1-3/4-oz.) can anchovy fillets, drained, chopped
2 garlic cloves, crushed
About 5 teaspoons finely chopped rosemary
Salt and black pepper to taste
1 cup milk

To Garnish:
Rosemary sprigs

Slice potatoes thinly and place in a bowl of cold water until ready to use. Preheat oven to 400F (205C).

In a skillet, melt 1/2 of butter. Fry onions a few minutes until softened; set aside.

Butter a gratin dish. Drain potato slices and dry on paper towels. Place a layer of sliced potatoes in dish; cover with onions. Sprinkle on some anchovies, garlic and rosemary. Season with salt and pepper and dot with part of remaining butter. Repeat until all potatoes and onions are used, finishing with a layer of potatoes.

Pour over milk and dot with remaining butter. Bake in oven about 40 minutes or until potatoes are cooked. Check occasionally and if browning too quickly, cover with foil

Serve straight from dish, garnished with rosemary sprigs.

Makes 5 to 6 servings.

Note: These potatoes make a good accompaniment to grilled meats or they can be served for lunch with crusty bread and a crisp green salad.

Stir-Fried Vegetable Nests

1 pound baking potatoes
1/2 teaspoon salt
1/2 cup plus 2 teaspoons cornstarch
Vegetable oil for deep-frying
1/4 Chinese cabbage
1 green bell pepper, cored and seeded
10 canned water chestnuts
5 stalks celery
3 carrots
1 fresh green chile
3 tablespoons peanut oil
1 garlic clove, crushed
1/4 cup water
3 tablespoons teriyaki sauce
2 tablespoons hoisin sauce

1. Finely grate potatoes into a colander; rinse well under cold running water. Drain well and thoroughly pat dry on paper towels. Place in a bowl. Add salt and 1/2 cup of cornstarch and mix well. Divide in 4 portions. Place 1 portion in a 4-inch metal sieve or basket. Spread potato to cover inside of sieve evenly. Place a slightly smaller sieve inside to keep shape during cooking.
2. Fill a wok or deep pan 2/3 full of vegetable oil and heat to 350F (175C). Lower sieve into hot oil and fry 4 minutes, until potato is golden; drain. Carefully loosen potato nest and keep warm. Cook remaining 3 nests in same way.
3. Shred cabbage. Dice bell pepper. Slice water chestnuts. Thinly slice celery. Peel and cut carrots in matchstick strips. Chop chile, discarding seeds. In a wok or skillet, heat peanut oil. Add garlic and vegetables; stir-fry 3 minutes.

Blend remaining cornstarch with water, teriyaki and hoisin sauces. Add to pan and cook 3 minutes, stirring constantly. Spoon into potato nests. Serve hot.

Makes 4 servings.

Scorzonera & Belgian Endive

8 ounces scorzonera or salsify
4 heads Belgian endive
1 tablespoon lemon juice
3 tablespoons butter
3 tablespoons all-purpose flour
2/3 cup milk
1/2 teaspoon Dijon-style mustard
1 to 2 tablespoons chopped fresh chervil
1 cup shredded Gruyère or Emmenthaler cheese (4 oz.)
Salt and pepper to taste
2 large slices cooked ham, halved
TO GARNISH:
3 small tomatoes
Sprigs of chervil

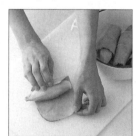 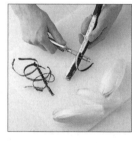 

1. Peel scorzonera and cut in 2-inch pieces. Place in a saucepan with whole Belgian endive, lemon juice and boiling water to cover. Simmer, covered, 10 minutes. Drain, reserving 1 cup liquor; set aside.
2. Preheat oven to 400F (205C). In a pan, melt butter. Stir in flour and cook 1 minute. Blend in milk and reserved liquor. Bring to a boil, stirring constantly. Simmer 2 minutes; stirring constantly. Remove from heat. Stir in mustard, chervil, 1/2 of cheese and salt and pepper.

Pat endive dry with paper towels.

Place scorzonera in 4 individual greased ovenproof dishes. Wrap endive in ham and place on top. Pour sauce over all and sprinkle with remaining cheese. Bake in preheated oven 25 minutes, until golden-brown.
3. To prepare tomatoes for garnish, insert a sharp pointed knife midway between stalk end and top of tomatoes. Cut all way around with a zigzag motion, through to center. Separate halves. Garnish dish with tomatoes and chervil.

Makes 4 servings.

Artichokes Dauphinoise

1-1/2 pounds Jerusalem artichokes
3 tablespoons butter
1 garlic clove, crushed
Salt and pepper to taste
2/3 cup half and half
2 tablespoons milk
1/2 cup shredded Gruyère cheese (2 oz.)
Freshly grated nutmeg
TO GARNISH:
Sprigs of sage

Glazed Vegetables with Madeira

6 medium-size zucchini
1 pound carrots
4 tablespoons unsalted butter
1 teaspoon green peppercorns, coarsely crushed
Salt to taste
Finely grated peel and juice of 1 lime
2 or 3 teaspoons Madeira wine
Vegetable oil for deep-frying
TO GARNISH:
8 large sprigs of fresh parsley
Lime twists

1. Scrub artichokes well in cold water, but do not peel. Parboil in boiling water to cover 8 to 10 minutes; drain well. Cool enough to handle, then peel and cut in thin slices.
2. Preheat oven to 350F (175C). Mix butter and garlic and use half to grease a 9-inch shallow ovenproof dish. Arrange 1/3 of artichoke slices in bottom of dish and season well with salt and pepper. Repeat layers, seasoning each layer.
3. In a small saucepan, heat half and half and milk until hot, but not boiling. Pour over artichokes. Sprinkle with cheese and nutmeg and dot with remaining garlic-flavored butter. Bake in preheated oven 45 minutes, until golden-brown. Serve hot, garnished with sage.

Makes 4 servings.

Variation: Use new potatoes when artichokes are unavailable—cooked this way they are extremely good.

1. Using a canelle knife, cut thin grooves down length of zucchini. Slice thinly and set aside. Peel carrots, slice thinly and cook in boiling salted water 3 minutes. Drain, refresh with cold water and drain again; set aside.
Rinse and dry parsley for garnish thoroughly on paper towels.
2. In a skillet, melt butter. Add zucchini and sauté 1 minute. Add carrots and cook 2 minutes, stirring frequently to glaze. Stir in crushed peppercorns, salt and lime peel and juice and heat through 1 minute.

Transfer to a warmed serving dish. Add wine to pan, deglaze and pour over vegetables. Keep warm while preparing parsley for garnish.
3. Half-fill a deep saucepan with oil and heat to 365F (185C) or until a cube of day-old bread browns in 45 seconds. Place parsley sprigs in a frying basket and submerge into hot oil; cook a few seconds until sizzling stops. Drain briefly. Garnish vegetables with parsley and lime twists.

Makes 4 to 6 servings.

French-Fried Celery Root

1 pound celery root
1 lemon slice
2 egg whites
2 cups fresh white bread crumbs
1/2 teaspoon dried mixed herbs
Vegetable oil for deep-frying
CHILI DIP:
2 tablespoons tomato paste
2 teaspoons chili sauce
1 garlic clove, crushed
1 teaspoon sesame oil
3 tablespoons water
6 tablespoons mayonnaise
1 teaspoon lemon juice
TO GARNISH:
Sprigs of flat-leaf parsley

Spiced Broccoli & Cauliflower

8 ounces broccoli spears
1/2 cauliflower
4 cardamom pods
4 tablespoons butter
1 small onion, thinly sliced and separated in rings
1/2 teaspoon cumin seeds
1/4 teaspoon ground coriander
1 (1/2-inch) piece gingerroot, peeled and grated
1/4 to 1/2 teaspoon turmeric
1 garlic clove, if desired, crushed
2 teaspoons lemon juice
Salt to taste
Plain yogurt, if desired
TO GARNISH:
Sprigs of cilantro

1. Peel and cut celery root in quarters, then slice in 1/4-inch slices. Place in a pan of boiling salted water with lemon slice and cook 5 minutes. Drain, return to pan and shake over low heat a few seconds to dry; cool.
2. To prepare chili dip, in a saucepan, combine tomato paste, chili sauce, garlic, sesame oil and water; simmer 2 minutes. Cool, then mix with mayonnaise and lemon juice. Spoon into a small serving bowl and chill until needed.
3. In a bowl, lightly beat egg whites until slightly frothy. On a plate, mix bread crumbs with herbs. Dip slices of celery root into egg whites. Allow excess to drain, then coat in bread crumb mixture, pressing on firmly with fingers. Half-fill a deep pan with oil and heat to 375F (190C) or until a cube of day-old bread browns in 40 seconds. Lower celery root slices into hot oil, a few at a time. Deep-fry about 3 minutes, until golden-brown and crisp. Drain on paper towels and keep warm while frying remainder. Serve hot, garnished with parsley and accompanied by chili dip.

Makes 4 to 6 servings.

1. Cut off broccoli flowerets and divide in even-size pieces. Cut stalks in half lengthwise, then cut in bite-size pieces. Divide cauliflower in even-size flowerets, discarding center stalk. Cook broccoli stalks in boiling salted water 3 minutes. Add cauliflower and broccoli flowerets and continue cooking 3 minutes until vegetables are barely tender; drain well.
2. Meanwhile, crush cardamom pods and remove seeds. In a large skillet, melt butter. Add onion, cumin seeds, coriander, gingerroot, cardamom, turmeric and garlic, if desired. Cook gently 5 minutes, stirring frequently. Add lemon juice and cook 3 minutes. Season with salt.
3. Add prepared broccoli and cauliflower to skillet. Toss gently in spiced butter and heat through 3 minutes, stirring gently. Spoon into a warmed serving dish. Drizzle with yogurt, if desired, and garnish with cilantro.

Makes 4 servings.

Fried Wild Rice & Vegetables

1/3 cup wild rice
2/3 cup Basmati rice
6 ounces bean sprouts
2 eggs
2 teaspoons water
Salt and pepper to taste
1-1/2 teaspoons butter
6 tablespoons corn oil
2 stalks celery, thinly sliced diagonally
1 leek, finely shredded
1 garlic clove, crushed
1 teaspoon sesame oil
2 to 3 teaspoons sake or dry sherry
1 to 2 tablespoons light soy sauce
6 cos or romaine lettuce leaves, finely shredded
Celery leaves to garnish

Sweet Potato Marquise

2 pounds sweet potatoes, peeled
6 tablespoons butter
Salt and pepper to taste
2 or 3 pinches of ground mace
2 egg yolks
3 tablespoons slivered almonds
4 ounces fresh green beans
1 tablespoon corn oil
3 shallots, finely chopped
2 tomatoes, peeled and chopped
1/3 cup frozen petits pois or green peas
1/4 cup chicken stock
6 to 8 long chives
TO GARNISH:
Sprigs of flat-leaf parsley

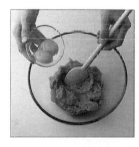

1. Rinse wild and Basmati rice separately under cold running water. Cook wild rice in boiling salted water 10 minutes. Add Basmati rice to pan and cook 20 minutes. Rinse and drain. Cool, then chill several hours or overnight.

Blanch bean sprouts in boiling water 30 seconds; drain.

2. Beat eggs with water and seasoning. In an 8-inch skillet, heat butter. Add eggs and cook until underside is golden and top is set. Turn out onto a flat surface; cool. Roll up, golden-side outside and slice thinly; set aside.

In a wok or skillet, heat 2 table-spoons of corn oil. Add celery, leek and garlic and stir-fry 2 minutes. Add bean sprouts and stir-fry 1 minute. Add 2 tablespoons corn oil, stir in rice and stir-fry 2 minutes.

3. Add sesame oil, sake or sherry and season; stir-fry 2 minutes. Spoon into a warmed serving dish; sprinkle with soy sauce. Heat remaining corn oil. Add lettuce and stir-fry about 2 minutes, until slightly wilted and glistening. Arrange around rice. Garnish with omelet slices and celery leaves.

Makes 4 servings.

1. Cut sweet potatoes in even pieces and cook in boiling salted water 15 to 20 minutes or until tender. Drain well, return to pan and shake over low heat a few seconds to dry off. Mash thoroughly. Add 4 tablespoons of butter and season with salt, pepper and mace. Stir in egg yolks and beat well.

2. Preheat oven to 400F (205C). Lightly grease a baking sheet. In a pastry bag fitted with a 1/2-inch plain nozzle, pipe 6 to 8 nests of potato mixture on baking sheet. Melt remaining butter and brush lightly over nests; stud with almonds. Bake on top shelf of preheated oven 15 to 20 minutes.

3. Meanwhile, trim green beans. Cut in half and cook in a steamer 8 to 10 minutes or until tender.

Meanwhile, in a saucepan, heat oil. Add shallots, tomatoes, petits pois and stock. Cover and cook gently 5 to 6 minutes. Season with salt and pepper and keep warm.

Transfer sweet potato mixture nests to a warmed serving plate and fill with vegetable mixture. Arrange bundles of beans attractively between nests. Garnish with parsley and serve hot.

Makes 6 to 8 servings.

Jansson's Temptation

1-1/2 pounds baking potatoes, peeled
4 tablespoons unsalted butter
1 large onion, quartered and thinly sliced
1/3 cup whipping cream
1/2 cup milk
1 (2-oz.) can anchovy fillets, drained
Salt and pepper to taste
6 tablespoons fresh white bread crumbs
TO GARNISH:
Sprigs of flat-leaf parsley

1. Preheat oven to 400F (205C). Cut potatoes in half lengthwise. Place flat-side down and cut in 1/8-inch slices, then cut slices in 1/4-inch matchstick strips. In a large skillet, melt 3 tablespoons of butter. Add onion and sauté gently 5 minutes, stirring occasionally.
2. Add potato sticks and continue frying gently 5 minutes, stirring frequently to prevent sticking. Remove from heat. Mix whipping cream and milk. Place 1/2 of onion and potato mixture in a shallow ovenproof dish. Chop 1/2 of anchovies and sprinkle over top. Season with salt and pep-

per. Pour 1/2 of cream mixture over top. Cover with remaining onion and potato mixture and press down firmly with a fish slice. Season again.
3. Sprinkle bread crumbs evenly over surface and press lightly. Pour remaining cream mixture over top. Melt remaining butter and drizzle over top. Bake in preheated oven 35 to 40 minutes, until golden-brown and cooked through. Cut remaining anchovies in half lengthwise and arrange in a lattice design over top. Garnish with parsley and serve hot.

Makes 4 servings.

Garlic-Baked Potatoes

1-1/2 pounds small even-size new potatoes
1 tablespoon corn oil
1 tablespoon butter
1 garlic clove, crushed
Salt and pepper to taste
2 sprigs of mint
4 bacon slices
4 green onions
TO GARNISH:
Sprigs of mint

1. Preheat oven to 350F (175C). Scrub potatoes well under cold water, but do not peel. Leave whole and pat dry on paper towels. Prick each potato twice with a fine skewer.
2. In a flameproof casserole dish, heat oil and butter. Add potatoes and fry 5 minutes to brown lightly, turning frequently. Stir in garlic and salt and pepper. Add 2 mint sprigs. Cover and bake in preheated oven 20 minutes or until almost tender.
3. Cut bacon in thin strips. Slice green

onions diagonally in thin slivers. Remove mint from casserole and stir in bacon and green onions. Cook, uncovered, 10 minutes, until bacon is crisp and potatoes are tender. Spoon into a warmed serving dish and garnish with mint sprigs.

Makes 4 servings.

Variation: Use 3 or 4 shallots instead of green onions. Thinly slice and separate in rings.

Desserts

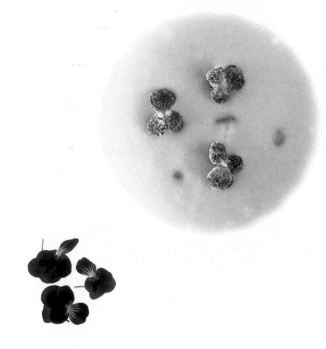

Rhubarb & Ginger Ice Cream

1 lb. rhubarb, cut in small pieces
1/3 cup superfine sugar
4 egg yolks
1-1/4 cups whipping cream
1 (2-inch) piece stem ginger in
   syrup, finely chopped
2 tablespoons ginger syrup

To Decorate:
Mint sprigs

To Serve:
**Langues de chats or ladyfinger
   cookies**

Put rhubarb and sugar in top half of a double boiler or a bowl set over a saucepan of simmering water. Cover and cook over low heat until tender. Puree in a blender or food processor or rub through a sieve; cool.

Place egg yolks and cream in top half of double boiler or bowl as before and whisk over low heat until thickened. Remove from heat immediately and continue whisking a few minutes; cool.

Stir rhubarb mixture into custard. Add ginger and ginger syrup; taste for sweetness—add a little more syrup if necessary. Pour mixture into container of an electric sorbetière and freeze according to manufacturer's instructions. Or pour into a freezer-proof container, cover and freeze about 3 hours, until firm. Stir several times during freezing to avoid ice crystals forming.

Scoop ice cream into chilled glass dishes and decorate with mint sprigs. Serve with langues de chats or ladyfinger cookies.

Makes 6 to 8 servings.

Variation: Use gooseberries instead of rhubarb.

Mascarpone with Violets

12 ladyfinger cookies
1 lb. mascarpone cheese
4 egg yolks
2 tablespoons Armagnac
1/3 cup superfine sugar
1/4 cup chopped candied angelica

Crystallized Violets:
1 bunch of violets
1 egg white, beaten
Superfine sugar

Line bottom of a serving dish with ladyfinger cookies, trimming to fit if necessary.

Sieve mascarpone into a bowl. Mix in egg yolks, Armagnac and sugar and blend well.

Set aside 2 to 3 teaspoons chopped angelica for decorations; stir remaining into mascarpone. Pour over cookies. Chill 2 to 3 hours.

To crystallize violets, hold by stem, dip into beaten egg white, then into sugar. Set on wire rack to dry.

Decorate dessert with reserved angelica and crystallized violets to serve.

Makes 6 servings.

Note: Mascarpone is a very rich smooth cream cheese, available from Italian delicatessens and some supermarkets. It is used primarily in desserts. For a less rich dessert with a grainy texture, use ricotta cheese.

Spiced Plums in Rum

1-1/3 cups dark rum
1 small cinnamon stick
1/2 vanilla bean
3 cloves
1/4 cup superfine sugar
12 dark plums

Sabayon Sauce:
3 egg yolks
3 tablespoons superfine sugar
2 tablespoons whipping cream

To Decorate:
Mint sprigs

Place rum, spices and sugar in a small saucepan and simmer over low heat 20 minutes. Flame to burn off any remaining alcohol.

Puncture plum skins 6 or 7 times with a sharp skewer or needle. Place in a bowl and pour over rum syrup. Chill at least 24 hours.

An hour before serving, remove bowl from refrigerator and let stand at room temperature. Pour off rum syrup and set aside; discard spices.

To make Sabayon Sauce, put egg yolks, sugar, cream and 1/4 cup of rum syrup in top part of a double boiler or a bowl set over a saucepan of simmering water. Whisk until light and frothy.

To serve, place 3 plums on each plate and spoon over Sabayon Sauce. Decorate with mint sprigs.

Makes 4 servings.

Note: These plums can be kept covered in the refrigerator for several months. They are equally delicious served plain with a little rum syrup as a sauce or with fresh whipping cream. Or they can be pitted, pureed and used to flavor homemade ice cream.

Lemon & Cardamom Cake

About 3 teaspoons shelled
cardamom seeds
2 lemons
1 cup ground almonds
1/2 cup dried bread crumbs
1/3 cup superfine sugar
4 eggs, separated
Pinch salt

To Serve:
Whipping cream, if desired
Shredded lemon peel, if desired

Preheat oven to 375F (190C). Butter a 6-1/2-inch springform pan.

Grind cardamom seeds in a mortar. Grate lemon peel and squeeze juice from lemons.

In a bowl, mix together ground almonds, 2 teaspoons of ground cardamom, bread crumbs and lemon peel and juice. Mix in sugar.

Beat egg yolks and add to almond mixture. Whisk egg whites with salt until stiff; carefully fold into mixture. Pour into prepared pan.

Bake in oven about 40 minutes or until a skewer inserted into center of cake comes out clean. Cool in pan.

Serve topped with piped whipped cream and shredded lemon peel, if desired.

Makes 6 servings.

Variation: Instead of lemons, this cake can be flavored with oranges. Substitute lemon juice and peel with orange juice and peel. Sprinkle with a few drops of orange flower water before serving.

Orange & Hazelnut Crepes

Batter:
1/2 cup all-purpose flour
1 small egg
2/3 cup milk
Pinch of freshly grated nutmeg
1 teaspoon vanilla extract
Finely grated peel of 1/2 orange
1 tablespoon vegetable oil

Topping:
8 ounces Grand Marnier cheese
1/4 cup crème fraîche
4 teaspoons finely shredded
marmalade
2 oranges, peeled, sectioned

Syrup:
2 tablespoons maple syrup
1/4 cup finely shredded marmalade

To Garnish:
Shredded orange and lemon peel
Chopped hazelnuts

To make batter, put all ingredients except oil in a blender or food processor fitted with the metal blade and blend until smooth. Heat a little oil in a small skillet and pour in enough batter to make a crepe 3 inches in diameter. Cook until bubbly on the surface and golden around the edge,

then turn and cook the other side until golden. Turn onto waxed paper and keep warm while cooking remaining batter to make 16 crepes in all.

To make topping, mix all ingredients, except the oranges, together in a bowl; set aside.

To make syrup, in a small saucepan, gently heat maple syrup and marmalade until melted and combined. Keep on low heat while assembling crepes.

Put 2 crepes on each of 4 individual plates. Spoon topping over crepes, arrange orange slices around each serving and pour syrup over topping. Decorate with orange and lemon peel and nuts, and serve immediately.

Makes 4 servings.

Note: If Grand Marnier cheese is unavailable, substitute 8 ounces cream cheese and 4 teaspoons Grand Marnier liqueur; omit the crème fraîche.

Store any leftover crepes, tightly wrapped, in the freezer.

Wild Strawberry Creams

1/2 cup whipping cream
3 tablespoons Framboise
1 tablespoon powdered sugar, sifted
3/4 cup fromage frais or plain yogurt
6 ounces wild strawberries

Frosted Leaves:
Strawberry leaves
1 egg white
2 tablespoons superfine sugar

In a bowl, whip cream, Framboise and powdered sugar together until it forms fairly stiff peaks. Fold in fromage frais and all but 12 strawberries. Spoon into 4 dessert dishes and refrigerate 30 minutes.

To make frosted leaves, brush leaves very lightly on both sides with a little egg white; sprinkle with super-

fine sugar, making sure they are completely coated. Leave in a warm place 30 minutes to dry.

Decorate the creams with remaining strawberries and frosted leaves. Serve with crisp wafer cookies.

Makes 4 servings.

Variations: Use ordinary strawberries instead of wild strawberries and slice them.

Raspberries may also be used in place of strawberries, with frosted raspberry leaves to decorate.

Note: Frosted leaves will last for up to 2 weeks in an airtight container if they are completely coated.

Blueberry Waffles

Topping:
4 ounces Petit Suisse cheese
2 tablespoons whipped cream
1/3 cup powdered sugar, sifted
1 cup blueberries

Batter:
3 cups all-purpose flour
Pinch of salt
1 teaspoon baking soda
1 teaspoon baking powder
2 large eggs
1 cup milk
About 1/2 cup cold water
1/2 cup butter, melted

First prepare topping. Blend together cheese, cream and powdered sugar in a small bowl; set aside.

To make batter, sift dry ingredients into a bowl. Beat eggs and milk together, then gently stir into dry ingredients to form a heavy batter.

Gradually add enough water to make a batter thick enough to coat the back of a spoon; add butter and mix to blend.

Heat an electric waffle iron and brush both sides with oil. Fill one side with batter, clamp down lid and cook until steam ceases to escape and waffles are golden brown and crisp. Remove from iron and keep warm while cooking next waffle.

To serve, put a spoonful of prepared topping on each waffle and cover with blueberries. Serve hot.

Make 2 to 3 servings.

Note: Non-electric waffle irons must be turned over halfway through cooking to ensure even results.

Pashka

1 cup cottage cheese
1/3 cup whipping cream
1 egg yolk
1/4 cup superfine sugar
1/4 cup raisins
1/4 cup finely chopped dried apricots
2 tablespoons chopped mixed nuts
  (walnuts, hazelnuts, almonds)
1 teaspoon vanilla extract
1/2 cup unsalted butter

To Decorate:
Fresh fruit in season

Press cottage cheese through a fine nylon sieve. Put into a large saucepan with remaining ingredients and heat gently 3 to 4 minutes, stirring constantly; do not boil. Remove from heat and let stand until thickened and completely cold.

Pour into prepared container (see below) and put on a rack in a dish, which is big enough to leave a space underneath to catch drips. Cover and refrigerate about 8 hours or until completely drained.

Turn out onto a serving dish and decorate with fresh fruit.

Makes 4 servings.

Note: Pashka is traditionally made in a flowerpot-shaped mold; use a new plastic or clay flowerpot. A sieve or strainer can be used to achieve the required rounding shape. Line chosen mold with cheesecloth or muslin, or use a clean dish towel.

Deep-Baked Cheesecake

1/2 cup butter or margarine
8 ounces graham crackers, finely
crushed
1/3 cup raspberry jam
3/4 cup fromage frais or plain yogurt
3/4 cup cottage cheese
4 eggs, separated
1/4 cup whipping cream
1/2 cup superfine sugar
1/2 cup all-purpose flour
Juice and grated peel of 1 small
lemon

To Decorate:
Lemon slices
Lemon peel strips

Preheat oven to 325F (165C).

In a small saucepan, melt butter; stir in crumbs. Press onto bottom of an 8-inch square cake pan. In a small saucepan, warm jam slightly to melt; spread over crumb base. Lightly butter sides of pan.

In a blender or food processor fitted with the metal blade, process cheeses, egg yolks, cream, sugar and flour until blended. Add lemon juice and peel and process briefly.

In a bowl, whisk egg whites until stiff; fold into cheese mixture. Pour onto crumb base and bake 45 minutes to 1 hour or until brown on top and firm to touch. Switch off heat; leave cake in oven 1 to 2 hours or until cool. Remove from oven and leave in pan until completely cold.

To serve, cut into 4 slices, then cut each slice in half. Decorate with lemon slices and lemon peel.

Makes 8 servings.

Chocolate Truffle Cheesecake

12 to 14 ladyfingers
2 tablespoons brandy or rum
1 (8-oz.) package cream cheese,
softened
1 cup whipping cream
1 teaspoon vanilla extract
12 ounces semisweet chocolate,
melted
2 egg whites

To Decorate:
2 ounces milk chocolate, melted
2 ounces white chocolate, melted
Rose leaves
1 teaspoon cocoa powder

Line the bottom of a 7-inch spring-form cake pan with waxed paper.

Arrange ladyfingers over paper, cutting them as necessary to fit as tightly as possible. Spoon brandy or rum over ladyfingers.

Beat together cream cheese and cream in a medium bowl until thick; stir in vanilla and chocolate and mix well.

In a bowl, whisk egg whites until stiff; fold into cheese mixture. Spoon into prepared pan; level the top. Cover and refrigerate at least 6 hours to set.

To prepare decoration, brush melted milk and white chocolate onto underside of rose leaves using a fine paintbrush. Place chocolate side up on waxed paper and let set. Apply a second coat and let dry. Carefully lift tip of leaves and peel away from chocolate.

Invert cake onto a serving plate. Using a fine sieve, dust cocoa powder around outside top edge. Arrange chocolate leaves over the top.

Makes 8 to 10 servings.

Note: This dessert is deceptively rich so serve small portions.

Pecan Pie

Pastry:
1-1/2 cups all-purpose flour
1/4 cup plus 3 tablespoons unsalted butter
1 tablespoon superfine sugar
1 egg yolk beaten with 1 tablespoon water

Filling:
2/3 cup maple syrup
1/2 cup light-brown sugar
3 eggs
2 tablespoons instant coffee granules dissolved in 1 tablespoon hot milk
1-1/2 cups pecans

Whipped cream or vanilla ice cream, if desired

To make pastry, sift flour into a bowl. Cut in butter until mixture resembles bread crumbs, then stir in superfine sugar. Stir in beaten egg yolk. Knead lightly to form a firm dough. Cover and chill 30 minutes.

Preheat oven to 375F (190C). On a lightly floured surface, roll out pastry and line an 8-inch flan or pie pan.

To make filling, in a saucepan, heat maple syrup and brown sugar until sugar has dissolved; cool slightly.

In a bowl, beat eggs and coffee-flavored milk; stir in maple syrup mixture and pecans. Pour into prepared pan and bake 30 to 40 minutes, until filling has set.

Serve warm or cold with whipped cream or vanilla ice cream, if desired.

Makes 6 to 8 servings.

Variation: Walnuts may be used in place of pecans and light corn syrup may be used instead of maple syrup.

Hot Soufflé & Coffee Sabayon

Soufflé:
3 tablespoons cornstarch
1 cup milk
4 (1-oz.) squares semi-sweet chocolate, broken in pieces
1 tablespoon crème de cacao
4 eggs, separated
1/4 cup superfine sugar

Coffee Sabayon:
2 eggs plus 3 egg yolks
1/3 cup superfine sugar
1 tablespoon plus 1 teaspoon instant coffee granules
2 tablespoons dry sherry
1 tablespoon brandy

To Decorate:
Powdered sugar, if desired

Preheat oven to 375F (190C). Butter a 4-cup soufflé dish; coat with superfine sugar.

To make soufflé, in a bowl, mix cornstarch with a little milk. In a saucepan, heat remaining milk and chocolate until chocolate has melted. Pour chocolate milk into cornstarch paste, stirring constantly. Return to pan and bring to a boil, stirring constantly. Simmer 1 minute. Remove from heat and stir in crème de cacao. Stir egg yolks, 1 at a time, into mixture. Cover surface closely with plastic wrap. Cool slightly.

In a bowl, whisk egg whites until beginning to form peaks. Gradually whisk in superfine sugar until stiff but not dry; stir a little into chocolate mixture, then fold in remainder. Pour into prepared soufflé dish and bake in oven 40 minutes.

Just before soufflé is ready, make coffee sabayon. In a heavy-bottom saucepan, combine eggs and egg yolks, superfine sugar, coffee, sherry and brandy. Cook over very low heat, whisking constantly, until thick and light.

Sift powdered sugar over soufflé, if desired, and serve with sabayon.

Makes 4 to 6 servings.

Note: If using individual soufflé dishes or bake about 15 minutes.

Baked Apricots

1 cup large dried apricots (about 18)
1 pot freshly made Earl Grey tea
3/4 cup ground almonds
1/3 cup powdered sugar, sifted
1/4 cup unsalted butter, melted
1 tablespoon lemon juice
18 blanched almonds
2 teaspoons sweet sherry
Chilled yogurt, if desired

Put apricots into a bowl. Strain hot tea over them and soak overnight.

Preheat oven to 400F (205C).

In a bowl, mix ground almonds, powdered sugar, all but 2 teaspoons of melted butter and lemon juice. Knead to a smooth paste.

Drain apricots; pat dry with paper towels.

Divide almond paste in 18 pieces; press each piece around an almond and use to stuff apricots.

Brush a baking dish with remaining butter. Put apricots into dish and sprinkle with sherry. Cover with buttered waxed paper and bake in oven 10 minutes.

Serve hot with yogurt, if desired.

Makes 6 servings.

Variations: Prunes or dried peaches may be used instead of apricots.

Different flavors of tea may be used to soak fruit.

Praline Coffee Ice Cream

Praline:
1/3 cup blanched almonds
1/4 cup superfine sugar

3 egg yolks
1/3 cup granulated sugar
1/2 cup water
2 cups whipping cream
2 tablespoons instant coffee granules
    dissolved in 1 tablespoon plus 1
    teaspoon hot water
1 tablespoon Kahlùa

To make praline, oil a baking sheet. In a heavy-bottom saucepan, gently heat almonds and superfine sugar, stirring frequently, until sugar has dissolved. Cook, stirring constantly, until rich golden-brown. Turn onto prepared baking sheet and let stand until completely cold and hard. Crush with a rolling pin or in a food processor. Set aside.

In a bowl, beat egg yolks until light and thick; set aside. In a saucepan, heat granulated sugar and water until sugar has dissolved. Increase heat and boil rapidly to thread stage (230F/110C). To test, dip fingers into cold water. Take a little syrup with a spoon then pull apart betwen thumb and forefinger. Syrup is ready when a 1-inch long thread of syrup forms. Cool 1 minute.

Pour syrup into beaten egg yolks, whisking until mixture is thick and mousse-like. In a bowl, whip cream until light, but not thick. Stir in cooled coffee and Kahlùa. Fold coffee cream into egg yolk mixture. Stir in praline.

Pour mixture into a 4-cup container. Freeze until mixture is half frozen, then transfer to a bowl and whisk. Return to freezer until firm.

Transfer ice cream to refrigerator 30 minutes before serving to soften. Scoop into chilled glass dishes to serve.

Makes 6 servings.

Chestnut & Coffee Bombe

Chestnut Ice Cream:
3 eggs, separated
1/3 cup superfine sugar
1/2 cup unsweetened chestnut puree
2 tablespooons brandy
1-1/4 cups whipping cream

Coffee Sorbet:
1/4 cup superfine sugar
1-1/4 cups water
3 tablespoons finely ground coffee
1/2 egg white

To Decorate:
Chocolate leaves

To make chestnut ice cream, in a bowl, whisk egg yolks and superfine sugar until thick and light. In another bowl, mix chestnut puree and brandy until smooth.

In a third bowl, whip cream until just holding its shape. Fold chestnut puree into egg yolk mixture, then fold in whipped cream. In a clean bowl, whisk egg whites until soft peaks form; fold into mixture.

Pour mixture into a freezerproof container and freeze 1-1/2 to 2 hours, until nearly firm, stirring twice. Turn into a chilled 5-cup bombe mold or bowl and press around bottom and side. Return to freezer.

To make coffee sorbet, put sugar and water into a saucepan and heat gently, stirring constantly, until sugar has dissolved. Bring to a boil and boil 4 minutes. Stir in ground coffee, remove from heat and let stand 10 minutes to infuse. Pour through a fine sieve into a freezerproof container. Cool, then freeze 1 to 1-1/2 hours, until slushy. Transfer to a bowl.

In a bowl, beat egg white until soft peaks form; beat into coffee mixture. Pour into center of bombe mold and freeze about 2 hours, until firm.

Transfer to refrigerator 30 minutes before serving to soften. Turn out onto a serving plate and decorate with chocolate leaves.

Makes 8 servings.

Jamaican Layer Ice Cream

Coffee Ice Cream:
1-1/4 cups half and half
1/3 cup freshly ground coffee
4 egg yolks
2/3 cup superfine sugar
1-1/4 cups whipping cream, whipped

Pineapple Ice Cream:
1/2 pineapple, peeled, cored
1 egg white
1/4 cup superfine sugar
2 tablespoons white rum
2/3 cup whipping cream, whipped

To Decorate:
Pineapple pieces

To make coffee ice cream, in a saucepan, heat half and half almost to boiling point. Add ground coffee, stir well and let stand 30 minutes.

In a bowl, whisk egg yolks and superfine sugar until thick and light. Reheat coffee-flavored cream until almost boiling. Strain through cheesecloth into egg yolk mixture. Set bowl over a pan of hot water and cook, stirring constantly, until mixture thickens. Cool, then fold in whipped cream.

Line a 9" x 5" x 3" loaf pan with plastic wrap. Spread 1/2 of coffee mixture in bottom of pan. Cover and freeze about 2 hours, until half-frozen. Set aside remaining coffee custard.

To make pineapple ice cream, in a blender or food processor, process pineapple to a puree. In a bowl, whisk egg white until soft peaks form. Gradually whisk in superfine sugar. Fold into pineapple puree with rum. Fold in whipped cream.

Spread over coffee ice cream in pan. Cover and freeze about 2 hours, until firm; freeze remaining coffee custard at same time. Stir coffee ice cream to soften slightly, spread over pineapple ice cream and return to freezer about 2 hours, until firm.

Turn out onto a serving plate and place in refrigerator 20 minutes before serving to soften. Serve in slices, decorated with pineapple pieces.

Makes 8 servings.

Amaretti Semifreddo

12 pairs amaretti cookies
1-3/4 cups plus 2 tablespoons
   whipping cream
2 tablespoons instant coffee granules
   dissolved in 1 tablespoon hot water
1 cup powdered sugar, sifted
4 egg whites
2 (1-oz.) squares semi-sweet chocolate

Crush amaretti cookies with a rolling pin or in a food processor.

In a bowl, mix whipping cream and cooled coffee, then stir in powdered sugar. Whip until beginning to thicken. Stir in crushed cookies.

In a bowl, whisk egg whites until soft peaks form; carefully fold into amaretti mixture. Transfer to a long narrow freezerproof container. Cover, seal and freeze about 2 hours, until quite firm.

Turn ice cream out onto a sheet of foil or plastic wrap and, using foil or plastic wrap as a guide, shape in a log. Wrap up firmly and return to freezer 2 to 3 hours, until firm.

Grate chocolate finely onto a flat surface. Unwrap ice cream. Roll ice cream in grated chocolate to coat completely. Keep in freezer until required. Serve cut in slices.

Makes 6 to 8 servings.

Note: If you do not have a long narrow container, freeze ice cream in 2 small loaf pans. Place side by side on foil to shape in a log.

This type of ice cream never sets completely solid so it is not necessary to soften before serving.

Variation: Stir grated chocolate into ice cream mixture and roll log in crushed amaretti cookies to coat.

Coffee Parfait

1/2 cup superfine sugar
2/3 cup water
3 eggs
1 tablespoon plus 1 teaspoon instant
   coffee granules dissolved in 1
   tablespoon boiling water
2/3 cup whipping cream

Chocolate Cups:
4 (1-oz.) squares semi-sweet chocolate,
   broken in pieces

To Decorate:
Chocolate leaves

Put sugar and water into a saucepan and heat until sugar has dissolved. Bring to a boil and boil steadily to 230F (110C) or until a little of syrup forms a thread when pressed between a wet thumb and forefinger when drawn apart.

In a bowl set over a pan of simmering water, whisk eggs until frothy. Pour syrup onto eggs and whisk, still over simmering water, until mixture is pale and thick and whisk leaves a trail when lifted. Stir in coffee. Remove from heat and set over a bowl of iced water. Whisk mixture until cool.

In another bowl, whip cream until just beginning to hold its shape; fold into coffee mixture. Turn into a freezerproof container. Cover, seal and freeze 2 to 3 hours, until firm.

To make chocolate cups, melt chocolate in a bowl set over a pan of hot water. Cool slightly. Spread melted chocolate evenly inside 12 to 16 double thickness of paper baking cups with a brush or spoon, coating bottom and side. Let stand until set. Add another layer of chocolate, if necessary. When set, carefully peel away paper cups.

Remove parfait from freezer 10 minutes before serving to soften. Scoop into chocolate cups and decorate with chocolate leaves.

Makes 6 to 8 servings.

Mocha Mousse in Filo Cups

3 sheets filo pastry
1 tablespoon unsalted butter, melted

Mousse:
4 (1-oz.) squares semi-sweet chocolate,
  broken in pieces
1 tablespoon plus 1 teaspoon instant
  coffee granules dissolved in 2
  tablespoons water
2 eggs, separated
2/3 cup whipping cream

To Decorate:
Powdered sugar

Preheat oven to 375F (190C). Cut each sheet of filo pastry in 12 (3-inch) squares.

Put a square of pastry in each of 12 cups of a muffin pan. Lightly brush pastry with butter. Put another square diagonally on top; brush with butter. Cover with a third square of pastry; brush with butter. Press a square of foil into each pastry cup and bake in oven 10 minutes or until pas-

try is crisp and golden. Cool on a wire rack.

To make mousse, put chocolate and cold coffee in a bowl set over a pan of hot water and let stand until chocolate has melted. Stir until smooth, then stir in egg yolks.

In a bowl, whip cream until soft peaks form. Fold whipped cream into chocolate mixture.

In a clean bowl, whisk egg whites until soft peaks form. Fold into chocolate mixture. Let stand until slightly thickened, then spoon into filo cups. Chill 15 minutes.

Sprinkle with powdered sugar before serving.

Makes 6 servings.

Note: Do not leave mousse in filo cups more than 30 minutes before serving as pastry softens quickly.

Vanilla & Coffee Bavarois

4 egg yolks
1/4 cup superfine sugar
1-1/4 cups milk
1 vanilla bean
1 (1/4-oz.) pkg. unflavored gelatin
  (1 tablespoon)
1 tablespoon strong coffee
Few drops vanilla extract
1-1/4 cups whipping cream

Coffee Sauce:
2/3 cup half and half
1 tablespoon strong coffee
1 teaspoon instant coffee granules

Lightly oil 6 (2/3-cup) molds.

In a bowl, whisk egg yolks and sugar until thick and pale.

In a saucepan, bring milk and vanilla pod slowly to a boil. Remove vanilla pod; slowly pour milk over egg yolk mixture, stirring well. Place over a pan of hot, but not boiling, water. Stir frequently until custard has thickened and coats back of a spoon. Sprinkle gelatin into mixture,

whisking well. When gelatin has dissolved, strain custard equally into 2 bowls. Stir coffee into 1 bowl and vanilla extract into other. Cover surface of custard closely with plastic wrap; cool.

When mixtures are on point of setting, whip cream lightly; fold 1/2 of whipped cream into each bowl. Divide coffee custard among oiled molds. Cover with vanilla custard. Chill at least 3 hours or until set.

To serve, invert molds onto serving plates.

To make sauce, in a bowl, combine all but 2 tablespoons of half and half with coffee; pour around molds. Carefully pour reserved cream in a thin line around sauce and feather into a design, using a skewer. Sprinkle with coffee granules just before serving.

Makes 6 servings.

Coffee Syllabub & Brandy Snaps

6 gingersnap cookies, crushed

Syllabub:
1/2 cup strong coffee
1 tablespoon brandy
1 tablespoon Tia Maria
1/4 cup superfine sugar
Pinch of grated nutmeg
1-1/4 cups whipping cream

Brandy Snaps:
1 tablespoon light corn syrup
2 tablespoons superfine sugar
2 tablespoons butter
3 tablespoons all-purpose flour
1/2 teaspoon ground ginger
1 teaspoon brandy

Divide cookie crumbs between 6 syllabub cups or tall glasses, reserving some for decoration.

To make syllabub, in a bowl, mix coffee, brandy, Tia Maria, sugar and nutmeg. Stir until sugar has dissolved. Whisk in cream until mixture thickens and holds soft peaks. Spoon over cookie crumbs. Refrigerate several hours or overnight, if desired.

To make brandy snaps, preheat oven to 350F (175C). Lightly grease 2 baking sheets.

In a heavy-bottom saucepan, slowly warm syrup, sugar and butter until sugar has dissolved and mixture is smooth. Remove from heat and sift in flour and ginger. Beat into mixture with brandy. Drop 18 half-teaspoonfuls of mixture onto baking sheets, allowing room for spreading. Bake in oven 10 minutes or until golden and lacy.

Remove from oven and cool 1 to 2 minutes. Remove brandy snaps from baking sheets and quickly roll each one around a thin stick (a chopstick is ideal). If they start to harden before rolling, return to oven 1 to 2 minutes. Let stand 1 to 2 minutes to set, then remove stick and transfer brandy snaps to a wire rack to cool.

Sprinkle reserved cookie crumbs on top of syllabubs. Serve with brandy snaps.

Makes 6 servings.

Caramel & Coffee Profiteroles

Choux Pastry:
2/3 cup bread flour
1/4 cup butter
2/3 cup water
2 eggs, beaten

Coffee Crème Pâtissière:
4 eggs, separated
1/4 cup superfine sugar
1/4 cup all-purpose flour
1-1/4 cups milk
1 teaspoon strong coffee
1 tablespoon plus 1 teaspoon whipping cream, whipped

Caramel Topping:
1/2 cup granulated sugar
1/4 cup water
1/4 cup hazelnuts, coarsely chopped, toasted

Preheat oven to 425F (220C).

To make choux pastry, sift flour onto a sheet of waxed paper. In a saucepan, gently heat butter and water until butter has melted, then bring to a boil. When boiling, add salt and flour all at once. Beat with a wooden spoon 1 minute until mixture forms a ball and leaves side of pan clean. Allow to cool a little.

Add eggs to mixture a little at a time, beating thoroughly. Mixture should be smooth and glossy and able to hold its own shape. Add a little more egg if necessary.

Drop teaspoonfuls of mixture onto dampened baking sheets. Bake in oven 10 minutes. Lower heat to 375F (190C) and bake 20 to 25 minutes more or until golden and crisp. Make a slit in side of each bun. Cool on wire racks.

Make and cool crème pâtissiere, following directions on page 148. Fold in whipped cream. Fill choux buns with cold crème pattisiere.

To make topping, in a small saucepan, gently heat granulated sugar and water until sugar has dissolved. Increase heat and cook rapidly until mixture is light golden-brown. Coat top of each bun with caramel. Quickly sprinkle with nuts. When caramel is hard, pile buns up in a serving dish. Serve within 2 hours.

Makes 20 buns.

Walnut & Coffee Roll

Roulade:
4 eggs, separated
1/2 cup superfine sugar
1 cup finely chopped walnuts
1 tablespoon strong coffee
Superfine sugar for dusting

Filling:
2/3 cup cream cheese, softened
1 tablespoon strong coffee
2 teaspoons brandy
2 tablespoons superfine sugar
2/3 cup whipping cream

Mocha Sauce:
4 (1-oz.) squares semi-sweet chocolate, broken in pieces
2 tablespoons unsalted butter
1/4 cup coffee

Preheat oven to 350F (175C). Line a jelly-roll pan with parchment paper.

In a bowl, whisk egg yolks and sugar until thick and light. Stir in chopped walnuts and coffee.

In a separate bowl, whisk egg whites until soft peaks form. Fold gently into walnut mixture. Spread in prepared pan and bake in oven 15 minutes, until firm. Cool in pan.

Meanwhile to make filling, in a bowl, combine cream cheese, coffee, brandy and sugar; beat until smooth. In a bowl, whip cream until it holds its shape, then fold into mixture.

Sprinkle a sheet of waxed paper with superfine sugar. Turn roulade onto paper; remove parchment paper. Spread filling over roulade, then roll up.

To make sauce, put chocolate, butter and cold coffee in a saucepan and heat gently until melted and smooth; cool.

Serve roulade cut in slices with mocha sauce poured around.

Makes 8 servings.

Tirami Su

Cake:
3 eggs
1/2 cup plus 1 tablespoon superfine sugar
3/4 cup all-purpose flour
1 tablespoon instant coffee granules, if desired

Filling:
12 ozs. mascarpone cheese
4 egg yolks
1/2 cup superfine sugar
2 tablespoons rum
2 egg whites

To Finish:
3/4 cup coffee
2 (1-oz.) squares semi-sweet chocolate, grated

To make cake, preheat oven to 350F (175C). Grease and line a deep 8-inch round cake pan with waxed paper.

In a bowl, whisk eggs and sugar until thick and light. Sift flour and coffee granules, if desired, over mixture, then fold in gently.

Spoon mixture into prepared pan and bake in oven 30 minutes, until golden and cake springs back when pressed in center. Turn onto a wire rack to cool.

To make filling, in a bowl, beat mascarpone until soft. In another bowl, whisk egg yolks and sugar until thick and light. Stir in mascarpone and rum. In a clean bowl, whisk egg whites until soft peaks form; fold into cheese mixture.

Cut cake horizontally in 3 layers. Put 1 layer on a serving plate. Sprinkle with 1/3 of coffee. Cover with 1/3 of filling. Repeat layers, finishing with a topping of cheese mixture. Chill overnight.

Sprinkle with grated chocolate to serve.

Makes 8 servings.

Brandy Alexander Pie

Pastry:
2 cups all-purpose flour
1/2 cup plus 2 tablespoons unsalted butter
3 tablespoons powdered sugar, sifted
1 egg yolk beaten with 2 tablespoons water

Filling:
1-1/2 (1/4-oz.) pkgs. unflavored gelatin (4-1/2 teaspoons)
2/3 cup double strength hot coffee
3 eggs, separated
1/4 cup superfine sugar
3 tablespoons brandy
2 tablespoons crème de cacao
2/3 cup whipping cream

Chocolate Caraque:
2 (2-oz.) squares semi-sweet chocolate, melted

To make pastry, sift flour into a bowl. Cut in butter until mixture resembles bread crumbs, then stir in powdered sugar. Stir in beaten egg yolk. Knead lightly to form a firm dough. Cover and chill 30 minutes.

Preheat oven to 400F (205C).

On a lightly floured surface, roll out pastry and line a deep 9-inch flan or pie pan. Bake blind 10 minutes. Lower temperature to 350F (175C) and bake 15 to 20 minutes, until pastry is golden; cool.

To make filling, sprinkle gelatin over hot coffee; stir until dissolved. In a bowl, whisk egg yolks and superfine sugar until pale and thick. Stir in coffee, brandy and crème de cacao. In a bowl, whip cream until thick but not stiff.

In another bowl, whisk egg whites until soft peaks form. Fold cream into coffee mixture. Gently fold in egg whites. Turn into crust and chill 2 to 3 hours.

To make chocolate caraque, pour chocolate onto a flat hard surface, spreading with a palette knife. Let stand until set. Holding blade of a knife at a 45° angle, push it along surface of chocolate to form curls. Lift caraque onto pie.

Makes 8 servings.

Mille-Feuilles

4 sheets filo pastry
Powdered sugar

Crème Pâtissière:
4 eggs, separated
1/4 cup superfine sugar
1/4 cup all-purpose flour, sifted
1-1/4 cups milk
2 teaspoons instant coffee granules
1 tablespoon plus 1 teaspoon whipping cream

To Serve:
Strawberry fans, below

Preheat oven to 400F (205C).

Fold each sheet of pastry to make 4 layers. Cut 3 (3-inch) circles through layers to make 48 circles. Put circles on baking sheets and bake in oven 2 minutes, until golden and crisp; cool.

To make crème pâtissière, in a bowl, beat egg yolks, sugar, flour and a little of milk. In a saucepan, heat remaining milk and coffee granules until almost boilng. Pour into egg yolk mixture, stirring constantly. Return to pan and cook gently 2 to 3 minutes. Cover and cool.

In a bowl, whip cream until thick; stir into custard. In a clean bowl, whisk egg whites until soft peaks form; fold into custard.

To assemble each mille feuille, put 2 pastry rounds on top of each other on a serving dish. Carefully spread with crème pâtissière. Repeat layers twice more. Put 2 more pastry rounds on top and dust thickly with powdered sugar. Repeat until you have 6 mille feuilles, each composed of 4 double layers of pastry and 3 layers of crème pâtissière.

With a very hot skewer, mark lines on powdered sugar.

Serve immediately, decorated with strawberry fans.

Makes 6 servings.

Note: To make strawberry fans, slice strawberries almost through to stalk end, then fan out.

Mille feuilles must be served as soon as they are assembled as pastry softens very quickly.

Mousseline Gâteau

5 eggs, separated
2/3 cup superfine sugar
1 tablespoon instant coffee granules
    dissolved in 1 tablespoon boiling
    water
1-1/4 cups ground almonds
1/3 cup ground rice

Mousseline Cream:
1/3 cup superfine sugar
3 tablespoons water
3 egg yolks
1/2 cup plus 2 tablespoons unsalted
    butter, softened
2/3 cup whipping cream

Topping:
6 (1-oz.) squares semi-sweet chocolate
2 tablespoons unsalted butter
2 tablespoons water

Preheat oven to 350F (175C). Grease and line 2 deep 8-inch round cake pans with waxed paper.

In a bowl, whisk egg yolks, sugar and coffee until thick and light. Fold in ground almonds and ground rice. In a separate bowl, whisk egg whites until soft peaks form; fold into mixture. Divide between prepared pans and bake in oven 20 to 25 minutes,

until well risen and firm to touch. Turn out onto a wire rack to cool.

To make mousseline cream, put sugar and water into a saucepan and heat gently until sugar has dissolved. Bring to a boil and boil steadily until syrup reaches 230F (110C) or until a little of syrup forms a thread when pressed between a wet thumb and forefinger and drawn apart.

In a bowl, whisk egg yolks. Pour syrup onto yolks in a steady stream, whisking constantly until thick and mousse-like. Whisk in butter, a little at a time. In another bowl, whip cream until soft peaks form; fold into egg yolk mixture. Chill 1 hour.

Cut cooled cakes in half horizontally and sandwich together with mousseline cream.

To make topping, put chocolate, butter and water into a bowl set over a pan of hot water. Stir until smooth. Pour over cake, spreading over top and side. Let stand until set.

Makes 8 servings.

Rich Cheesecake Gâteau

Cake:
3 eggs
1/2 cup plus 2 tablespoons superfine
    sugar
1/4 cup all-purpose flour
1 tablespoon instant coffee granules,
    if desired

Filling:
1/2 cup unsalted butter, softened
1 cup light-brown sugar
3 eggs, separated
1 tablespoon plus 1 teaspoon instant
    coffee granules dissolved in 2
    tablespoons water
7/8 (8-oz.) pkg. cream cheese, softened
1-1/4 cups whipping cream

To Decorate:
Sifted powdered sugar

Preheat oven to 350F (175C). Grease and line a deep 9-inch round cake pan with waxed paper.

To make cake, in a bowl, whisk eggs and superfine sugar until thick and light. Sift flour and coffee granules, if desired, over mixture, then fold in gently.

Spoon mixture into prepared pan and bake in oven 25 minutes, until golden and cake springs back when pressed in middle. Turn onto a wire rack and cool.

Wash and dry cake pan. Line bottom and side with waxed paper.

To make filling, in a bowl, cream butter and brown sugar until light and fluffy. Beat in egg yolks, coffee and cream cheese.

In a bowl, whip cream until it just holds its shape. Fold whipped cream into cheese mixture.

In a bowl, whisk egg whites until stiff, fold into mixture.

Cut cake in half horizontally. Put 1 layer into prepared pan, spread filling on top, then cover with other layer. Chill overnight.

Carefully turn cake out onto a serving plate and dust with powdered sugar to serve.

Makes 12 to 15 servings.

Apricots with Orange

8 ounces apricots
2/3 cup orange juice
1-1/4 cups boiling water
2 tablespoons Cointreau
3 oranges
1/4 cup pistachios (1 ounce)

1. Put apricots, orange juice and water in a saucepan and soak 2 hours. Bring to a boil, cover and simmer gently 10 minutes. Transfer to a bowl, add Cointreau and cool.
2. Cut 4 thin strips of orange peel with a vegetable peeler and cut into needle-fine shreds. Blanch in boiling water 1 minute; drain and dry on paper towels. Set aside.
3. Peel oranges with a serrated knife

and cut into sections, removing all membrane. Add to apricots and mix gently. Transfer to individual serving dishes and sprinkle with pistachios and shredded orange peel to serve.

Makes 4 servings.

Variation: Use 8 ounces strawberries in place of oranges.

Syrian Fruit Salad

1-3/4 cups dried apricots
2/3 cup prunes
1/3 cup raisins
1/4 cup pine nuts, toasted
1/4 cup pistachios (1 ounce), roughly chopped
1/4 cup slivered almonds, toasted
1 tablespoon rose water
1 pomegranate

1. Put apricots, prunes and raisins in a medium-size bowl, cover with 3 cups water and soak overnight.

Pour fruit and soaking liquid into a saucepan, bring to a boil, reduce heat, cover and simmer 15 minutes; cool.
2. Transfer to a serving bowl and sprinkle with pine nuts, pistachios, almonds and rose water.
3. Halve pomegranate and scoop out

seeds using a teaspoon; sprinkle over fruit salad. Cover and refrigerate until required. Serve the fruit salad with plain yogurt.

Makes 6 servings.

Variation: Use dried peaches and figs instead of the apricots and prunes if you prefer.

Crème aux Pruneaux

10 ounces fromage frais or 1/4 cup plain yogurt and 1
(8-oz.) package cream cheese, softened
1 tablespoon honey
2/3 cup whipping cream
PRUNE SAUCE:
2/3 cup pitted prunes
1-7/8 cups apple juice
TO DECORATE:
2 tablespoons half and half
Lemon balm sprigs

  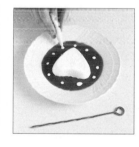

1. Mix fromage frais or yogurt and cream cheese and honey together until smooth. Whip cream until it forms soft peaks; fold into cheese mixture.
2. Line 6 heart-shaped molds with cheesecloth; spoon in cheese mixture and smooth the tops. Put on a plate and refrigerate overnight. Soak prunes in apple juice overnight too.
3. To make sauce, put prunes and apple juice into a medium-size saucepan, bring to a boil, reduce heat, cover and simmer 15 minutes. Cool

slightly, then transfer to a blender or food processor fitted with the metal blade and process to a puree; pour into a pitcher and allow to cool.

Unmold hearts out on individual plates; pour prune sauce around. Put half and half into a plastic bag and drop small dots of half and half into the sauce around the heart. Swirl with a skewer into an attractive design. Decorate with lemon balm to serve.

Makes 6 servings.

Figs with Praline

2/3 cup whipping cream
8 figs
PRALINE:
1/4 cup whole unblanched almonds
2 tablespoons superfine sugar
MELBA SAUCE:
8 ounces raspberries
2 tablespoons powdered sugar, sifted
TO DECORATE:
Mint leaves

1. First make praline: put almonds and sugar in a small saucepan and heat until sugar has melted. Cook, shaking saucepan occasionally, until a good caramel color. Turn onto an oiled baking sheet and cool until hard. Crush with a rolling pin and set aside.
2. Whip all but 2 tablespoons cream until it holds its shape; fold in praline.

Cut a deep cross in the top of each fig and open out slightly. Put a generous spoonful of praline cream in the center of each fig; set aside.

3. To make Melba sauce, put raspberries and powdered sugar in a blender or food processor fitted with the metal blade and process to a puree; rub through a sieve to remove seeds.

Pour a pool of Melba sauce onto 4 individual plates. Put dots of remaining cream on sauce and swirl into a pattern with a skewer. Arrange 2 figs on each plate and decorate with mint to serve.

Makes 4 servings.

Petits Vacherins aux Abricots

MERINGUE:
2 egg whites
3/4 cup light brown sugar
1/2 cup pecans, ground
FILLING:
1/2 cup dried apricots, soaked overnight
1 cup whipping cream
2 tablespoons apricot brandy
TO FINISH:
8 pecans

Hazelnut Galettes with Mango

6 tablespoons butter
1/3 cup light brown sugar
1 cup all-purpose flour, sifted
2/3 cup hazelnuts, toasted and ground
1-1/4 cups whipping cream
MANGO SAUCE:
4 ounces dried mango, soaked overnight
2 passion fruit, halved
TO DECORATE:
Pineapple mint sprigs

1. Preheat oven to 275F (135C). Line 2 baking sheets with parchment paper and draw 8 (3-inch) circles and 8 (2-inch) circles on the paper.

Whisk egg whites until stiff; gradually whisk in sugar. Carefully fold in ground nuts with a large metal spoon.

2. Put meringue in a pastry bag fitted with a 1/2-inch plain tip and pipe onto the circles to cover completely. Bake 1-1/2 to 2 hours. Transfer meringue rounds to a wire rack to cool.

To prepare filling, put apricots and soaking liquid in a small saucepan, bring to a boil, cover and cook 20 minutes. Drain, chop and set aside.

3. Whip cream and apricot brandy together until it forms stiff peaks; put a quarter of the cream in a pastry bag fitted with a large fluted tip. .Fold apricots into remaining cream and spread over the larger meringue circles. Cover with the smaller circles. Pipe a whirl of cream on top of each vacherin and decorate with a pecan.

Makes 8 servings.

1. Preheat oven to 350F (175C). In a bowl, cream butter and sugar together until light and fluffy; stir in flour and hazelnuts and mix to a firm dough, using your hand.

On a floured surface, knead lightly until smooth, then roll out thinly and cut out 8 (3-inch) circles and 8 (2-inch) circles. Place on a baking sheet and bake 12 to 15 minutes, until golden. Transfer to a wire rack to cool.

2. To make sauce, put mango and soaking liquid in a saucepan, cover and cook 15 minutes. Drain, reserving liquid; chop mango and set half aside. Put half the mango pieces and 1/3 to 1/2 cup reserved liquid in a blender or food processor fitted with the metal blade and process to a thin puree. Sieve passion fruit and add juice to mango sauce.

3. Whip cream until it forms stiff peaks; put one-fourth in a pastry bag fitted with a large fluted tip. Mix the reserved chopped mango with remaining cream; spread over the large pastry rounds. Cover with smaller rounds and pipe a rosette of cream on top. Spoon 2 tablespoons mango sauce onto 8 serving plates and place a galette on each. Decorate with mint.

Makes 8 servings.

Almond & Apricot Cornets

COOKIE MIXTURE:
1/4 cup all-purpose flour
1/4 cup sugar
1 egg white
2 tablespoons butter, melted
2 tablespoons slivered almonds
FILLING:
1-1/3 cups dried apricots, soaked overnight
2/3 cup whipping cream
1/4 cup crushed Amaretti cookies
TO DECORATE:
Frosted mint leaves

Red Currant & Nut Tartlets

1 cup all-purpose flour
1/4 cup butter, chilled
1 tablespoon plus 2 teaspoons sugar
1/2 cup hazelnuts, ground
1 to 2 tablespoons milk
FILLING:
1 (8-oz.) package cream cheese, softened
1 tablespoon sugar
Grated peel and juice of 1/2 lemon
SAUCE:
12 ounces red currants
1/4 cup sugar
TO DECORATE:
Frosted leaves

1. Preheat oven to 400F (205C). Grease and flour 3 baking sheets.

Put flour and sugar in a bowl; make a well in the center, add egg white and butter and beat until smooth. Put dessertspoons of the mixture onto prepared baking sheets, spread out thinly into 5-inch rounds, and sprinkle with almonds. Bake 6 to 7 minutes, until pale golden; only bake 3 at a time or they will begin to set before you roll them up.

2. Remove from baking sheet with a thin spatula and curl around cornet molds, holding in position until set; remove from molds.

3. To prepare filling: put apricots and their soaking liquid in a saucepan and cook 20 minutes; drain, reserving liquid. Put two-thirds of the apricots and 3/4 cup reserved liquid in a blender or food processor fitted with the metal blade and process to a puree. Chop remaining apricots. Whip cream and fold in chopped apricots and Amaretti crumbs. Spoon into prepared cornets.

Decorate with frosted leaves and serve with apricot sauce.

Makes 6 servings.

Note: The cookie mixture makes 9 cornets, which allows for breakages.

1. Sift flour into a bowl and cut in butter until mixture resembles bread crumbs. Stir in sugar and hazelnuts; add enough milk to mix to a firm dough. Knead lightly on a floured surface; refrigerate 15 minutes.

2. Preheat oven to 400F (205C). On a lightly floured surface, roll out pastry thinly and use it to line 12 patty pans; prick bottoms with a fork, press a square of foil into each tartlet case and refrigerate 15 minutes. Bake 10 minutes; remove foil and cook 5 minutes.

3. To make filling, mix cheese, sugar, lemon peel and juice in a bowl; spoon into tartlets.

To make sauce, put the red currants in a saucepan with the sugar and 2 tablespoons water. Cover and simmer 5 minutes. Set aside one-fourth of the red currants for decoration. Rub the remainder through a sieve and cool.

Arrange a few red currants on top of each tartlet and decorate with frosted leaves. Spoon the red currant sauce onto 6 individual plates and arrange 2 tartlets on each plate to serve.

Makes 6 servings.

Fruit Parcels & Brandy Cream

1 eating apple
1/4 cup mincemeat
1 teaspoon grated orange peel
1 sheet filo pastry
1 tablespoon butter, melted
Vegetable oil for deep-frying
BRANDY CREAM:
2/3 cup half and half
3 tablespoons brandy
TO DECORATE:
Powdered sugar for sprinkling
Candied orange peel

1. Quarter, core and chop apple; put in a small bowl with the mincemeat and orange peel and mix together thoroughly.
2. Cut filo pastry into 24 (3-inch) squares; pile on top of each other and cover with a clean towel to prevent pastry from drying out. Take one pastry square, brush with butter and lay another square on top; brush with butter. Set aside. Repeat with remaining pastry.
3. Put a small mound of mincemeat mixture in the center of each pastry square, then bring up edges of pastry and pinch together into a "money bag" shape; the butter will help the

pastry to stick.
 In a deep pan, heat oil until a cube of bread turns brown in 60 seconds. Put 3 parcels in a frying basket and deep-fry 1 minute, until crisp and golden-brown, turning once; drain thoroughly on paper towels. Repeat with remaining parcels.
 To make brandy cream, mix half and half and brandy together; put 2 tablespoons on each serving plate. Place 3 fruit parcels on each plate and sprinkle with powdered sugar. Decorate with candied orange peel.

Makes 4 servings.

Chestnut Tulips

COOKIE MIXTURE:
1/4 cup all-purpose flour, sifted
1/4 cup sugar
1 egg white
2 tablespoons butter, melted
2 ounces semisweet chocolate, chopped
CHESTNUT FILLING:
4 ounces semisweet chocolate, in pieces
1/3 cup half and half
8 ounces peeled, cooked chestnuts, sieved
2 tablespoons Grand Marnier
2/3 cup whipping cream
TO DECORATE:
Chocolate rose leaves

1. Make and cook cookie mixture, as for Almond Cornets (see page 153), omitting almonds. Remove from baking sheets with a thin spatula and invert each one over the bottom of an upturned glass. Mold to give wavy edges, let harden, then remove carefully.
2. Put chocolate in a dish over a saucepan of hot water until melted. Dip the wavy edge of each biscuit into the chocolate, rotating until coated; set aside to dry.
3. To make filling, heat chocolate and half and half in a pan, until

melted. Put in a blender or food processor fitted with the metal blade with chestnuts and Grand Marnier and process until smooth; turn into a bowl. Whip whipping cream and carefully fold into chestnut mixture.
 Spoon filling into cookies just before serving and decorate with chocolate rose leaves.

Makes 6 servings.

Note: The cookie mixture makes 9 cookies; this allows for 3 breakages, as they are delicate.

Mango Brûlée with Nut Curls

1/2 cup dried mango, soaked overnight
3/4 cup whipping cream
3/4 cup plain yogurt
1/3 cup light brown sugar
NUT CURLS:
3 tablespoons butter
2 tablespoons plus 2 teaspoons sugar
1/4 cup all-purpose flour, sifted
1/4 cup slivered almonds

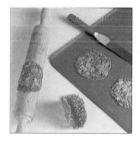

1. Put mango and soaking liquid in a saucepan, bring to a boil, and cook 5 minutes; drain thoroughly. Whip cream until soft peaks form, then fold in yogurt. Add mango and stir to combine.
2. Turn into 4 ramekins or other individual ovenproof dishes and sprinkle thickly with brown sugar. Preheat oven to 375F (190C).
3. To make nut curls, in a small bowl cream butter and sugar together until light and fluffy; stir in flour and almonds and mix well. Place 12 to 14 teaspoons of the mixture well apart on baking sheets and flatten with a spatula. Bake 6 to 8 minutes, until pale golden. Cool 1 minute, then remove with a spatula and place on a rolling pin to curl, until set.

Put the mango creams under a preheated hot broiler 1 to 2 minutes, until caramelized. Serve with the nut curls.

Makes 4 servings.

Hazelnut Ice & Chocolate Sauce

1 cup fresh whole-wheat bread crumbs
1/4 cup light brown sugar
2/3 cup hazelnuts, ground
3 egg whites
1/2 cup sugar
1-1/4 cups whipping cream
CHOCOLATE SAUCE:
4 ounces semisweet chocolate, chopped
1-1/4 cups half and half

1. Mix bread crumbs, brown sugar and ground hazelnuts together on a baking sheet; broil under medium heat until golden-brown, stirring occasionally to ensure the mixture browns evenly. Cool.
2. Whisk egg whites until stiff; gradually whisk in sugar. Whip whipping cream. Carefully fold hazelnut mixture and cream into egg white mixture; turn into a freezerproof container, cover, seal and freeze 4 hours, until firm.

To make sauce, put chocolate and all but 2 tablespoons half and half in a saucepan and heat very gently until melted. Stir to mix; leave to cool.
3. One hour before serving, scoop out balls of ice cream, using a melon baller; place on a baking sheet and return to freezer until required. Spoon chocolate sauce onto 6 individual plates. Fill a paper pastry bag with remaining half and half, snip off the end and drizzle a spiral on each pool of sauce. Use a skewer to create feathered designs. Arrange hazelnut ice cream balls on the sauce and serve immediately.

Makes 6 servings.

Glacé Fruit Bombes

2 ounces crystallized papaya
2 ounces crystallized pineapple
1 ounce angelica
2 ounces glacé pears
1/3 cup glacé cherries
2 ounces glacé apricots
3 tablespoons brandy
3 egg yolks
1/3 cup sugar
1-1/4 cups half and half
1-1/4 cups whipping cream
TO DECORATE:
Slivers of glacé pear or apricot

Duet of Sorbets

PEAR SORBET:
8 ounces dried pears, soaked overnight
1/4 cup sugar
2 tablespoons pear liqueur
1 egg white
MANGO SORBET:
6 ounces dried mango, soaked overnight
1/4 cup sugar
2 passion fruit, halved and sieved
1 egg white
TO DECORATE:
Frosted mint leaves (see below)

  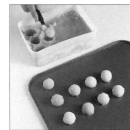

1. Chop papaya, pineapple and angelica; core and chop pears; quarter cherries; pit and chop apricots. Put papaya, pineapple and angelica in a bowl, add boiling water to cover and leave 10 minutes to soften and remove excess sugar. Drain thoroughly, then put in a bowl with remaining glacé fruits. Add brandy and soak 2 hours.
2. Beat egg yolks and sugar together until creamy. Bring half and half to a boil and pour onto egg mixture, mixing vigorously. Pour into a double boiler over a saucepan of simmering water and heat gently until thickened. Strain and cool.
3. Whip whipping cream until fairly thick and fold into the cooled custard. Pour into a rigid freezerproof container, cover, seal and freeze 2 hours, until half-frozen. Stir well, then fold in soaked fruit with any brandy that has not been absorbed. Press into a 2-cup bombe mold, cover with a lid or foil and freeze 2 to 3 hours until firm. Cut into wedges and decorate with glacé fruit.

Makes 6 servings.

1. To make pear sorbet, put pears in a saucepan with 1-3/4 cups of the soaking liquid, cover and simmer gently 15 minutes; stir in sugar. Pour into a blender or food processor fitted with the metal blade and process until smooth. Pour into a rigid freezerproof container and leave to cool. Add liqueur, cover, seal and freeze about 3 hours, until half-frozen.
2. Whisk egg white until stiff. Add half-frozen sorbet and whisk together until smooth. Return to freezerproof container, cover, seal and freeze 2 hours, until firm.
　Make mango sorbet as above, substituting mango for pears, and passion fruit for liqueur.
3. One hour before serving, scoop out balls of each sorbet, using a melon baller; put on a baking sheet and return to the freezer until required. (Press down any remaining sorbet in container and keep for another occasion.) Arrange a mixture of sorbet balls on chilled individual plates and decorate with mint to serve.

Makes 8 to 10 servings.

Frosted mint leaves: Brush leaves with egg white, dip into sugar to coat evenly. Shake off excess sugar and allow to dry.

Chocolate & Chestnut Dessert

8 ounces semisweet chocolate, in pieces
1/4 cup cold water
1/2 cup butter, softened
3/4 cup light brown sugar
1 (15-oz.) can unsweetened chestnut purée
3 tablespoons brandy
TO DECORATE:
1/2 cup whipping cream
8 chocolate rose leaves (see below)

1. Grease an 8" x 4" loaf pan. Put chocolate and 1/4 cup cold water in a small saucepan over low heat until melted; cool. Put butter, sugar and chestnut puree in a blender or food processor fitted with the metal blade and process until smooth; add chocolate and brandy and process again. Turn into prepared pan, smooth the surface with a spatula, cover and refrigerate overnight.
2. To make chocolate rose leaves, choose leaves with clearly marked veins. Coat the underside of each leaf

with melted chocolate, using a fine paint brush. Allow to set, chocolate side up, then paint on a second coat and allow to set. Carefully lift the tip of the leaf and peel away from the chocolate.
3. Whip cream until stiff; put into a pastry bag fitted with a fluted tip. Turn out dessert, cut into slices and arrange on individual serving dishes. Decorate with piped cream rosettes and chocolate rose leaves to serve.

Makes 8 servings.

Chestnut & Orange Roll

1 large orange
8 ounces peeled, cooked chestnuts, sieved
or 1 (15-oz.) can unsweetened chestnut puree
3 eggs, separated
3/4 cup light brown sugar
2 tablespoons powdered sugar
1-2/3 cup whipping cream
1/4 cup Cointreau

1. Preheat oven to 350F (175C). Grease and line a 13" x 9" baking pan, extending paper 1/2 inch above sides.
Cut a few strips of peel from the orange, cut into shreds and blanch 1 minute; drain and set aside. Squeeze juice from orange. In a blender or food processor fitted with the metal blade, process 2 tablespoons orange juice with sieved chestnuts, chestnut puree, egg yolks and brown sugar. Turn into a large bowl.
2. Whisk egg whites until fairly stiff; fold 2 tablespoons into chestnut mixture to lighten it, then carefully fold in remainder. Turn into prepared pan and spread evenly. Bake 20 to 25

minutes, until firm. Cool slightly, then cover with a clean damp towel and cool.
3. Sift powdered sugar onto a sheet of waxed paper; turn cake onto it, then peel off lining paper. Whip 1 cup whipping cream with 2 tablespoons Cointreau, spread over cake and roll up like a jellyroll.
To make sauce, mix remaining Cointreau and orange juice with grated peel and remaining whipping cream. Pour onto individual plates, place a slice of cake on top and decorate with orange peel shreds.

Makes 8 servings.

Apricot & Almond Flan

ALMOND PASTRY:
1-1/2 cups all-purpose flour
6 tablespoons butter or margarine, chilled
1/2 cup ground almonds
2 tablespoons sugar
1 egg yolk
APRICOT FILLING & SAUCE:
1-1/3 cups dried apricots, soaked overnight
1-1/4 cups apple juice
1 egg
1/4 cup butter, softened
3 tablespoons superfine sugar
1-1/4 cups ground almonds
2 drops almond extract
2 tablespoons apricot brandy
Powdered sugar

1. Sift flour into a bowl and cut in butter until mixture resembles bread crumbs; stir in ground almonds and sugar. Add egg yolk and 2 to 3 tablespoons water, mixing to a firm dough. Knead lightly on a floured surface until smooth; cover and refrigerate 20 minutes. Roll out three-quarters of the dough and use to line an 8-inch flan pan placed on a baking sheet. Refrigerate 30 minutes.
2. Preheat oven to 400F (205C). To make filling, drain apricots and cook in apple juice 10 minutes; drain, reserving 6 tablespoons liquid, and chop. In a bowl, beat egg, butter, sugar, ground almonds and almond extract together until smooth. Put half the apricots in prepared flan pan; spoon almond mixture over top.
3. Roll out remaining pastry thinly, cut into strips and use to make a lattice pattern over filling, moistening edges. Bake 15 minutes; reduce temperature to 375F (190C) and bake 15 to 20 minutes, until firm to the touch and golden. Cool.

To make sauce, blend remaining apricots, reserved liquid and brandy in a blender until smooth. Remove flan from pan, sprinkle with powdered sugar and serve with apricot sauce.

Makes 8 servings.

Praline & Apricot Cake

3 eggs, separated
1/2 cup sugar
Grated peel and juice of 1 lemon
1/3 cup semolina
1/4 cup ground almonds
PRALINE:
1/3 cup whole unblanched almonds
1/4 cup sugar
FILLING:
2/3 cup dried apricots, soaked overnight
1-1/4 cups whipping cream
TO DECORATE:
Candied apricot slices

1. Preheat oven to 350F (175C). Grease, line and flour an 8-inch cake pan.

Beat egg yolks with sugar, lemon peel and juice until thick; stir in semolina and ground almonds. Whisk egg whites until stiff; carefully fold into mixture. Turn into prepared pan and bake 25 to 35 minutes, until firm in center. Turn onto a wire rack to cool.
2. Make praline as for Figs with Praline (see page 151); crush with a rolling pin. To make filling, put apricots and soaking liquid in a saucepan, bring to a boil, cover and cook 15 minutes. Drain, chop and cool. Whip cream until thick; set two-thirds aside. Fold apricots and 2 tablespoons praline into remaining cream.
3. Split cake in half horizontally and sandwich together with the apricot and praline cream. Spread a thin layer of cream over side of cake and coat with praline. Cover top with a thin layer of cream.

Put remaining cream in a pastry bag fitted with a large fluted tip and pipe lines at 1/2-inch intervals on cake. Spoon remaining praline in between. Decorate with candied apricot slices.

Makes 8 servings.

Avocado Ice Cream

2 large avocados
2/3 cup packed light-brown sugar
3 cups whipping cream
1 teaspoon vanilla extract
3 ripe bananas, chopped
3 egg whites
TO DECORATE:
Sliced kiwifruit
Halved strawberries

Lemon & Raspberry Bombe

Finely grated peel of 2 lemons
Juice of 3 lemons
2 eggs, separated
1 cup superfine sugar
1 cup whipping cream
6 ounces raspberries
Grated peel and juice of 1 orange
2 egg whites
TO DECORATE:
Raspberries
Shredded orange peel

  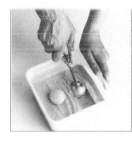

1. Peel avocado and chop pulp in cubes. Puree in a blender or food processor with brown sugar, whipping cream, vanilla and bananas.
2. In a large mixing bowl, whisk egg whites until stiff. Gently fold avocado puree into egg whites. Transfer to a rigid plastic container, seal and freeze 1 hour or until mixture is frozen at edges. Turn into a bowl, beat thoroughly, then return to container and freeze 2 to 3 hours or until softly frozen through. Beat again, then freeze overnight.
3. Transfer to refrigerator 1 hour before serving. Serve scooped in balls and decorated with sliced kiwifruit and halved strawberries.

Makes 6 to 8 servings.

1. In a small bowl, mix lemon peel and juice. In a large bowl, whisk 2 egg whites until stiff. Gradually whisk in 1/2 of sugar, then beat in egg yolks. In a separate bowl, whip 1/2 of cream until thick, then add lemon peel and juice and whisk until firm; fold into egg mixture. Pour into a rigid freezerproof container, cover and freeze until firm.
2. Put raspberries into a saucepan with remaining sugar and orange peel and juice; cook gently 5 minutes. Remove 1/2 of raspberries with a slotted spoon; set aside. Press remaining fruit and juice through a sieve into a bowl; cool. Whip remaining cream until thick and fold in whole raspberries and puree. Whisk remaining 2 egg whites until stiff and fold into mixture. Pour into a rigid freezerproof container, cover and freeze until firm.
3. Chill a bombe mold, then line with lemon ice cream. Cover and freeze 30 minutes. Spoon raspberry ice cream into center of mold, level surface, cover and return to freezer until firm.

To turn out, rub mold with a cloth wrung out in hot water until bombe drops out. To serve, cut in wedges and decorate with raspberries and shredded orange peel.

Makes 6 to 8 servings.

Grapefruit & Mint Sorbet

3/4 cup superfine sugar
1/2 cup water
Juice of 2 grapefruit
Juice of 1 lime
1 tablespoon finely chopped mint leaves
2 egg whites
3 kiwifruit
TO DECORATE:
Sprigs of mint

Sapote Sorbet in Baskets

SORBET:
About 3 pounds sapotes
1 cup superfine sugar
3/4 cup water
2 egg whites
1 tablespoon lemon juice
GINGER BASKETS:
3 egg whites
3/4 cup superfine sugar
1 teaspoon ground ginger
1/2 teaspoon ground cinnamon
Generous pinch of grated nutmeg
1 teaspoon finely grated gingerroot
1/4 cup plus 2 tablespoons unsalted butter, melted,
cooled
TO DECORATE:
Sprigs of mint

1. In a saucepan, heat sugar and water gently until sugar is dissolved, then boil 5 minutes; cool. Strain grapefruit and lime juices into a bowl. Stir in cooled syrup and chopped mint. Turn into a freezerproof container, cover and freeze 2 to 3 hours, until half-frozen.
2. Whisk egg whites until stiff, then fold into half-frozen mixture. Return to freezer until just firm, then beat thoroughly and freeze until required.
3. Peel kiwifruit and puree in a blender or food processor; sieve to remove seeds, if desired.

To serve, cover plates with kiwi puree. Using 2 dessert spoons, shape ovals of sorbet and arrange three on each plate. Decorate with mint sprigs and serve immediately.

Makes 4 servings.

1. To make sorbet, halve sapotes and scoop out 2 cups pulp. In a heavy saucepan, heat sugar and water over low heat until sugar is dissolved. Increase heat and simmer 5 minutes, then cool. Beat egg whites until stiff. Fold sapote pulp, egg whites and lemon juice into cooled syrup.

Turn into a rigid plastic container, seal and freeze 1 hour or until just set. Turn into a bowl and beat 2 minutes until mixture is light and fluffy. Return to container and freeze 2 to 3 hours or until solid.
2. To make ginger baskets, preheat oven to 400F (205C). Grease 2 large baking sheets. In a bowl, beat egg whites and sugar with a fork 30 seconds. Add remaining ingredients and mix thoroughly. Spread mixture in 6 to 8 (6-inch) circles on greased baking sheets, spacing well apart.
3. Bake in oven 8 to 10 minutes. Using a palette knife, carefully lift each circle and place inside a muffin cup or over bottom of a glass. Frill edges and cool, then carefully remove.

Transfer sorbet to refrigerator 30 minutes before serving. Scoop sorbet into ginger baskets and decorate with mint sprigs.

Makes 6 to 8 servings.

Cherries Jubilee

1/3 cup superfine sugar
Finely shredded peel of 1/2 orange
Juice of 1 orange
1-1/4 cups water
1 pound dark sweet cherries, pitted
1 (2-inch) cinnamon stick
1 tablespoon arrowroot
TO SERVE:
Vanilla ice cream
1/4 cup brandy
Sprigs of mint

1. Put sugar, orange peel, 1/2 of orange juice and water into a saucepan. Heat gently, stirring occasionally, until sugar has dissolved. Add cherries to pan and cook over low heat about 5 minutes, until they begin to soften. Using a slotted spoon, transfer cherries to a bowl; discard orange peel.
2. Add cinnamon stick to syrup in pan. Bring to a boil, then boil 3 minutes; discard cinnamon stick. Mix arrowroot with remaining orange juice and stir into syrup. Simmer, stirring constantly, until mixture thickens and becomes clear. Return cherries to pan and heat through.
3. Divide ice cream among 4 individual dishes. Heat brandy in a large metal ladle over an open flame, light and as soon as it flames, pour over cherries. When flames have died down, spoon cherries over ice cream and serve immediately, decorated with mint sprigs.

Makes 4 servings.

Oriental Fruit Salad

1 small watermelon
1/2 ogen melon
1/2 honeydew melon
1 pound rambutans
1 pound lychees
3 mangosteens
1 starfruit (carambola)
1/2 cup plum wine, saké or dry sherry

1. Sketch out a design for the side of the watermelon on a piece of paper; try to find a Chinese or Japanese symbol to copy. Using a non-toxic felt-tip pen, draw a design on skin of watermelon.

Cut off top 1/3 of watermelon, then using a melon baller, scoop out pulp in balls and place in a large bowl. Scoop out any remaining pulp with a large spoon.
2. Using a small sharp knife, carefully carve out design on skin of watermelon, making sure only dark-green skin is removed so that the lighter pith shows through.
3. Shape ogen and honeydew melon pulp in balls and add to bowl. Peel rambutans, lychees and mangosteens. Slice starfruit; add to melon balls. Add honey and plum wine, saké or sherry and mix gently. Spoon fruit into carved watermelon shell. Serve chilled.

Makes 6 to 8 servings.

Note: For a professional finish, leave a 1-inch strip of skin attached over watermelon to make a handle. Decorate with flowers.

If rambutans are unavailable, substitute lychees.

Nectarine Tart

1-1/2 cups all purpose flour
Pinch of salt
1/2 cup butter, diced
1 egg yolk
1 teaspoons superfine sugar
1 tablespoon lemon juice
1 tablespoon water
FILLING:
1/4 cup plus 2 tablespoons butter, softened
1/3 cup superfine sugar
2 eggs, beaten
3/4 cup ground almonds
1/4 cup plus 1 tablespoon apricot jam
2 nectarines
1 tablespoon lemon juice

Mixed Berry Tartlets

1-1/2 cups all-purpose flour
Pinch of salt
1/3 cup superfine sugar
3 egg yolks
1/4 cup plus 3 tablespoons butter, softened
1 pound mixed berries (such as strawberries, raspberries,
red currants, black currants, blackberries)
1/4 cup red currant jelly
1 tablespoon water
CRÈME PATISSIÈRE:
2 egg yolks
1/4 cup superfine sugar
1 tablespoon all-purpose flour
1 tablespoon cornstarch
1-1/4 cups milk
1 tablespoon kirsch

1. Sift flour and salt into a bowl, then cut in butter. Make a well in center. In another bowl, beat egg yolk with sugar, lemon juice and water. Pour into well, then mix. Knead lightly to form a smooth dough. Wrap in plastic wrap and chill 30 minutes. Roll out pastry thinly and line an 8-inch loose-bottom flan pan.
2. Preheat oven to 375F (190C). To make filling, in a large bowl, beat butter and sugar until light and fluffy. Gradually beat in eggs, then stir in ground almonds.
Spread 3 tablespoons of jam over bottom of pastry. Spread almond mixture over jam. Bake in oven 45 minutes, until top is light-golden. Cool slightly in pan, then transfer to a wire rack to cool completely.
3. Peel, pit and slice nectarines. Arrange in a spiral pattern on top of tart. In a small saucepan, gently warm remaining apricot jam with lemon juice. Sieve, then brush over nectarine slices. Serve tart cold, cut in wedges.

Makes 6 servings.

1. Sift flour onto a cool flat surface and make a well in center. Add salt, sugar, egg yolks and butter to well. Using fingertips, work ingredients, gradually drawing in flour. Knead lightly to form a smooth dough. Wrap in plastic wrap and chill 1 hour.
2. Preheat oven to 400F (205C). Roll out pastry thinly and line 8 (3-inch) tartlet pans. Prick bottoms and chill 20 minutes. Bake in oven 10 minutes. Using fingertips, press puffed up pastry back in shape. Return to oven 5 to 10 minutes or until pastry is crisp and golden. Cool slightly in pans, then turn out.
To make crème patissière, in a bowl, mix egg yolks, sugar, flour and cornstarch. Mix in a little milk. Bring remaining milk to just below boiling point, then gradually add to egg mixture, stirring constantly. Pour back into pan; whisk over low heat until thickened. Cover with dampened waxed paper; let stand until cold.
3. Stir kirsch into cold crème patissière, spread in pastry cups, then arrange berries on top. Heat red currant jelly with water. Brush over fruit and let stand 2 hours to set before serving.

Makes 8 tartlets.

Baked Apple Bundles

1/4 cup mincemeat
1 tablespoon chopped pecans
1 tablespoon chopped angelica
1/4 cup calvados or brandy
4 large Cox's Orange Pippins or similar eating apples
8 sheets filo pastry
2 tablespoons butter, melted
2 tablespoons powdered sugar

1. Preheat oven to 350F (175C). Put mincemeat, pecans and angelica into a bowl. Stir in calvados or brandy and let stand 1 hour.

Grease a baking sheet. Core apples and place on a greased baking sheet. Spoon mincemeat mixture into apple cavities. Bake in oven 15 to 20 minutes. Remove and cool.
2. Lay 4 sheets of filo pastry on a flat surface. Brush liberally with melted butter, then cover each greased sheet of filo with another sheet of filo at a 45° angle.
3. Place an apple in center of each filo pile and gather up pastry around apple to make an 8-pointed bundle. Tie with string and place on baking sheet. Bake in oven 10 to 15 minutes. Remove string, dust with powdered sugar and tie with a ribbon. Serve immediately.

Makes 4 servings.

Orange Crepes with Pistachios

CREPES:
1 large egg, lightly beaten
2 tablespoons butter, melted
1-1/3 cups milk
1 cup all-purpose flour
Pinch of salt
1 tablespoon superfine sugar
Finely shredded peel of 1 orange
FILLING & SAUCE:
1 cup plain yogurt
2 teaspoons orange flower water
1/2 cup chopped pistachios
2 sweet oranges
1/4 cup honey
2 tablespoons Grand Marnier liqueur

1. To make filling, place yogurt in a bowl and stir in orange flower water. Add 1/2 of chopped pistachios. Chill.

To make sauce, peel and section orange. In a small saucepan, heat honey gently. Add orange sections and heat through gently 2 minutes. Stir in liqueur.
2. To make crepes, in a small bowl, mix egg, butter and milk. Sift flour and salt into a large bowl, then stir in sugar and orange peel. Make a well in center and add liquid mixture. Using a wire whisk, gradually mix liquid into flour to form a batter. Let stand 30 minutes.

Heat a 7-inch crepe pan over moderately high heat, then oil pan with a few drops of oil. Pour in about 2 tablespoons of batter and tilt pan to coat bottom evenly. Cook 1 to 2 minutes, until underside is golden-brown. Toss crepe and cook 20 seconds. Continue making crepes in this way, stacking them with waxed paper on a warmed plate as they are cooked; keep hot.
3. Just before serving, spoon a little filling onto each crepe and fold to form a triangle, enclosing filling. Arrange on individual plates. Pour sauce over crepes and sprinkle with remaining pistachios to serve.

Makes 4 to 6 servings.

Kiwi & Passion-Fruit Pavlova

MERINGUE:
4 egg whites
Pinch of salt
1 cup superfine sugar
1 teaspoon cornstarch
1 teaspoon white-wine vinegar
FILLING:
2 cups whipping cream
2 tablespoons superfine sugar
6 passion fruit
6 kiwifruit, peeled, sliced

1. Preheat oven to 275F (135C). Line a baking sheet with parchment paper. Draw a 9-inch circle on paper. To make meringue, beat egg whites with salt until stiff peaks form. Gradually beat in superfine sugar, then continue to beat 5 minutes. Fold in cornstarch and vinegar. Using a palette knife, spread meringue mixture evenly over circle on prepared baking sheet.

Bake in oven 10 minutes. Lower heat to 225F (105C) and cook 45 minutes more. Turn off heat and leave meringue in oven to cool slowly 1 hour. Remove from oven and carefully transfer to a plate.

2. To make filling, whip cream with sugar until thick. Cut passion fruit in half and scoop out pulp into a bowl. Fold pulp and 1/2 of kiwifruit slices into cream mixture.

3. Carefully spoon cream mixture over meringue, smoothing with a palette knife. Decorate top with remaining kiwi slices. Serve immediately cut in wedges.

Makes 6 to 8 servings.

Wild Strawberry Cheesecake

1-1/4 cups finely crushed graham crackers
1/2 cup finely chopped hazelnuts
1/4 cup plus 2 tablespoons butter, melted
1-1/2 cups cottage cheese
1/4 cup superfine sugar
3 eggs, separated
Finely grated peel and juice of 1 lemon
1 (.25-oz.) envelope unflavored gelatin (1 tablespoon)
1-1/4 cups whipping cream
12 ounces wild strawberries
3 tablespoons red currant jelly
2 teaspoons water

1. In a bowl, mix graham cracker crumbs and hazelnuts; stir in melted butter. Spoon into a deep 8-inch springform pan and chill until firm.

2. In a bowl, beat cottage cheese with sugar, egg yolks and lemon peel. Dissolve gelatin in lemon juice, then stir into cheese mixture. Whip cream until stiff peaks form; fold into mixture. Whisk egg whites until stiff, then fold in. Cover and chill 10 minutes, until beginning to set.

3. Spoon 1/2 of cheese mixture over crust. Sprinkle 2/3 of strawberries evenly over cheese mixture. Cover with remaining cheese mixture. Chill 2 hours.

Remove cheesecake from pan and arrange remaining strawberries on top. Warm red currant jelly with water over low heat. Cool until thick enough to coat back of a spoon, then brush over top of cheesecake and strawberries. Let stand until set.

Makes 6 servings.

Exotic Fruit Brûlée

3 peaches
3 apricots
3 oriental persimmons
1 tablespoon plus 2 teaspoons finely chopped preserved
stem ginger
1 tablespoon rose water
1-1/4 cups whipping cream
1 tablespoon powdered sugar
1/3 cup superfine sugar

Strawberries Romanoff

1 quart strawberries
3 tablespoons powdered sugar
Grated peel and juice of 1 orange
1-1/4 cups whipping cream
1/2 cup Cointreau or other orange-flavored liqueur
2 tablespoons brandy
TO DECORATE:
6 to 12 strawberries
Shredded orange peel

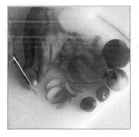  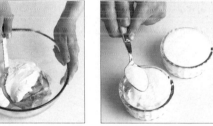    

1. Peel peaches and apricots. Discard pits; slice peaches and apricots thinly and place in a bowl. Peel persimmons and slice thinly; add to bowl with chopped ginger. Pour over rose water and mix gently.

2. In a separate bowl, whisk cream with powdered sugar until stiff; gently fold into fruit mixture. Spoon into 6 ovenproof ramekin dishes. Cover with plastic wrap and chill 2 hours.

3. Preheat broiler. Sprinkle superfine sugar over top of each dish. Place ramekins on a broiler rack under hot broiler 2 to 3 minutes or until sugar has caramelized. Cool and serve cold.

Makes 6 servings.

Note: If oriental persimmons are unobtainable, use a ripe mango instead.

1. Put strawberries in a large bowl and sprinkle with 2 tablespoons of powdered sugar. Add orange peel and juice and liqueur. Mix gently. Cover bowl with plastic wrap and refrigerate 30 minutes.

2. In another bowl, whisk whipping cream, brandy and remaining powdered sugar until fairly stiff. Cover with plastic wrap and refrigerate 30 minutes.

3. Spoon strawberries with juice into 6 individual glass serving dishes. Top with brandy-flavored cream and decorate with strawberries and shredded orange peel. Serve immediately.

Makes 6 servings.

Note: Crisp thin shortbreads or langue de chat cookies are ideal served with this dessert. Serve any remaining brandy-flavored cream in a separate bowl.

Citrus Mousse

2 eggs
2 egg yolks
1/2 cup superfine sugar
Finely grated peel and juice of 1 lemon
Finely grated peel and juice of 1 lime
Finely grated peel and juice of 1 large orange
2 tablespoons Cointreau or other orange-flavored liqueur
2 cups whipping cream
1 (.25-oz.) envelope unflavored gelatin (1 tablespoon)
3 tablespoons water
TO DECORATE:
Shredded lemon, lime and orange peel

Pear Mousse & Chocolate Sauce

1/2 cup medium-dry white wine
1/3 cup superfine sugar
2 pared lemon peel strips
3 Bartlett or Conference pears
3/4 cup fromage frais or ricotta cheese
2 eggs, separated
1-1/4 cups whipping cream
2 tablespoons Poire William liqueur
2 (.25-oz.) envelopes unflavored gelatin (2 tablespoons)
3 tablespoons water
4 (1-oz.) squares semisweet chocolate
12 rose leaves
2 to 3 tablespoons strong black coffee

1. Put eggs, egg yolks, sugar and grated peel in a bowl set over a pan of gently simmering water. Whisk until thick. Remove from heat and continue whisking until cool. Strain fruit juices into a measuring cup to make 3/4 cup; add extra orange juice if necessary. Gradually whisk juice into egg mixture, then whisk in liqueur. Whip 1-1/4 cups cream until it forms soft peaks; fold into mousse.
2. Dissolve gelatin in water, then fold into mousse mixture. Set bowl over iced water and stir until beginning to set, then turn into a glass serving dish. Chill 2 hours until set.
3. Whip remaining cream until stiff enough to pipe. Decorate mousse with piped cream rosettes and shredded lemon, lime and orange peel. Serve as soon as possible.

Makes 4 to 6 servings.

1. Put wine, 2 tablespoons of sugar and lemon peel into a saucepan; stir over low heat until sugar is dissolved. Peel, core and slice pears; add to syrup and poach gently 15 minutes. Cool and discard lemon peel. Strain mixture through a sieve, pressing pear pulp through back of a wooden spoon.
2. Drain fromage frais, then beat in egg yolks, and remaining sugar. Beat in 3/4 cup of cream, liqueur and pear puree. Dissolve gelatin in water. Stir a little pear mixture into dissolved gelatin, then stir gelatin into rest of pear mixture. Whisk egg whites until stiff, then fold into pear mixture. Divide among 6 ramekins and chill 6 hours.
3. Melt chocolate in a small bowl set over a pan of hot water. Brush underside of each rose leaf with melted chocolate; place on waxed paper in a cool place; reserve remaining chocolate. When chocolate leaves have set, carefully peel away rose leaves.

Warm reserved chocolate, if necessary, until melted, then stir in coffee and remaining cream to make a thin sauce; cool.

Turn mousses out on to individual plates, top with chocolate leaves and pour sauce around.

Makes 6 servings.

Index

ANISSA
June 1 93
FROM WoodBridge